Critical Essays on Robert Penn Warren

Critical Essays on Robert Penn Warren

William Bedford Clark

G. K. Hall & Co. • Boston, Massachusetts

Copyright © 1981 by William Bedford Clark

Library of Congress Cataloging in Publication Data

Critical essays on Robert Penn Warren.

(Critical essays on American literature)
Includes bibliographical references and index.
1. Warren, Robert Penn, 1905-   —Criticism and
interpretation—Collected works. I. Clark, William
Bedford. II. Series.
PS3545.A748Z66   813'.52   80-28716
ISBN 0-8161-8424-0   AACR1

CRITICAL ESSAYS ON AMERICAN LITERATURE

This series seeks to collect the most important previously printed criticism on writers and topics in American literature along with, in various volumes, original essays, interviews, bibliographies, letters, manuscript sections, and other materials brought to public attention for the first time. William Bedford Clark's volume on Robert Penn Warren is the most comprehensive collection of criticism ever assembled on this important American writer, who is at once a leading novelist, poet, and critic. It contains reprinted essays by such leading scholars of modern literature as Malcolm Cowley, John Crowe Ransom, Henry Nash Smith, and Carlos Baker along with an important introduction by Professor Clark and an original analysis of *Brother to Dragons* by Richard G. Law. We are confident that this collection will make a permanent and significant contribution to American literary study.

JAMES NAGEL, GENERAL EDITOR

Northeastern University

*To My Mother
and
To the Memory of My Father*

CONTENTS

Articles and Essays

INTRODUCTION

The speaker in Robert Penn Warren's poem "Homage to Emerson, On Night Flight to New York" struggles against a sense of his own abstractness, a feeling of vacuity born of his condition: hurtling through dark space in the pressurized cabin of a plane cruising at 38,000 feet. He tries to fix upon fugitive memories from his past in an effort to preserve his individuation, and, in Section IV ("One Drunk Allegory"), he focuses at length upon an episode that took place late one night in the French Quarter in New Orleans. In front of the Old Absinthe House a drunken cripple loses his balance and falls flat on his "you-know-what," amid a flurry "of flying crutches/Like a Texas tornado. . . ." The speaker props the man against a lamp post, only to have him collapse a second time. The cripple declines further assistance, observing that his situation is as good as any other for contemplating the stars—"*Until, of course, the cops come.*" Here, couched in grotesque humor, is a succinct image of Warren's characteristic vision of the human condition. Imperfect man, finding himself in a predicament that is at once painful and absurd, longs for transcendence, knowing all the while that he will eventually be called to account for being who and what he is. In a literary career that has spanned well over half a century, Warren has perennially explored the implications of this vision in poetry and fiction as well as in his criticism and historical and social commentary. A rich critical heritage has evolved in response to Warren's work. Neil Nakadate has traced it in detail in *Robert Penn Warren: A Reference Guide*.[1] What follows is a selective overview, in narrative form, of the critical reaction to Warren's writing, and such a survey has a two-fold purpose. From his days as a junior member of the Fugitives at Vanderbilt through the period of his editorship of the prestigious *Southern Review* to the present, Warren has been a highly visible presence on the American literary scene. Consequently, he has drawn attention from some of the most distinguished men and women of letters in this century, and the history of critical reaction to Warren's career can be read, in certain respects, as a barometer of American literary politics and tastes from the 1930s on as well as for the light it sheds on the Warren canon.

Warren's first book, *John Brown: The Making of a Martyr* (1929), was a biography informed by his interest in Agrarianism and his temperamental distrust of abstract idealism. His treatment of his subject was therefore anything but pietistic, and this seems to have disturbed Gorham Munson, who was also offended by Warren's penchant for split infinitives.[2] Avery Craven gave the book a mixed review, but another distinguished historian, Allan Nevins, while noting that Warren was quite

1

"harsh" on Brown, found his "final verdict" sound and saw Warren's speculations regarding the intent of the Harper's Ferry raid as investing Brown's actions with "a new dignity."[3] Warren's regional identification with the South was already well-established by this point. Despite the attention given *John Brown*, however, he was regarded primarily as a poet, and his first collection of verse, *Thirty-six Poems* (1935), was greeted as something of an event by Morton Dauwen Zabel, who reviewed it in the pages of *Poetry*.[4] Zabel commended the "exacting craftsmanship" of Warren's verse, and noted that he had obviously profited from his association with the Fugitives without being circumscribed by the biases peculiar to that "school." Despite strained elements in some of his poems, Warren was, in Zabel's view, "one of the most serious amd gifted intelligences of his generation." The anonymous reviewer for *The Nation*, however, was disturbed by what he regarded as Warren's excessive intellectualism.[5] He felt that Warren's tendency towards "ratiocination" hampered his lyrical gifts, a recurring objection many readers would voice regarding the "metaphysical" elements in Warren's poetry in subsequent years. Warren's friend and sometime collaborator, Cleanth Brooks, was of course much more in tune with what the poet was up to, and he elaborated upon the virtues of Warren's idiom at some length in *Modern Poetry and the Tradition*.[6] In Brooks's view, the very inclusiveness (and resulting inner tensions) of Warren's poetry formed the basis of its strength.

In 1939, Warren made his debut as a novelist with *Night Rider*, a book based on the "tobacco wars" in his native Kentucky. It was generally praised as an especially promising first novel, though the praise was mingled with reservations. Herbert J. Muller termed *Night Rider* "a notable achievement," and admired the way in which the author "fully *rendered* his story" rather than simply telling it. Nevertheless, Muller found Warren's women characters altogether "forgettable" and the novel's concluding chapters overly long. He also expressed misgivings about the handling of the protagonist, Perse Munn.[7] Christopher Isherwood had trouble with Munn as well, but regarded him as the only flaw in an otherwise "powerful and profound novel." Isherwood noted Warren's talent for portraying minor characters and for evoking a strong sense of time and place, even in the mind of a foreign reader like Isherwood himself.[8] In keeping with the 1930s preoccupation with the "politics" of a writer, one might have expected Phillip Rahv, who reviewed *Night Rider* for the Marxist *Partisan Review*, to have denounced the work as too reactionary. Instead, Rahv ranked it first among the seven novels he considered in his review, a list that included Steinbeck's *The Grapes of Wrath*. Unlike Muller and Isherwood, Rahv found Perse Munn "wholly convincing," and he asserted that, on the basis of this first novel, Warren had "attained at one bound a leading position among American novelists."[9] Further early testimony to the importance of *Night Rider* came from Kenneth Burke, who discussed aspects of the book in *The Philosophy of Literary Form: Studies in Symbolic Action.*[10]

Eleven Poems on the Same Theme (1942) gave ample evidence of Warren's continuing poetic development, and John Frederick Nims praised it highly in *Poetry*. Although he felt that Warren's "intellection" sometimes resulted in a "loss of immediacy," Nims nevertheless stated that the book was "distinguished" and far superior to the work of another poet-critic, R. P. Blackmur.[11] Warren's second novel, *At Heaven's Gate* (1943), likewise received attention from some notable quarters. In "The Pattern of Dry Rot in Dixie," [12] Maxwell Geismar relished Warren's portrayal of the moral bankruptcy of the New South, but failed to see any positive "alternative" offered to it. Malcolm Cowley liked the novel, but thought that Warren had tried to tell "too many stories in too many styles." Unlike Geismar, however, Cowley sensed the importance of Ashby Wyndham as a foil to the other characters.[13] Andrew Lytle wrote a penetrating, though abbreviated, analysis of *At Heaven's Gate* for *The Sewanee Review*,[14] and another of Warren's Southern friends, Caroline Gordon, reviewed the novel, calling it "one of the most profound interpretations that has yet been made of Southern life."[15]

On the basis of his work as a "new critic," the success of his first two novels, and his growing body of poetry, by the mid-1940s Warren was regarded as a literary triple-threat. Something of his stature is suggested by the fact that his volume *Selected Poems, 1923–1943* (1944) was reviewed by critics like Arthur Mizener, William Arrowsmith, Dorothy Van Ghent, Lionel Stevenson, Louise Bogan, and F. O. Matthiessen.[16] Elizabeth Drew called Warren's poems a "blend of alert and subtle intelligence, emotional precision and rigorous craftsmanship."[17] John Crowe Ransom, Warren's undergraduate mentor at Vanderbilt, also had high praise for the *Selected Poems*. He emphasized Warren's strong sense of "Original Sin" and noted his vital regional roots. Ransom preferred Warren's poetry to his fiction, which he found a bit too steeped in naturalism for his taste. However, he regretted the presence of the "naturalistic method" in *The Ballad of Billie Potts*, a poem that would remain a controversial part of the Warren canon.[18] Ransom's reservations about Warren's work, although decidedly minor, point toward an interesting fact: even those reviewers who were most enthusiastic about Warren's writing seldom failed to qualify their praise. Still, Warren had clearly arrived as a major American writer, and he began to be the subject of full-length critical essays in his own right. Irene Hendry, in "The Regional Novel: The Example of Robert Penn Warren,"[19] investigated Warren's regionalism and his interest in psychology, and she pointed out the central role that the theme of self-knowledge played in his fiction. W. P. Southard, in "The Religious Poetry of Robert Penn Warren,"[20] an eccentric and disjointed (though perceptive) essay, likewise identified the search for self as one of Warren's principal thematic concerns. Southard saw Warren's religious sense, though hardly orthodox in a denominational way, as profound and far-reaching, and he argued that Warren's vision was more Judaic than Christian. Taken together, Hendry's and Southard's essays represented an auspicious beginning for what would eventually become a full-fledged Warren "industry" among academic critics.

In 1946, Warren brought out *All the King's Men*, a novel that went on to win the Pulitzer Prize and a work that is generally regarded as his finest piece of fiction. It was widely reviewed, but not always favorably. Most reviewers noted obvious parallels between Willie Stark, the novel's focal character, and Huey Long, and residual fears of the late Long may well have colored some reviewers' estimation of Warren's book. Writing for the Jesuit periodical *America*, Harold C. Gardiner lambasted what he regarded as the unsavory aspects of the novel with a surprising degree of moral fastidiousness.[21] Leo Kirschbaum, reviewing the novel for *Commentary*, pronounced it an outright failure.[22] Elizabeth Hardwick, in *The Partisan Review*, found it "a mystifying book,"[23] and Diana Trilling argued that the novel was quite "remarkable" for its "sheer virtuosity," but marred by "ethical and political confusion."[24] (Subsequent commentary on *All the King's Men* tends to suggest that perhaps it was Miss Trilling who was confused in this instance.) On the other hand, Henry Rago gave the novel a detailed and sympathetic reading, praising its power and craftsmanship. Rago recognized the centrality of Jack Burden to the novel and the note of hope on which it concluded, and he stressed Warren's skillful use of language to control the pace of his story: ". . . One sees how Thomas Wolfe would have written if he had had flair and coherence."[25] It is also interesting to note how William Faulkner reacted, privately, to *All the King's Men* in a letter to a Harcourt, Brace editor who had sent him an advance copy for his comments: "The Cass Mastern story is a beautiful and moving piece. That was his [Warren's] novel. The rest of it I would throw away." However, Faulkner went on to admit that the rest of the novel was indeed "good solid sound writing," and he conceded that "maybe the Cass story made the rest of it look thinner than it is."[26] Given what we know of Faulkner's temperament, such a concession, coupled with his genuine enthusiasm for the Cass Mastern episode, was something akin to high praise.

In spite of its mixed reception among reviewers, *All the King's Men* was an immense popular success, and it gradually emerged as a significant critical triumph as well, though this proved in time to be a mixed blessing since Warren's subsequent novels would be inevitably, and at times unfairly, compared with it. Still, for better or worse, *All the King's Men* represented an obvious watershed in Warren's career, and, almost immediately, it generated a good deal of substantial literary criticism, although much of that criticism was initially polemical. In "Anatomist of Monsters,"[27] for example, Oscar Cargill traced Warren's modernist preoccupation with grotesques, but blamed him for not treating his Southern demagogue in *All the King's Men* with the scorn John Dos Passos and Sinclair Lewis had brought to bear on their fictional dictators. On the other hand, Robert B. Heilman set out to defend the novel from the hostility of the critics in a lengthy and insightful essay-review entitled "Melpomene as Wallflower: or, The Reading of Tragedy."[28] For Heilman, the book represented a "recovery," in modern dress, of the traditional tragic sense of the Greeks and Elizabethans.

In the midst of such critical attacks and counter-attacks, Norton R. Girault published a particularly perceptive analysis of *All the King's Men*. Girault argued that the novel was a "dramatic monologue on a grand scale"; unlike many earlier commentators, he was much less concerned with Willie Stark than with Jack Burden, the novel's narrator and, in Girault's view, its real "protagonist."[29] The obvious importance of *All the King's Men* to the Warren canon prompted two other critics to survey the author's achievement up to that point. John L. Stewart noted Warren's early Agrarian affiliation and emphasized his recurring theme of the protagonist's flight from, and eventual return to, the problem of evil, an evil Stewart saw as "primitivistic," not sociological, in conception.[30] Eric Bentley likewise noted the importance of the motif of *return* in Warren's fiction, and he stressed the central role the issue of self-knowledge played in the novels. Bentley regarded Warren's vision as sharing much with the world-view set forth by Christian orthodoxy, and while admitting that Warren's writing was occasionally "faulty," he found it forceful nonetheless. Bentley especially admired the way in which Warren held his essentially "romantic genius" in check through artistic self-discipline.[31]

In the meantime, Warren himself was engaged in the art of literary criticism, contributing a lengthy essay on Coleridge's *Rime of the Ancient Mariner* to a new edition of that poem which featured the fanciful illustrations of Alexander Calder. Harvey Breit, R. P. Blackmur, and Kenneth Burke all questioned, to varying degrees, Warren's speculative reading of Coleridge's text,[32] but whatever its value as Coleridge criticism, "A Poem of the Pure Imagination" was unquestionably valuable as an implicit gloss on Warren's own work. Warren also brought out a collection of his shorter fiction, *The Circus in the Attic* (1947). Henry Nash Smith reviewed these stories and observed that the author's imagination had largely "nourished itself upon Proustian exploration of a remembered world of childhood in Northwestern Tennessee." Smith felt, however, that shorter fiction did not, generally speaking, give Warren sufficient space to develop his themes as adequately as he might, though he regarded the title story in the collection a distinct success.[33] William Van O'Connor, on the other hand, argued that the stories, given the limitations of the genre, compared quite respectably with the level of achievement represented by Warren's novels. O'Connor suggested that *The Circus in the Attic* had certain affinities with Joyce's *Dubliners*, in spite of the obvious differences in setting between the two.[34]

Warren's *World Enough and Time*, a self-styled "romantic novel" based on the "Kentucky Tragedy" that once had appealed to the imaginations of nineteenth-century Southern writers like Poe and William Gilmore Simms, was published in 1950. Malcolm Cowley called it "the longest and richest" of Warren's novels, but he felt that the author had "given us more of a feast than we can easily digest," having presented ample material for "four" novels in a single book.[35] The talented historical-novelist A. B. Guthrie also reviewed *World Enough and Time*. Guthrie was not so much disturbed by Warren's straying from the precise facts of the infamous Beauchamp case as he was troubled by the machinery of the novel, the presentation of past events as data to be understood by a modern consciousness. This, argued Guthrie, resulted in a loss of immediacy in Warren's account of Jerry Beaumont's life and times because the reader was removed from a sense of direct involvement in the story. (Subsequent commentators would see the role of Warren's historian/narrator as thematically important.) Still, if *World Enough and Time* was not the kind of "historical" novel Guthrie preferred, it was, he wrote, a "distinguished book," one not easily forgotten.[36] Arthur Mizener published a sympathetic essay-review of *World Enough and Time*, though he, like Guthrie, thought that Warren's commentary on the events of his story was unnecessary. Mizener nevertheless pointed out the significance of the book as a "romantic novel," and he analyzed at some length Jerry Beaumont's struggle to reconcile the ideal and the real levels of human experience.[37]

As was the case following the publication of *All the King's Men*, the appearance of *World Enough and Time* prompted several critics to attempt an overall evaluation of Warren's career. Richmond C. Beatty, something of a kindred spirit, praised Warren in no uncertain terms: ". . . Excellence amounting to genius is present in almost everything he has published since his university days."[38] In "Mr. Warren's Albatross,"[39] however, W. M. Frohock, while acknowledging Warren's command of technique, was less than enthusiastic, though he did establish the extent to which Warren's work was all of a piece. Joseph Frank used Warren's essay "Pure and Impure Poetry" as a point of departure for his article "Romanticism and Reality in Robert Penn Warren."[40] Frank saw *World Enough and Time* as a pivotal work in Warren's development of a viable "religious" vision, and he correctly predicted that Warren's future writing would likely move more in the direction of symbolism. In "Robert Penn Warren: The Symbolic Journey,"[41] Sam Hynes noted the centrality of a "moral statement" to all of Warren's major works, and he systematically traced the implications of the theme of "withdrawal-and-return" that earlier commentators on Warren had noted. John M. Bradbury and Charles R. Anderson likewise wrote essays designed to view Warren's first four novels as a thematically unified achievement.[42]

Brother to Dragons, a book-length "tale in verse and voices" based on a sordid episode involving the murder of a slave by two of Thomas Jefferson's nephews, was published in 1953. Among the most interesting reviews were those of Randall Jarrell, Delmore Schwartz, and Robert Lowell, representatives of a generation of poets who had come into their own under the shadow of men like Warren and Allen Tate. The admiration these men felt for *Brother to Dragons* was very real. Jarrell called it "Warren's best book" and went on to praise Warren's "miraculous," if somewhat overt, rhetorical gifts.[43] Schwartz saw the book as a "realization of the dominant tendency of modern literature to be narrative poetry, no matter how often the works in question are entitled novels." He regarded the "violent brutality" of *Brother to Dragons* as symbolic of modern evils like the concentration camps, and he praised Warren's "mastery" of blank verse, comparing the power of the work with that of Melville.[44] Robert Lowell was somewhat more circumspect, but he was no less impressed by the grand scale of *Brother to Dragons*. Though the poem was "tactless" in certain regards, it was, said Lowell, "alive," and he placed it in the company of Eliot's *Four Quartets*, Williams's *Paterson*, and Pound's *Pisan Cantos*. Warren's work was, in Lowell's view, "slighter, lighter and less in earnest," but he did not see this as a serious objection. He compared the book quite favorably to Browning's "story poems," and he noted Warren's debt to the Elizabethans. Like Jarrell, Lowell regarded *Brother to Dragons* as Warren's "best book," the work in which he most nearly approached the "power" of Melville and Faulkner.[45] The reaction of the flamboyant critic Leslie Fiedler to *Brother to Dragons* was enthusiastic in its own way. Fiedler was struck by the archetypal "terror" and surrealistic power of Warren's vision, though he stated that the rhetorical tone of the poem, a Senecan "straining of language," threatened at times to approach the "ridiculous." Still, Fiedler defended Warren's use of "bombast and melodrama," arguing that such literary devices answered a basic human need and that Warren handled them with a "skill and courage" to be commended.[46]

Many readers, however, were less disposed to respond to Warren's "melodrama" and rhetoric in a positive way, and Wallace W. Douglas stated the "high-brow" case against him in "Drug Store Gothic: The Style of Robert Penn Warren."[47] Though Douglas admitted that Warren was "enormously sophisticated" in his use of melodramatic clichés, he blamed him for an "academicism" that coupled classic literary devices with the conventions of Hollywood films, the formulae of hard-boiled detective fiction, and a general rhetorical portentousness. The publication of the panoramic *Band of Angels* (1955), Warren's version of the intrinsically melodramatic myth of the tragic mulatto, added more fuel to the fire. Maxwell Geismar, in a caustic review entitled "Agile Pen and Dry Mind,"[48] labelled Warren a "derivative" talent, a writer steeped in "Faulknerian decadence," and he saw *Band of Angels* as the "low point" in Warren's career. The novel was, in Geismar's words, little more than "a sophisticated revival of the Southern romances of the 1900's." Leslie

Fiedler, however, found affinities between Warren and Faulkner without suggesting that Warren was merely imitative. Indeed, in Fiedler's view, Warren was a decidedly original talent, capable of reviving the old-fashioned "Historical Romance" for "sophisticated and strategic ends."[49] Carlos Baker likewise saw more than melodrama at work in *Band of Angels*. He viewed it as a philosophical "parable of slavery and freedom," and while he felt that it did not surpass *All the King's Men*, he nevertheless called it "a good book on a serious and important subject."[50] *Band of Angels* and its author found a particularly able champion in F. Cudworth Flint, who surveyed the reaction to the novel, with special words of blame for Geismar and of praise for Fiedler.[51] Flint himself found at least one aspect of *Band of Angels* disappointing, however. He regretted the absence of a character like Ashby Wyndham in *At Heaven's Gate*.

Warren had long held an interest in the question of race relations in his native South (his contribution to the Agrarian symposium *I'll Take My Stand* had dealt with the issue), and this interest took on a renewed intensity following the Supreme Court's 1954 decision in the case of "Brown vs. The Board of Education," which ordered the desegregation of the nation's public schools "with all deliberate speed." The result was *Segregation: The Inner Conflict in the South* (1956), a book that found an especially congenial reader in Ralph McGill, the liberal Southern journalist. In "A Southerner Talks with the South,"[52] McGill described *Segregation* as "a cry of anguish," a book that accurately set forth the turmoil of a divided people, both black and white. But Warren's attention to fiction and to social issues in th mid-1950s did not distract him from poetry. In 1957, he published *Promises*, a volume that earned him his second Pulitzer Prize, and a work that in many ways marked a shift from his earlier verse style.

Babette Deutsch reviewed the book and evoked the names of Yeats and D. H. Lawrence, while M. L. Rosenthal was less receptive in "Out There in the Dark."[53] Rosenthal saw Warren's regionalism as a liability, but George Garrett argued that Warren had made good use of his Southern "gifts" and that *Promises* was evidence of its author's maturity as a poet.[54] In "The Founding Fathers," [55] Leonard Casper discussed the Gabriel and Rosanna segments of the book in terms of the complementary images which provided the volume with its implicit unity.

Meanwhile, the body of scholarly and critical writing devoted to Warren and his work continued to grow. Frederick P. W. McDowell published seminal essays on *Brother to Dragons* and *World Enough and Time*, as well as on Warren's criticism.[56] Seymour L. Gross explored analogues between *The Heart of Darkness* and *All the King's Men* in "Conrad and *All the King's Men*,"[57] and Floyd C. Watkins wrote an analysis of *The Ballad of Billie Potts* entitled "Billie Potts at the Fall of Time."[58] William Wasserstrom, in "Robert Penn Warren: From Paleface to Redskin,"[59] saw Warren as the American writer who best bridged the gap between high and low culture. *All the King's Men* remained the focal point of most discussions of Warren's work, however, and 1957 saw the publication of an important collection of new articles on that book, *All the King's Men: A Symposium.*[60] Warren's own *Selected Essays* was issued in 1958, and Alfred Kazin, reviewing the book, saw Warren as more flexible than his fellow Southern critics Tate and Brooks, yet committed to the same essentially "Christian" set of values.[61]

Warren's connection with the Fugitives and Agrarians was treated at length by John M. Bradbury in *The Fugitives: A Critical Account.*[62] Bradbury devoted a chapter each to an assessment of Warren's poetry and fiction, but he recognized that an overall evaluation of Warren's work was premature. "It would appear," said Bradbury in classic understatement, "that Warren's career as a poet is not complete in the mid-fifties." In *The Fugitive Group: A Literary History,*[63] Louise Cowan also dealt with Warren's early relationship with men like Ransom and Tate, an association that determined in many ways the course his literary career had taken.

The end of the 1950s saw the publication of a new Warren novel, *The Cave* (1959), and a new book of poems, *You, Emperors, and Others* (1960). *The Cave* attracted the same widespread attention from reviewers that had become customary for a Warren novel, and as usual opinion was divided sharply between those who regarded Warren's fiction as vulgar and overly rhetorical and those who admired the author's technique and imaginative powers. Arthur Mizener, already well established as a champion of Warren's work, noted the "beautifully intricate and unobstrusive structure" of the novel, though he concluded his review with faint reservations about the explicit nature of Warren's rhetoric.[64] However, John Edward Hardy found *The Cave*, like *Band of Angels*, "discouraging."[65] Likewise, in "You, Robert Penn Warren,"[66] Hardy regarded *You, Emperors, and Others* as decidedly inferior to *Promises*, though he described himself as "a long-time enthusiast" of Warren's writing.

Apparently undaunted by negative criticism, Warren continued to work at a surprising rate, and the decade of the 1960s would be one of his most productive. 1961 marked America's observation of the centennial of the Civil War, and Warren responded to the spirit of the times with *The Legacy of the Civil War*, a book-length essay, and with his seventh novel, *Wilderness.* Warren's friend and colleague, the historian C. Vann Woodward, was struck by Warren's insight into the "inwardness" of the war, and he discussed *The Legacy* at length in his own "Reflections on a Centennial: The American Civil War."[67] *Wilderness* received the usual praise and blame, but at least one of Warren's former detractors was converted by Warren's "tale" of the Civil War. Fr. Harold C. Gardiner praised the novel as a blend of "gossamer and steel."[68] Granville Hicks commented on the obvious departure *Wilderness* represented from Warren's previous novels, but he saw it as a vital summation of what its author had learned "about the nature of man and the character of life."[69]

The Warren "industry" among academic critics continued to expand. A special Robert Penn Warren Number of *Modern Fiction Studies* included seven new essays on the range of Warren's work, including Everett Carter's "The 'Little Myth' of Robert Penn Warren," Elizabeth M. Kerr's "Polarity of Themes in *All the King's Men*," Leonard Casper's "Journey to the Interior: *The Cave*," and Joe Davis's "Robert Penn Warren and the Journey to the West."[70] In the same year, Leonard Casper brought out the first book-length study of Warren, *Robert Penn Warren: The Dark and Bloody Ground*.[71] Casper's book was structured along both biographical and critical lines and began by pointing out the short-sightedness of many of Warren's detractors. Casper noted the range of Warren's appeal, his ability to reach both "the groundling and the box seat," and he identified the informing dialectic of Warren's work as "Socratic" rather than naturalistic and "Marxist." Casper tended to treat Warren's fiction, poetry, criticism, and social commentary as part of a unified body of writing, but despite his effort to deal with the Warren corpus as a whole, he devoted over twice as much space to considering the fiction as he did to discussing the poetry, an indication of the extent to which Warren's role as a novelist was seen as preeminent at the time.

In keeping with this tendency to examine Warren's fiction in detail, Alan S. Ryan wrote an important article on the first of the novels, "Robert Penn Warren's *Night Rider*: The Nihilism of the Isolated Temperament,"[72] and A. L. Clements explored the topic "Theme and Reality in *At Heaven's Gate* and *All the King's Men*."[73] Clements argued that Warren's "tripartite theme of time, self-knowledge and responsibility" was founded upon an awareness that reality was "ironic, paradoxical, and profoundly interrelated." James H. Justus, who was to become one of the most astute of Warren critics, studied the novelist's imaginative use of an historical source in "Warren's *World Enough and Time* and Beauchamp's *Confession*,"[74] and Chester E. Eisinger devoted over 30 pages in his *Fiction of the Forties*[75] to a consideration of Warren as a "conservative" voice in American literature. Cleanth Brooks, admittedly a friend and staunch supporter, included a chapter on Warren in *The Hidden God*,[76] placing him in the company of Eliot, Yeats, Hemingway, and Faulkner. Although Brooks had some interesting things to say about *All the King's Men* and its theme of the importance of the past, he was especially drawn to Warren's poetry, seeing *Brother to Dragons* as the work in which Warren challenged "most directly some of the liberal secular ideas of our time." Brooks also brought his critical powers to bear on several of Warren's shorter poems. Warren's preoccupation with history was treated perceptively by William C. Havard in "The Burden of the Literary Mind: Some Meditations on Robert Penn Warren as Historian."[77] Havard defined Warren as "a novelist who accepts historical experience as fundamental to philosophical understanding as that understanding is unfolded through the creative imagination."

At this time, a second book-length study of Warren and his work appeared on the scene, *Robert Penn Warren* by Charles H. Bohner.[78] Avowedly an "introduction," Bohner's book was much more than that. He discussed Warren's major thematic concerns (the problem of evil, the significance of history, man's propensity for violence and his corresponding need for self-knowledge and self-fulfillment), and he coupled his chronological survey of Warren's career with critical observations that were often judicious, if seldom definitive. Bohner considered "The Return" as the best of Warren's earlier lyrics, and though he thought that *The Ballad of Billie Potts* was seriously flawed, he argued that it was essential to any understanding of Warren's work. He also questioned Malcolm Cowley's assumption that *At Heaven's Gate* was a kind of *roman à clef* and pointed out Warren's debt to Dante in that novel. In Bohner's view, "Blackberry Winter" was "one of the great stories of American literature," and *Brother to Dragons* was a "more personal" work than Warren's earlier books. Bohner discussed *Promises* as a unified whole, and he found the note of affirmation sounded in *Promises* and *You, Emperors, and Others* echoed in *The Cave* and *Wilderness*. His concluding judgment that Warren was a writer who "remains unpredictable" was a prophetic understatement, for in the same year, 1964, Warren brought out his eighth novel, *Flood*.

Flood did not receive a warm reception from reviewers. Even some of the same readers who had reacted favorably to Warren in the past voiced their disappointment, notably Granville Hicks and Carlos Baker.[79] This prompted Warren's perennial defender Arthur Mizener to write a lengthy *apologia*, "The Uncorrupted Consciousness."[80] Mizener pointed out that *Flood* was explicitly subtitled *A Romance of Our Time*, and as a "philosophical romance," it could hardly be expected to follow the rules for a straightforward realistic novel. "One may or may not share Mr. Warren's vision," he wrote, "but one ought to recognize its depth and inclusiveness." John Lewis Longley, Jr. also wrote a defense of the novel, "When All is Said and Done: Warren's *Flood*," in which he called it "a powerful and moving Divine Comedy of art, Daedalian man, holy and profane love, damnation and redemption." Longley's essay was part of his *Robert Penn Warren: A Collection of Critical Essays*,[81] a book that reprinted many of the most perceptive articles on Warren up to that time. Longley's collection also included Warren's *Paris Review* interview, conducted by Ralph Ellison and Eugene Walter, and a new piece by George P. Garrett, "The Recent Poetry of Robert Penn Warren." Garrett traced Warren's development as a poet up to *You, Emperors, and Others*, and he looked forward to more poems. He would not be disappointed.

A more ambitious survey of Warren's poetic achievement was Victor H. Strandberg's *A Colder Fire: The Poetry of Robert Penn Warren*.[82] Strandberg approached the poetry in more-or-less chronological sequence, devoting entire chapters to *Brother to Dragons*, *Promises*, and *You, Emperors, and Others*. He used Jungian psychology as a point of departure for much of his commentary, and if at times Strandberg's application of such principles seemed forced, it nevertheless gave his reading of Warren's poetic canon a unified coherence. John L. Stewart also had much to say about Warren's poetry, as well as his fiction, in *The Burden of Time: The Fugitives and Agrarians*.[83] Although Stewart was not temperamentally well-suited for reading Warren's sometimes idiosyncratic poems on their own terms, he nevertheless conceded that parts of *Promises* were "incomparably better" than most of the American poetry of the same period. Stewart noted that Warren was a very independent writer, but he still regarded him as the "most Agrarian" of the major figures in the movement. In Stewart's estimation, the Warren canon was "deeply flawed," but nonetheless imbued with "a greatness that survives all." In yet another study of the Agrarians, *Tillers of a Myth: Southern Agrarians as Social and Literary Critics*,[84] Alexander Karanikas dealt with Warren's views on matters like race and the artist's relationship to society, but he approached his subject from an ideological stance that biased many of his judgments.

Warren's continuing interest in social questions, especially the race issue, bore fruit in a remarkable experiment in journalism, *Who Speaks for the Negro?* (1965). It was widely reviewed and attracted favorable attention from C. Vann Woodward and from Joseph Epstein, who was intimately involved in the Civil Rights struggle at the time.[85] In 1966, Warren published a new edition of *Selected Poems*, and a new book of verse, *Incarnations*, appeared in 1968. Shortly thereafter, Warren brought out a book-length verse meditation entitled *Audubon* (1969). The poet Stanley Plumly commented on the latter two volumes in "Robert Penn Warren's Vision."[86] Although a sympathetic reader of Warren's poetry, Plumly was occasionally troubled by the "language" of *Incarnations*, while he praised the "pure," "rich," and "finely textured" language of *Audubon*. Monroe K. Spears was another writer who was particularly sensitive to what Warren was doing as a poet in the late 1960s. In "The Latest Poetry of Robert Penn Warren,"[87] Spears pointed out Warren's suggestive use of the second person pronoun in his verse, and he described *Incarnations* as a "plateau" in Warren's development as a poet. For Spears, some of the "most effective" poems in that volume dealt with sexuality. He discussed Warren's vision of man's "moral and physical" communion with the world of plants and animals and his essentially "anti-Marvellian" use of nature imagery, concluding with the observation that the new *Selected Poems* and *Incarnations* made clear "the magnitude of Warren's achievement."

On a more formal level, Warren's sense of man's communion with Being and Time was the subject of an important essay by Victor Strandberg, "Warren's Osmosis."[88] James Justus traced Warren's use of an "ancient mariner" figure in his fiction in "The Mariner and Robert Penn Warren,"[89] and he contributed another essay, "All the Burdens of Warren's *All the King's Men*," to Warren French's collection of criticism *The*

Forties: Fiction, Poetry, Drama.[90] During this same period, important essays on *All the King's Men* by Ladell Payne, Arthur Mizener, and Christopher G. Katope also appeared,[91] and Allen Shepherd, whose appreciation of Warren's work was guarded, published a series of articles on Warren's fiction.[92] Among the studies that linked Warren's work with the influence of Dante was L. Hugh Moore's "Robert Penn Warren and the Terror of Answered Prayer."[93]

Moore also published a book-length study of Warren's novels, *Robert Penn Warren and History: 'The Big Myth We Live,'*[94] in which he analyzed Warren's use of historical "facts" as the raw material for philosophical meaning and examined Warren's well-known assertion that history is morally neutral while man is not. Moore devoted a chapter to Warren's preoccupation with tradition and myth, and he argued that *Wilderness* was the successful culmination of Warren's efforts as an historical novelist, "a novel that perhaps comes closer to realizing Warren's artistic and philosophical intentions than any he has written." In an impressive study of the Southern historical sensibility, *The Myth of Southern History*,[95] F. Garvin Davenport also offered insight into Warren's sense of the past and of the meaning of history, and he drew perceptive parallels between Warren's vision and that of another "border-state" thinker, the Protestant theologian Reinhold Niebuhr.

Warren's ninth novel, *Meet Me in the Green Glen*, was published in 1971 and met with the usual range of critical response. While some readers may have regarded it as evidence of Warren's declining powers as a writer of fiction, others had high praise for the book. James Boatwright, reviewing it for the *New York Times Book Review*,[96] found it a "splendid" novel, "astonishing in its vividness and power." In "The Enormous Spider Web of Warren's World,"[97] John W. Aldridge coupled his discussion of the novel with a survey of Warren's major concerns as a writer, and particularly as a Southerner. Aldridge noted that *Meet Me in the Green Glen* was a much tighter piece of fiction than Warren's previous two novels and that it shared a certain kinship with his poetry, but Michael Cooke went even farther: he credited Warren with creating a new genre in *Meet Me in the Green Glen*, the "neohexameral novel."[98]

Meet Me in the Green Glen was also the subject of a chapter in Barnett Guttenberg's *Web of Being: The Novels of Robert Penn Warren*.[99] Guttenberg viewed the novel as Warren's "most explicit" treatment of the problem of "true being" and his most detailed investigation into the nature of love. *Web of Being* was itself an ambitious book, and its author read the Warren novels as a running "indictment of the modern world" with its characteristic "alienation of the self from itself." Guttenberg examined Warren's fiction in the light of existentialist thought, particularly in terms of Heidegger's notion of "authenticity" and Martin Buber's description of the "I" and "Thou" relationship. Though necessarily limited by his thesis, Guttenberg's approach to the novels was consistent and revealing. However, like earlier critics who had attempted to survey Warren's career as a novelist in its entirety, Guttenberg was a bit premature. In 1977, Warren published a tenth novel, *A Place to Come To*, thus rendering all previous efforts at a comprehensive assessment of his fictional achievement inconclusive.[100]

Although the decade of the 1970s saw the appearance of two new Warren novels, it was Warren's verse that left the greatest impression on his critics. In 1974, he published *Or Else—Poem/Poems, 1968-1974*—as its title suggests, a further experiment in presenting a collection of shorter poems as a unified work—and *Selected Poems, 1923-1975* appeared in 1976. Hilton Kramer greeted the publication of the new *Selected Poems* with a laudatory review in the *New York Times Book Review*,[101] writing that it confirmed Warren's place "among the finest poets of our time" as "one who speaks to us with a moral intensity few others have even attempted." Stanley Plumly saw the volume as a remarkable demonstration of Warren's "profound capacity for growth,"[102] and Willard Spiegelman noted the thematic consistency of Warren's poetic canon.[103] The range of Warren's achievement in verse was the subject of Victor H. Strandberg's *The Poetic Vision of Robert Penn Warren*,[104] a book that superseded his earlier study of the poetry and an important addition to the body of commentary on Warren's work. Strandberg surveyed the history of critical reaction to Warren's verse, and he examined Warren's "poems of passage" and the abiding sense of "mysticism" at the core of his vision. Although Strandberg endeavored to make his book as inclusive and up-to-date as possible (even to the point of citing unpublished poems), Warren was once again ahead of his critics. In 1978, he published *Now and Then*, a new book of poetry that made something of a "convert" of Harold Bloom and earned Warren a third Pulitzer Prize.[105] In certain respects, Warren's literary career had come full circle by the late 1970s. Although he maintained his currency as a practicing novelist and essayist—his Jefferson Lectures appeared in 1975 as *Democracy and Poetry*—Warren was once more preeminently a poet. Robert Lowell, who had literally gone to school to Warren during the halcyon days at Louisiana State University, hailed him as "an old master still engaging the dazzled disciple."[106]

As the preceding pages testify, much has been written about Warren and his work, but much remains to be done. Recent essays on *All the King's Men* by Richard Law, Luther Stearns Mansfield, and Mark Royden Winchell demonstrate that the novel still lends itself to close critical scrutiny and suggest that it may continue to be the most frequently discussed of Warren's works.[107] *Brother to Dragons*, however, has also attracted its share of serious critical attention in recent years,[108] and its central importance to the canon was underscored when Warren brought out a carefully reworked "new version" of his "tale in verse and voices" in 1979. It is likely that future commentators will continue to find it a fruitful source for critical inquiry. *Meet Me in the Green Glen* and *A Place to*

Come To have yet to receive adequate attention, and the earlier novels likewise deserve further analysis of the kind Richard Law has brought to bear on *Night Rider* and James Justus has demonstrated in his essay on *At Heaven's Gate*.[109] The structuralist approach that Simone Vauthier has applied to *All the King's Men* opens up a new range of critical possibilities for examining Warren's work,[110] and critics of like persuasion will find the Warren canon a rich field for similar explorations. Students of the South and its culture will no doubt continue to reexamine Warren's regional consciousness in the manner of Louis D. Rubin, Jr. and Louis P. Simpson,[111] but there is even more to be done in the area of hard scholarship. A dependable biography is sorely needed, and detailed assessments of Warren's contributions as an editor, teacher, and dramatist are long overdue. Warren's correspondence, when and if it is edited, will be an important boon to our understanding of his role in the history of American letters. Meanwhile, his place of eminence in our literary history seems secure. Few American writers have enjoyed so lengthy and consistently productive a career, and perhaps none has achieved so much in so many different ways.

William Bedford Clark

Notes

1. (Boston: G. K. Hall, 1977). Nakadate's annotated bibliography is an invaluable source for the serious student of Warren's work, and the present editor owes him a sincere debt of gratitude for making the history of critical response to Warren so readily accessible.

2. *The Bookman* (March, 1930), p. 114.

3. See Craven's review in the *New York Herald Tribune Books*, 12 Jan. 1930, p. 17. Nevins's review, entitled "Martyr and Fanatic," appeared in *The New Republic*, 19 March 1930, pp. 134–35.

4. "Problems of Knowledge," *Poetry*, April 1936, pp. 37–41.

5. *The Nation*, 25 March 1936, p. 391.

6. (Chapel Hill: Univ. of North Carolina Press, 1939).

7. "Violence upon the Roads," *Kenyon Review*, 1 (1939), 323–24.

8. "Tragic Liberal," *New Republic*, 31 May 1939, p. 108.

9. "A Variety of Fiction," *Partisan Review*, 6, No. 3 (1939), 106–13.

10. (Baton Rouge: Louisiana State Univ. Press, 1941).

11. "Two Intellectual Poets," *Poetry*, Dec. 1942, pp. 505–08.

12. *New York Times Book Review*, 22 Aug. 1943, p. 4.

13. "Luke Lea's Empire," *New Republic*, 23 Aug. 1943, p. 258.

14. *Sewanee Review*, 51 (1943), 599–602.

15. "Passionate Southern Eloquence," *New York Herald Tribune Weekly Book Review*, 22 Aug. 1943, p. 5.

16. For annotated citations, see Nakadate, pp. 24–30.

17. *New York Herald Tribune Weekly Book Review*, 25 June 1944, p. 11.

18. "The Inklings of 'Original Sin,' " *Saturday Review*, 20 May 1944, pp. 10–11.

19. *Sewanee Review*, 53 (1945), 84–102.

20. *Kenyon Review*, 7 (1945), 653–76.

21. "Why Put Him Together?" *America*, 25 Aug. 1946, p. 503.

22. "Leading Pulitzer Contender," *Commentary*, Oct. 1946, pp. 392–94.

23. "Fiction Chronicle," *Partisan Review*, 13 (1946), 583–84.

24. *The Nation*, 24 Aug. 1946, p. 220.

25. "Books of the Week," *Commonweal*, 4 Oct. 1946, pp. 599–600.

26. *Selected Letters of William Faulkner*, ed. Joseph Blotner (New York: Vintage, 1978), p. 239.

27. *College English*, 9 (1947), 1–8.

28. *Sewanee Review*, 55 (1947), 154–66.

29. "The Narrator's Mind as Symbol," *Accent*, 7 (1947), 220–34.

30. "The Achievement of Robert Penn Warren," *South Atlantic Quarterly*, 47 (1948), 562–79.

31. "The Meaning of Robert Penn Warren's Novels," *Kenyon Review*, 10 (1948), 407–24.

32. For annotated citations, see Nakadate, pp. 40–41.

33. "Proustian Exploration," *Saturday Review*, 31 Jan. 1948, pp. 14–15.

34. *Western Review*, 12 (1948), 251–53.

35. *New York Herald Tribune Book Review*, 25 June 1950, p. 1.

36. "Virtue Plundered in Kentucky," *Saturday Review*, 24 June 1950, pp. 11–12.

37. "Amphibium in Old Kentucky," *Kenyon Review*, 12 (1950), 697–701.

38. "The Poetry and Novels of Robert Penn Warren," *Vanderbilt Studies in the Humanities*, 1 (1951), 142–60.

39. *Southwest Review*, 36 (1951), 48–59.

40. *Hudson Review*, 4 (1951), 248–58.

41. *University of Kansas City Review*, 17 (1951), 279–85.

42. Bradbury, "Robert Penn Warren's Novels: The Symbolic and Textural Patterns," *Accent*, 13 (1953), 77–89; Anderson, "Violence and Order in the Novels of Robert Penn Warren," *Hopkins Review*, 6 (1953), 88–105.

43. "On the Underside of the Stone," *New York Times Book Review*, 23 Aug. 1953, p. 6.

44. "The Dragon of Guilt," *New Republic*, 14 Sept. 1953, pp. 17–18.

45. "Prose Genius in Verse," *Kenyon Review*, 15 (1953), 619–25.

46. "Seneca in the Meat-House," *Partisan Review*, 21 (1954), 208–12.

47. *College English*, 15 (1954), 265–72.

48. *The Nation*, 1 Oct. 1955, p. 287.

49. "Romance in the Operatic Manner," *New Republic*, 26 Sept. 1955, pp. 28–30.

50. "Souls Lost in a Blind Lobby," *Saturday Review*, 20 Aug. 1955, pp. 9–10.

51. "Mr. Warren and the Reviewers," *Sewanee Review*, 64 (1956), 632–45.

52. *New York Times Book Review*, 2 Sept. 1956, pp. 1, 13.

53. Deutsch, *New York Herald Tribune Book Review*, 25 Aug. 1957, p. 4; Rosenthal, *The Nation*, 18 Jan. 1958, pp. 56–57.

54. *Georgia Review*, 12 (1958), 106–08.

55. *Western Review*, 22 (1957), 69–71.

56. "Psychology and Theme in *Brother to Dragons*," *PMLA*, 70 (1955), 565–86; "The Romantic Tragedy of Self in *World Enough and Time*," *Critique*, 1, No. 2 (1957), 34–48; "Robert Penn Warren's Criticism," *Accent*, 15 (1955), 173–96.

57. *Twentieth Century Literature*, 3 (1957), 27–32.

58. *Mississippi Quarterly*, 11 (1958), 19–28.

59. *Prairie Schooner*, 31 (1957), 323–33.

60. (Pittsburgh: Carnegie Institute of Technology).

61. *Partisan Review*, 26 (1959), 312–16.

62. (Chapel Hill: Univ. of North Carolina Press, 1958).

63. (Baton Rouge: Louisiana State Univ. Press, 1959).

64. "In the Darkness They Found Light," *New York Times Book Review*, 23 Aug. 1959, p. 1.

65. "Robert Penn Warren's Double-Hero," *Virginia Quarterly Review*, 36 (1960), 583–97.

66. *Poetry*, Oct. 1961, pp. 56–62.

67. *Yale Review*, 50 (1961), 481–90.

68. *America*, 11 Nov. 1961, p. 206.

69. "Crusader in a World of Chance," *Saturday Review*, 18 Nov. 1961, p. 19.

70. *Modern Fiction Studies*, 6 (1960), 1–88.

71. (Seattle: Univ. of Washington Press, 1960).

72. *Modern Fiction Studies*, 7 (1961), 338–46.

73. *Criticism*, 5 (1963), 27–44.

74. *American Literature*, 33 (1962), 500–11.

75. (Chicago: Univ. of Chicago Press, 1963).

76. (New Haven: Yale Univ. Press, 1963).

77. *South Atlantic Quarterly*, 62 (1963), 516–31.

78. (New York: Twayne, 1964).

79. Hicks, "Fiddlers Before the Flood," *Saturday Review*, 25 April 1964, pp. 29–30; Baker, rev. of *Flood*, *New York Herald Tribune Book Week*, 26 April 1964, pp. 6, 10.

80. *Sewanee Review*, 72 (1964), 690–98.

81. (New York: New York Univ. Press, 1965).

82. (Lexington: Univ. of Kentucky Press, 1965).

83. (Princeton: Princeton Univ. Press, 1965).

84. (Madison: Univ. of Wisconsin Press, 1966).

85. Woodward, "Warren's Challenge to Race Dogma," *New Republic*, 22 May 1965, pp. 21–23; Epstein, "Down the Line," *Commentary*, Oct. 1965, pp. 101–05.

86. *Southern Review*, NS6 (1970), 1201–08.

87. *Sewanee Review*, 78 (1970), 348–57.

88. *Criticism*, 10 (1968), 23–40.

89. *Texas Studies in Literature and Language*, 7 (1966), 117–28.

90. (Deland, Florida: Everett/Edward, 1970).

91. Payne, "Willie Stark and Huey Long: Atmosphere, Myth or Suggestion?" *American Quarterly*, 20 (1968), 580–95; Mizener, "Robert Penn Warren: *All the King's Men*," *Southern Review*, NS3 (1967), 874–94; Katope, "Robert Penn Warren's *All the King's Men*: A Novel of Pure Imagination," *Texas Studies in Literature and Language*, 12 (1970), 493–510.

92. See for example "Robert Penn Warren as a Philosophical Novelist," *Western Humanities Review*, 24 (1970), 157–68, and "The Poles of Fiction: Warren's *At Heaven's Gate*," *Texas Studies in Literature and Language*, 12 (1971), 709–18.

93. *Mississippi Quarterly*, 21 (1967), 29–36.

94. (The Hague and Paris: Mouton, 1970).

95. (Nashville: Vanderbilt Univ. Press, 1970).

96. 7 Nov. 1971, p. 6.

97. *Saturday Review*, 9 Oct. 1971, pp. 31–32, 35–37.

98. *Yale Review*, 61 (1971), 599–609.

99. (Nashville: Vanderbilt Univ. Press, 1975).

100. Here, as elsewhere with Warren's work, the comments of reviewers offer an interesting point of departure for more systematic criticism. See David M. Wyatt, "Robert Penn Warren: The Critic as Artist," *Virginia Quarterly Review*, 53 (1977), 475–87, and Richard Howard, "A Technician's Romance," *Saturday Review*, 19 March 1977, pp. 30, 34.

101. 9 Jan. 1977, pp. 1, 26.

102. "Warren Selected: An American Poetry, 1923–75," *Ohio Review*, 18, No. 1 (1977), 37–48.

103. "The Poetic Achievement of Robert Penn Warren," *Southwest Review*, 62 (Autumn 1977), vi–vii, 411–15.

104. (Lexington: Univ. of Kentucky Press, 1977).

105. See Bloom's review of *Now and Then*, *New Republic*, 30 Sept. 1978, pp. 34–35.

106. See Lowell's poem "Louisiana State University in 1940," in *Day by Day* (New York: Farrar, Straus and Giroux, 1977), pp. 25–26. Dave Smith, a poet of the present generation, paid tribute to Warren in an essay-review entitled "He Prayeth Best Who Loveth Best," *American Poetry Review*, 8, No. 1 (1979), 4–8.

107. Law, " 'The Case of the Upright Judge': The Nature of Truth in *All the King's Men*," *Studies in American Fiction*, 6 (1978), 1–19; Mansfield, "History and Historical Process in *All the King's Men*," *Centennial Review*, 22 (1978), 214–30; Winchell, "O Happy Sin!: Felix Culpa in *All the King's Men*," *Mississippi Quarterly*, 31 (1978), 570–85.

108. Dennis Dooley,"The Persona RPW in Warren's *Brother to Dragons*," *Mississippi Quarterly*, 25 (1971), 19–30; Neil Nakadate, "Voices of Community: The Function of Colloquy in Robert Penn Warren's *Brother to Dragons*," *Tennessee Studies in Literature*, 21 (1976), 114–24; Richard G. Law, "*Brother to Dragons*: The Fact of Violence vs. the Possibility of Love," *American Literature*, 49 (1978), 560–79.

109. Law, "Warren's *Night Rider* and the Issue of Naturalism: The 'Nightmare' of Our Age," *Southern Literary Journal*, 8, No. 2 (1976), 41–61; Justus, "On the Politics of the Self-Created: *At Heaven's Gate*," *Sewanee Review*, 82 (1974), 284–99.

110. "The Case of the Vanishing Narratee: An Inquiry into *All the King's Men*," *Southern Literary Journal*, 6, No. 2 (1974), 42–69.

111. Rubin and Simpson are two of the most perceptive students of the Southern literary mind writing at the present time. See Rubin's chapter on Warren in *The Wary Fugitives: Four Poets and the South* (Baton Rouge: Louisiana State Univ. Press, 1978), pp. 327–61, and Simpson's brief, but suggestive, discussion of Warren's fiction in *The Harvard Guide to Contemporary American Writing*, ed. Daniel Hoffman (Cambridge: Harvard Univ. Press, 1979), pp. 167–73.

REVIEWS

"Martyr and Fanatic"
[*John Brown: The Making of a Martyr*]

Allan Nevins*

To admirers of the Abolitionists, John Brown will always be a hero, for he carried Abolitionist principles to their furthest and most dramatic extreme. It is no accident that the most thorough and scholarly biography of the man is by a grandson of William Lloyd Garrison. The Great New Englanders filled with the Abolitionist spirit—Emerson, Whittier, Wendell Phillips—lost no time in apotheosizing Brown as their martyr; and under the spell of their eloquent words, historians long attributed to him more influence on events than he exerted. But today the Abolition movement is viewed with increasing coldness. It was to some extent useful in the thirties and early forties in helping to awaken an active moral repugnance to slavery and bring the question to the front. After that, much of it was a pernicious hysteria which hindered instead of helped the real movement against slavery—the free-soil movement led by Lincoln, Seward and Chase, which aimed at the immediate restriction and ultimate destruction of the slave system. It is entitled to very little real praise for freeing the Negro; it is entitled to less than none for the maintenance of the Union, which many Abolitionists would have rent asunder. As Abolitionist credit has fallen till, in such a book as Beveridge's "Lincoln," it approaches zero, the credit of John Brown has fallen also. His real historical importance was small.

Nevertheless, he remains an intensely interesting figure. Mr. Warren's capable volume drives a path almost midway between the hostile treatment by Mr. H. P. Wilson and the laudatory treatment by Mr. O. G. Villard. Mr. Wilson pictured John Brown as a crafty, unscrupulous soldier of fortune, an adventurer who gambled with the money and lives of other men merely to gain riches and fame, and did not halt at the meanest crimes. In Mr. Villard's far abler and more careful book, he is pictured as an enthusiast whose motives were wholly unselfish, who aimed always at the freeing of a race; who committed murder at Pot-

* Reprinted with permission from *The New Republic*, 19 March 1930, pp. 134–35. Copyright © 1930, The New Republic, Inc.

21

tawatomie and other crimes elsewhere, but who atoned at Harper's Ferry
by the nobility of his philosophy and by his sublime readiness to give his
life for his principles. Mr. Wilson oversimplified John Brown's character
and motives; Mr. Villard seemed to many to take too much the position of
Brown's pleader. To weigh the evidence on both sides and attempt to
render impartial judgment was a useful enterprise.

Mr. Warren is severe on John Brown. He is much harsher than Mr.
Villard, harsher even than Rhodes, in dealing with Brown's misdeeds—his embezzlements or at least reckless carelessness with his
employer's money, his chicanery, his cruelty, his bloody violence. Yet his
final verdict is not very different from that of such cool writers as Rhodes.
The crux of the matter is the question of Brown's sincerity. Many of the
acts which he committed were atrociously wrong—there is no doubt of
that. The chief aim he kept in view, the freeing of the slaves, had moral
grandeur—there is equally little doubt of that. Was he sincere in holding
that his noble end justified his ignoble means? Mr. Warren answers this
by saying that he was no hypocrite, but a man of enormous and criminal
egotism. He was convinced that he was an instrument of Providence, that
his will was God's will, that God had said to him, as to Joshua and Gid-
eon, "Go forth and slay." He stole money, but not for himself, for he lived
like an anchorite—it was for his cause. He killed innocent men, again for
his cause. Mr. Warren, almost in spite of himself, admits that he always
had an inner conviction that he was right. It did not fail him when he sat
in his Virginia cell reading for the last time his cheap Bible.

> From the time when inflamed eyes stopped his ambition
> of becoming a minister—the usual career of the more in-
> telligent and ambitious frontier youth—until the time when he
> rode a murdered man's horse out of the Pottawatomie valley,
> every effort had ended in some unpredictable failure. Superb
> energy, honesty, and fraud, chicanery, charity, thrift, en-
> durance, cruelty, conviction, murder and prayer—they all
> had failed, only to leave him surer than before that he was
> right and that his plans were "right in themselves."

In short, he was a fanatic. Mr. Warren is no doubt right in saying that he
was not insane, and was as responsible for his deeds as are the general run
of those we call criminals. But what other men regarded as crimes he
regarded as the execution of a divine mandate.

Apart from this reading of Brown's character, and its brisk and
dependably accurate recital of Brown's career, Mr. Warren's book is
notable for its interpretation of the last act in the grim fanatic's life. His
raid at Harper's Ferry is interpreted by Mr. Villard as primarily a foray
for the liberation of slaves, without intention of causing a general slave in-
surrection. Mr. Warren believes that it was a good deal more than a
foray. He concludes that Brown hoped and expected not merely to bring

about a servile revolt, but to hasten the imminent conflict between North and South. His raid was to be the spark which should cause the whole border to blaze up as Kansas had blazed in 1856, and should lead to a general war. Necessarily he could not make any elaborate plans. But his scheme was not to take a few slaves and retreat to the Maryland hills; it was to seize the arsenal, arm hundreds of Negroes, march southward organizing the blacks, and wait for the aroused North to follow him. This theory is hard to reconcile with some of Brown's own statements, but Mr. Warren believes he made these statements in order to lead on his men till they could not turn back. If so, this was an insanely impracticable scheme, but also one of striking grandiosity. Mr. Warren's theory gives to the last great coup of John Brown a breadth and daring that lift it to a new dignity.

"Problems of Knowledge"
[*Thirty-six Poems*]

Morton Dauwen Zabel*

The scruples of Mr. Warren's talent are first announced in the fact that his first book of thirty-six poems is the work of ten years. They are next apparent in the exacting craftsmanship he has spent on all its entries; nothing unconsidered or unfelt has been given a place here, and nothing untested by severely examined personal values and decisions. But the most compelling sign of his worth as a poet appears in the independence he has shown in growing beyond his studious youthful efforts at style and the formidable influences that supervised them. To belong to the Fugitives was one of the best fortunes that could befall, in America at that moment, any young poet interested in craft and its uses. But schools of style offer as much risk as benefit; a premature forcing of the intellectual manner, while essentially more profitable than the flaccid impressionism encouraged among most beginners, can breed as deluding and pretentious an ambition in a poet as the visionary arrogance or lyric softness which it aims to correct. It has been the misfortune of several Fugitive followers (perhaps all but the two who have survived as remarkable poets) that in becoming disciples they did not resist being stultified by their models, their ambitious critical and historical ideas, and particularly by the mannerisms of literary irony and erudition which—whether studied in Eliot, Yeats, Ransom, or the classic models of these men—seldom admit of safe transmission to other hands.

*Reprinted from *Poetry*, April 1936, pp. 37–41, by permission of the editor and Mrs. Alta Fisch Sutton. Copyright © 1936, The Modern Poetry Association.

Mr. Warren has survived his privileges without concealing them. There is no mistaking the echo of his affiliations in earlier poems:

> . . . A certain weight of cunning flesh devised
> So hunger is bred in the bitter bone
> To cleave about this precious skeleton
> Held mortmain of her womb and merchandised
>
> Unto the dark: a subtile engine, propped
> In the sutured head beneath the coronal seam
> Whose illegal prodigality of dream
> In shaking the escheat heart is quick estopped.

Here it is not difficult to trace almost every phrase to its use in other writers, or to recognize in the calculated complexity of tone and meaning a now very obvious way of refracting the poem's pathos through the elaborate precosity of the writer. The labor of developing an idea has not been subdued to the idea's own intense sincerity; the best proof that the latter exists is shown by the fact that this poem (*Letter of a Mother*), in spite of its transparent mechanics, still compels sympathy, and remains one of the most poignant in the book. Some of the more recent poems show similar passages:

> Slow film of rain creeps down the loam again
> Where the blind and nameless bones recline.
>
> they are conceded to the earth's absolute chemistry
> they burn like faggots in—of damp and dark—
>   the monstrous bulging flame—
> calcium phosphate lust speculation faith treachery
> it walked upright with habitation and a name
> *tell me its name.*

One can immediately see here (in *The Return*) how firm lyric feeling has been afflicted with another, but artificial, kind of firmness, and with what strenuous effort the phrases are made to encompass more than their context allows. They never succeed in concealing the strain of forcing a poetic theme with too many stimulants. The method is a valuable one; dryness of irony and omniscience is combined with humor or compassion in an extremely effective way, but it is a way that easily falls into its own kind of banality. The feeling of the poem is enervated to the point of exhaustion; a serious method has declined into personal convention and victimized its author. An extreme example of such miscalculation comes in *Toward Rationality* which, in spite of three fine images and an excellent vein of wit, becomes unbearably elephantine in its brainy and overplotted ingenuity.

It is, however, in recognizing two sources of poetic sincerity that Mr. Warren shows unmistakable strength; they are present in different degrees in the above poems, but are not fully employed until poems which I take to be some of his most recent work—*The Last Metaphor, Pacific Gazer, Calendar, Garden Waters,* and an exquisite reflective lyric, *The Garden.* In another form they appear in poems of more realistic content—the sequence of descriptive and lyric episodes called *Kentucky Mountain Farm, Letter from a Coward to a Hero,* and two sardonic tales drawn from the more sinister aspects of Southern life—*Genealogy* and *Pondy Woods.* The first of these sources is a really critical sense of a local ideal—the culture of the South stated neither as sentiment nor as argument, but in terms of a tragic vision that defines a faith without dictating it and presents it with so intense a feeling that local images and symbols become the natural medium of the sense. The best evidence of this lies in Mr. Warren's detail and metaphor; they manage to convey their shock and brilliance without becoming exotic or forced, and they build up a strong and authentic atmospheric pathos in the volume. Even in those poems most obviously plotted in thought, visual contact and penetration supply a sharpness of detail so invariably tempered by the right sense of situation and tone that extravagance and mere decorative cleverness are avoided. This might be illustrated by isolated images: "the faithless yellow flame" of wheat, "the sunshine of consent's good season," and "the blue tense altitudes" of the buzzards over Pondy Woods; but obviously a fuller presentation of context than is possible here would be necessary to make their quality apparent.

The second source is Mr. Warren's emphasis on his own conflict of spirit, writing it down without making it vulgarly personal, but insisting that it rescue him from the elaborate subterfuges and disguises of his literary education. Many of these poems are on directly personal themes; that alone would not give them personal authority, and in fact several are too obviously intimate or hortatory to be convincing. But the persistence in them of an increasing lyric clarity, and of a tonal richness that includes serious mental habits without overwriting them, is evidence of how soundly instructed the personal discipline has been. The poems in free-verse best describe the course of this discipline, but its real fruits appear in *The Last Metaphor, To a Face in the Crowd, The Garden,* and two fine examples of the right kind of austere craftsmanship, *Pacific Gazer* and *Calendar.* These are the work of a poet who honors his school by requiring no comparison with it, and of a writer who more and more shows himself, in both his verse and prose, one of the most serious and gifted intelligences of his generation.

"Tragic Liberal" [*Night Rider*]

Christopher Isherwood*

The action of this novel passes in Kentucky, around the beginning of the present century. It opens with the return of Perse Munn, a young lawyer, to his native town. Perse, seen on the threshold of his career, seems to have everything in his favor. He is happily married to May, a charming and devoted wife. He wins his first case, a murder charge against a young farmer named Bunk Trevelyan, by a flash of brilliant intuition. Bunk's life is saved, and Perse Munn's reputation securely established.

But already the future is piling up its storm-clouds. For Munn has become one of the leaders of the Association of Growers of Dark Fired Tobacco, a local coöperative organization which has recently been founded to fight the prices and demands of the foreign buyers. From the first, the Association has a hard struggle. The farmers are obstinate or timid; many of them refuse to join. The coöperative fails to impose its terms; the buyers buy elsewhere; funds run low. Step by step, Munn and his friends are driven towards acts of violence. Step by step, they find themselves compelled to establish an illegal, terroristic organization. At first, the Night Riders confine themselves to small punitive raids on non-coöperating farmers—the victims are compelled to destroy their own crops. But inevitably, violence breeds greater violence; murder is committed; petty sabotage is followed by big armed raids on the enemy warehouses. Munn's own life begins to follow the pattern of his public acts. His wife leaves him; he is drawn into a passionate, unhappy love affair with the daughter of his principal associate, Mr. Christian. The story ends, as it had to end, with Munn's death: he is shot while trying to escape from the troops whom Big Business has called in to protect its threatened interests.

Both in design and execution, this is a large-scale novel: it must be judged by large-scale standards. The publishers, and Mr. Allen Tate, are certainly of my opinion—they even go so far as to invoke Tolstoy's name on the cover. Very well, let us seriously ask ourselves the question: Is this a masterpiece? I believe not. Why? Because, I feel, Mr. Warren has failed in his presentation of the chief character. Perse Munn is conceived as a figure of tremendous significance: he is the noble liberal gone astray in a world of power politics. Maneuvered by the logic of events from his democratic platform, he tries to use Force, and Force uses him. Such a man must be very vividly and subtly described by his creator—from the inside as well as from the out. He must be an individual, not a mere type. Perse Munn, as I see him, is the weakest character in this book.

*Reprinted with permission from *The New Republic*, 31 May 1939, p. 108. Copyright © 1939, The New Republic, Inc.

In fact, he embodies the only weakness in a very brilliant, powerful and profound novel. All the minor characters in "Night Rider" are well done. Mr. Christian fairly bulges out of the page; Bunk Trevelyan is an original and convincing Judas. And Mr. Warren has, to a high degree, the conspicuous American literary virtue of being able to make people talk. Not only the big dramatic scenes—the trial, the murder of Trevelyan, the burning of the warehouse—but equally the little moments of everyday life are vividly evoked. From the very first sentences you begin to hear and see and smell the Kentucky of forty years ago. Mr. Warren reconstructs an entire world. That he has reconstructed it for myself, a foreigner, without previous knowledge of the social background, is a measure of his great success. Indeed, so important is the theme of this novel and so considerable its achievement, that I almost wish he would rewrite it—as George Moore used to—ten years from now, when the powers already apparent in this first attempt have come to full maturity.

"Luke Lea's Empire"
[At Heaven's Gate]

Malcolm Cowley*

This is one of the very few serious American novels I have read since we entered the war. That, I suppose, is pretty faint praise at a time when most novels have been careless or trivial or written with one eye on the headlines, but there is more to be said about "At Heaven's Gate." It is full of interesting characters, some of them new to contemporary fiction. Its background, which is a Southern city at the end of boom years, is freshly observed and convincing. Its author is Robert Penn Warren, a talented poet and story writer who has worked for years over this second novel, with the result that it is full of surprises for the reader; some of the passages are better written than anything else in recent fiction. Because of all these virtues, the book has to be judged by extremely strict standards. Here is an injustice that reviewers ought to explain and serious writers have to accept. Fourth and fifth-rate books get praised because they try to do so little that they could hardly fail. The almost first-rate books get severely blamed for trying to do much, even if they partially succeed.

I should say, for example, that Warren succeeds with his heroine. Sue Murdock is not one of his new characters; essentially she is the lost girl of the 1920's, the girl in the green hat, the heroine of "The Sun Also Rises" and "Butterfield 8." Warren's portrait of her is less moving than Hemingway's and less accurate in details than John O'Hara's, but he does one

*Reprinted with permission from The New Republic, 23 Aug. 1943, p. 258. Copyright © 1943, The New Republic, Inc.

thing the others fail to do—that is, he gives a satisfactory explanation of how she came to be lost and what she has tried to escape. She is rebelling against her father; that is why she plunges into a series of love affairs and why two of them end abruptly when she finds that her lover is taking her father's place. There is Freud in the novel; there is also a good deal of high finance. Sue's father, Bogan Murdock, makes you think of Luke Lea, the banker and promoter whose empire used to extend over the Middle South. Her first lover, Jerry Calhoun, is a farm boy who becomes a football star and then a vice-president of a big Murdock bank. Her second lover is a self-centered esthete with no interest in financial affairs, but the third is a labor leader directing a strike against one of the Murdock industries. The most sympathetic portrait in the book is that of Ashby Wyndham, a mountain evangelist who, simply by being a sincere Christian, puts a sudden end to Murdock's reign.

Each of these portraits is convincing and some of them are brilliant, considered by themselves. The trouble with the novel as a whole is that it tells too many stories in too many styles. Here is a series of quotations that might easily have come from five different novels:

> 1. The river . . . came gleamingly out of the haze of distance to the south, and the tributaries converged toward it across the land. He knew the names, Big Duck, Little Duck, Holly Mill Creek, Still Deer, Pine-Away, and had heard, years back, or so it seemed, the ripple of their waters at dams, at fords, over stones, had felt it upon his wrists or about his ankles, and had called to friends across their easy widths.

> 2. Dust, it lays on the floor, under the goin forth and the comin in, and ain't nothin, and gits stirred up in the trompin, but a sunbeam come in the dark room and in that light it will dance and shine for heart joy.

> 3. "On this shoal water of morality, criticism, even when flying the Jolly Roger of estheticism, has foundered whenever it has undertaken to investigate the tragic theme."

> 4. He reckoned if you'd been around that baby much and had a dose of the hogwash he put out under the label of soothing syrup, it'd take you more than a pissing-spell to come to grips with reality and face the challenge and roll up your sleeves and spit in the palms of your hand.

> 5. . . . and they put me to bed at dark every night and it was the man with the eyes always wet and sad behind the glasses and he said, my dear, it won't hurt, it won't hurt a bit, it—

The first of these quotations is supposed to represent Jerry Calhoun's stream of consciousness, but actually it is Warren writing a poem, and a good one, about the land he loves. The second is part of Ashby

Wyndham's long story, the best narrative writing in the novel. The third is Slim Sarrett, the esthete, composing an essay that might have been printed in The Southern Review. The fourth is a meditation by Sweetie Sweetwater, the labor leader, and seems to me completely false; the spit on his palms smells dry and bookish. The fifth is Sue Murdock in a drunken stupor, just before her death; she has nightmares like those of Faulkner's novels. In presenting each of these five people, Warren asks us to look at him through a different pair of glasses. The book lacks a unifying medium; it might have been written by five authors in collaboration, but also in violent disagreement.

The one element that holds it together is not a character or an idea or a point of view. It is a city, one that anybody can recognize as Nashville, Tennessee, with a few traits borrowed from Memphis—let us simply call it a state capital in the Middle South during a period of economic revolution. Warren lets us see all sides of it. Here is the social crowd; here are the politicians; here are the dispossessed farmers and the underpaid workmen; here is the university, which might be Vanderbilt, and the intellectuals who might have belonged to the Fugitive group; and here, dominating the others, is the dishonest but far-sighted promoter working to transform the whole region—to carry it from an area of agriculture and small handicrafts straight into the age of finance capitalism. Almost everybody suffers morally from the change; nobody feels at home; but even after Luke Lea's empire is destroyed, the city cannot go back to its old ways. That is the real subject of Warren's book, though I doubt that he ever regarded himself as a social historian.

[At Heaven's Gate]

Andrew Lytle*

The characters in this book never see over the high walls of heaven. All are turned away from the gate. The unknowable will of God pursues great and small with the mysterious, almost vindictive, vehemence we are accustomed to attach to the pagan Fates. The locality for the action is of great importance. It is not background but a society in which those who determine the idea and the image no longer entertain belief. It may still be called a Christian society, but the spirit is gone out of it, except in that common reservoir of any society's strength, the peasantry, or what goes for a peasantry in this country. Here there is belief; but the belief and the pursuit of salvation are ignorant and misguided, as must be the case when those whose function it is to direct and preserve the complex forms of

*Reprinted with permission from the Sewanee Review, 51 (1943), 599–602. Copyright © 1943, The University of the South.

tradition are perverted. The rich and the powerful, deprived of form and spiritual purpose but possessing the energy of their natures, become monsters as this energy operates to no proper end. Like the Spartan boy they cloak the wolf as it gnaws their vitals. But this last stage of Western Puritanism, the Renaissance's last gasp, is a more sinister thing than the Spartan ordeal. Only the will is left, unsupported by faith. In a Christian state the will only has meaning as it is related to the struggle for salvation. It resists or does not resist all obstacles which bar the gates of Paradise to the pilgrim. Operating, as it does in this book, in a spiritual vacuum, it turns upon itself; consequently the senses and the matter of this world, once the occasion of the great drama of the human soul, go through a self-devouring process of exploitation and meaningless waste. The irony of the title and the basic irony of the catastrophe, almost a holocaust, depend upon just this.

There is an upper level of action moving about Bogan Murdock, a powerful and unscrupulous financier, and a lower level which involves Ashby Wyndham, son of a simple farming family, who sins, knows he has sinned, not only knows but feels his degradation and his peril and sets out on a pilgrimage of salvation. At the crucial moment his failure precipitates the denouement by accidentally confronting the two levels of experience, that which believes and that which aimlessly uses the forms of belief. The fraud and utter inadequacy of stock-jobbing finance is exposed through the only person it has corrupted, a boy hero from the hills who has allowed his reputation to be used to sell out the people who made him. The other characters are beyond corruption. Ashby's people are exploited and reduced to squalor. Acted upon, not acting, they are free of temptation. Those who belong to financial circles cannot properly be called corrupt. They are the damned, or the betrayed who were taken at birth into a world where all had reached emptiness and dissolution.

This prevents the book from reaching tragic proportions, since the tragedy is one of a whole society. The actors in the top reaches of its hierarchy are denied the qualities necessary either to pity or fear. Bogan Murdock, the strong man of the piece, lacks sensibility as well as belief. He is all will and vanity, so that when the end comes he meets it as if nothing had happened. If he has any feeling about anything, it is his imbecile father, who years ago shot a political opponent for exposing his perfidy. The son uses his power to have a park set aside as a monument of esteem to one who belonged in the penitentiary. The meaning of this is the lack of meaning in the act, and it is symbolic of Murdock's life. He and his kind know that the forms are empty but they do lip service to them, for without this pretense their false stewardship of power would fall apart. That it functions without meaning or any good to those who should profit by it is corollary to the fact that, empty as they are, these forms still have some force as the only means which pulls the whole together. The irony of the situation is pointed up by the old father's imbecile condition. What he had done had meaning for the society of his day and therefore for him. The knowledge of his real dishonor destroyed his mind. The dreadful commentary which follows is that nothing can destroy the son.

This introduces a consideration about the limitations put upon the author by his viewpoint. The Fate which overtook the Greek protagonist, certainly in Aeschylus, overtook a protagonist who believed. In this fine book the actors flee their parents, not gods. In this flight there is hate and a sense of shame. The fathers represent some failure or betrayal of what they should be, as persons and as symbols of their place in society: Bogan Murdock, the financial and country club substitute for a genuine aristocracy; Mr. Calhoun, the father of the girl's first lover, who becomes immersed in the decay of a distinguished house; the intellectual with Greek tastes who creates for the girl a romantic parenthood to forget his actual bourgeois surroundings. And there is a labor agitator, nauseated by the betrayal of the tradition through his father's sentimental version of it. His nausea must have come from the knowledge that his father, who had fought through the Civil War, knew the truth.

The girl's flight from her father, Murdock, is not a flight but a search for the satisfaction a woman must ask of a man. She is the real heroine of the piece, and it would seem to be Mr. Warren's intention to use her and Ashby Wyndham as the two basic elements of the social situation which reflect the state of society. The girl flees the house of will and takes one lover after another. They all fail her and they fail from a fundamental lack of manhood. One has predominately will, another sex, another erudite conversation, another violence, but none can give her what she wants because of this obsession which pursues and makes him impotent. Her murder and the goaling of Ashby, the undoing of the two forces which reflect the state of social order, together properly force the end.

This analysis does not do full justice to the book, to the technical brilliance, nor to the ordering and rendering of the scenes. It has been limited to the meaning which seems to lie behind the treatment. It is neither allegory nor sociology, the usual and limited methods which are now current in handling of such material. It does not make tragedy for the reasons suggested, and the question arises whether the obsessions of the actors would persist and not be changed by the dramatic complications. It seems a little forced that the labor agitator would return to violence after he has found something outside himself, that something which he pretends to be looking for. This makes the murder of the girl appear fortuitous in the light of the immense complexities which always intrude where life, and not an idea, is concerned.

"The Inklings of 'Original Sin' " [Selected Poems, 1923-43]

John Crowe Ransom*

Of more than seasonal magnitude is the literary event which gives to the public the whole staple of Robert Penn Warren's poetry. For ten years my head has rung with magnificent phrases out of the five poems which he contributed to a Special Poetic Supplement in *The American Review* of March, 1934. I felt they must have made a great commotion (as I knew they had not) and established him at once as a ranking poet; they were so distinctive, those poems of twenty lines each, with their peculiar strain of horror, and their clean-cut eloquence and technical accomplishments. But evidently the rating of the poet waits upon the trial of his big book. The five poems are in the present book, and serve very well as its center, though some later ones may define a little better the special object of this poet's tragic sense.

For a text I will try the easiest of the five, "Aubade for Hope." The speaker (or hero: sometimes he is in the third person) appears to be an adapted and adult man waking, in the company of his bride it would seem, in the Kentucky farmhouse on a winter morning:

> Dawn: and foot on the cold stair treading or
> Thump of wood on the unswept hearthstone is
> Comment on the margin of consciousness,
> A dirty thumb-smear by the printed page.
>
> Thumb-smear: nay, other, for the blessed light
> Acclaimed thus, as a ducal progress by
> The scared cur, wakes them that wallowed in
> The unaimed faceless appetite of dream.
>
> All night, the ice sought out the rotten bough:
> In sleep they heard. And now they stir, as east
> Beyond the formal gleam of landscape sun
> Has struck the senatorial hooded hill.
>
> Light: the groaning stair; the match aflame;
> The Negro woman's hand, horned gray with cold,
> That lit the wood—oh, merciless great eyes
> Blank as the sea—I name some things that shall
>
> As voices speaking from a further room,
> Muffled, bespeak us yet for time and hope:
> For Hope that like a blockhead grandam ever
> Above the ash and spittle croaks and leans.

*Reprinted from the *Saturday Review*, 20 May 1944, pp. 10–11. Copyright © *Saturday Review*, 1944. All rights reserved.

The waking is out of a dream in which the speaker was faced with some nameless evil, and he is glad to be woken; and the dawn to which he wakes is a symbol of hope though sadly short of brilliant in its accessories and triumphant. The waking or rational world does not altogether displace the dark world of the unconscious. The "merciless great eyes" that are addessed in parenthesis bring a difficulty of identification; they are new in the present version, having displaced some less telling original item. But in the light of other poems I should hazard that they belong to an ancestor, or a ghostly mentor, and survive from the dream as a counterpoise to hope, and attend their victim much as the Furies would attend the Greek hero under a curse. We feel they will not be propitiated though the citizen start punctually on his round of moral daylight activities.

But what is his curse? "Aubade for Hope" is of the very type of the Warren poems, whose situations are always fundamentally the same. It is true that the poet is fertile, and I find quite a few titles to suggest his range of variation upon the one tragic theme; as, "Terror," "Pursuit," "Crime," "Letter from a Coward to a Hero," "History," "End of Season," "Ransom," "Aged Man Surveys Past Time," "Toward Rationality," "To a Friend Parting," "Eidolon," "Revelation," "Variation: Ode to Fear," "Monologue at Midnight," "Picnic Remembered," "Man Coming of Age," and the Marvellian "The Garden." It is the quality of a noble poetry that it can fixate powerful living images of the human crisis, and be received of us with every sense of the familiar, yet evade us badly if we would define its issue; and that is why poetry, intuitive in its form like religion, involves us in endless disputation when we try to philosophize it. I proceed with peril, but I rely on a conviction that Warren's version of horror is not only consistent, but more elemental and purer than that of other poets. For there was Poe, for example, with whom it was almost vulgarly "literary" and supernatural; and Baudelaire, for whom it recorded his implication with the monstrous and obscene, and his detestation and disgust. The terror they felt was perhaps chiefly for crazy breaches of the common moral code, but ours here is stranger and yet far more universal than that.

The recent poem, "Original Sin: A Short Story," furnishes us with a philosophical term, or at least a theological one; which we should use provided we remember that the poet has not put all his secrets into one word.

Nodding, its great head rattling like a gourd,
And locks like seaweed strung on the stinking stone,
The nightmare stumbles past, and you have heard
It fumble your door before it whimpers and is gone:
It acts like the old hound that used to snuffle your door and moan.

You thought you had lost it when you left Omaha,
For it seemed connected then with your grandpa, who

> Had a wen on his forehead and sat on the verandah
> To finger the precious protuberance, as was his habit to do,
> Which glinted in sun like rough garnet or the rich old brain bulging
>   through.

But this nightmare, the vague, inept, and not very presentable ancestral ghost, is not to be exorcised. It appears even in Harvard Yard, for the victim's handsome secular progress has led him so far, where the ghost is ill at ease indeed. But you must not think the illusion of the ghost is the form of the speaker's simple nostalgia, for that is painful, too, but goes away:

> You were almost kindly then in your first homesickness,
> As it tortured its stiff face to speak, but scarcely mewed;
> Since then you have outlived all your homesickness,
> But have met it in many another distempered latitude:
> Oh, nothing is lost, ever lost! at last you understood.

This ghost will not be laid. Yet it is an ineffectual ghost, unlike that portentous apparition of Hamlet the Elder, which knew so much about "theatre," including how to time and how to make an entrance: our ghost does not interfere with the actions of the living.

> But it never came in the quantum glare of sun
> To shame you before your friends, and had nothing to do
> With your public experience or private reformation:
> But it thought no bed too narrow—it stood with lips askew
> And shook its great head sadly like the abstract Jew.

> Never met you in the lyric arsenical meadows
> When children call and your heart goes stone in the bosom:
> At the orchard anguish never, nor ovoid horror,
> Which is furred like a peach or avid like the delicious plum.
> It takes no part in your classic prudence or fondled axiom.

We must return to the title, and take its consequences: Original Sin. And here it may be of some moment that we ourselves have had dire personal inklings of Original Sin, hustled and busybody creatures as we are yet perhaps painfully sensible of our treachery to some earlier and more innocent plan of existence; or, on the other hand, that we know it by theology and literature. The poets and priests who dramatize it in Adam's Fall seem to have known it precisely in the same sense with Warren's protagonist; and historically it has proved too formidable an incubus to rate as an idle "metaphysical" entity, for it can infect the whole series of our human successes with shame and guilt. Briefly, Original Sin is the betrayal of our original nature that we commit in the interest of our rational evolution and progress. Anthropologists may well imagine—if they are imaginative—that the guilt-feeling of Original Sin, though it opposes no specific adaptation or "conditioning" of the pliant human spirit, might yet have some business on the premises as an unassimilated core of resistance and therefore stability; so precarious would seem the unique biological experiment of equipping an animal species with reason instead of the law of its own nature. Original Sin obtains a sort of poetic justification when we consider the peculiar horror to which the strict regimen of medieval monks exposed them; acedia; the paralysis of will. Or, for that matter, the horror which has most shaken the moderns in their accelerating progress: the sense of psychic disintegration, that is, of having a personality which has been casually acquired, and is still subject to alteration, therefore hollow and insincere.

By the present account Original Sin seems to be nearly related to the Origin of Species—of that species at least which is most self-determining of its behavior. It may be tempting to assume, and dogmatic theology at its nadir of unrealism is apt to assume, that the blame falls only on Adam, and we are answerable only in some formalistic sense to Adam's ghost. But here we should take into account the phenomenon of "recapitulation"; for it is understood that individually we re-enact the evolution of species. We do it physiologically, but there is a conscious side to it too. We have a nature, and proceed to "condition" it; and more and more, from age to age, are subjected to the rule of reason, first the public reason which "educates" us, and then, when we have lost our native spirits, our own reason, which draws corollaries to the public reason. If we may venture now upon a critical impertinence, and commit the biographical fallacy, we will refer the nightmare of our poet's verse to the admirable public datum of his life, to see what edification it will bring. As follows. The South Kentucky country of his nativity is distinctive among landscapes, and the sense of it is intimate and constitutive in the consciousness of its inhabitants; and his breed, the population of that country, acknowledges more firmly than another the two bonds of blood and native scene, which individuate it. If then the ancestral ghost really haunts the mature poet, as the poetry professes, it might be said to have this excuse, that the circumstance of his origin is without visible consequence upon his social adaptiveness, which is supple and charming, or upon his capacity for such scholarship and industry as his professional occasions may demand, which is exemplary. The poetic torment of his sensibility is private, and yet here it is, published. But we need not think it something very special. The effect is universal as philosophers use that term: it is the way a fine native sensibility works, in those who have the sensibility and keep it.

Besides the poetry, Warren has a well-known body of fiction, including an important recent novel; the aforesaid nightmare of Original Sin showing in the fiction too. But the poetry, I think, is superior to the fiction, for a curious reason. Warren has fallen in increasingly with the vogue of the "naturalistic" novel; and this means that he likes to take low life, or at any rate life with a mediocre grade of vitality, for his material. His characters are mean, and inarticulate too, though their futilities and defeats furnish him faithfully with documents of the fateful Original Sin. But they do not know what tune they are playing, and the novelist has the embarrassment of having to speak for them. In the recent novel, "At Heaven's Gate," he has to contrive a quaint though marvelously realized rural saint, to furnish a significant commentary; and it is not very organically connected with the action of the plot.

I mention this because Warren begins to import the naturalistic method into his verse; as in the Kentucky ballad of "Billie Potts," the most substantial poem in the present volume. With great skill he expands the primitive ballad form (in this case the loose and vernacular American form) without quite breaking it down, though he goes much farther than Coleridge did in his "Ancient Mariner." The story is of how Young Billie left Old Billie (and his old mother too) behind in Kentucky, and went West to make his fortune on his own power (and his own reason) with scarcely a backward look. The Pottses, incidentally, are most unsympathetic characters; they are a nest of Kentucky rattlesnakes. But after ten years' success Young Billie has a sort of "conversion," and returns to the ancestral rooftree; where his parents promptly kill him; for one cannot return. It is true that they do not recognize him, but the accident is at least the symbol of the intention. To interpret all this in terms of his thesis Warren uses long parentheses, filled with his own matter and language, and that is a gloss far more implausible than that which Coleridge wrote upon his margins.

I suggest that this is not the best strategy of composition. And I would add something else, which for me is of paramount importance: I wish we had a way of holding this poet, whose verse is so beautiful when it is at his own height of expression, to a level no lower than this height.

[All the King's Men]

Henry Rago*

The publication of "All the King's Men" assures Robert Penn Warren of a place among the handful of novelists in America worth taking seriously. His story moves chiefly through the fabulous but completely credible political career of Willie Stark, a Southern demagogue whose personality and language are a terrifying mixture of good and evil, the scripture and blasphemy, purity and cynicism. But Mr. Warren's hero, to my mind, is not Willie Stark, but the conscience of a people—the novel is about the South, about America, and about all men in "the terrible division" of modern society—and he brings this conscience to its point of

*Reprinted with permission from *Commonweal*, 4 Oct. 1946, pp. 599–600. Copyright © 1946, Commonweal Publishing Co.

greatest awareness in Jack Burden, who is with the Boss day in and day out as intellectual hatchet-man and stooge. It is Jack Burden who tells the story and who suffers in it. Burden (the name is good allegory) is a former newspaperman; he is heir to a respected family tradition in the community; he is deeply sensitive; one of Mr. Warren's skilful touches is in the startling differences in language between Burden's speeches and his thoughts. Burden knows from the beginning that the frustration which drives him to live on Willie Stark's energy worsens in an obscure guilt. But there *is* energy in Willie Stark, there is life there, for good or for bad. And so Burden exchanges the conflict which stifles all action in him for the paradoxes of good and evil in Willie Stark. Values do not conflict in Willie; they destroy each other. His personality is the destructive element in which things are made neutral. There is no value except the dionysiac one of the brute personality itself. Values for Willie are always "just a couple of jumps behind what [we need] to do business on." So Jack Burden suffers from betrayal at the outset, and the story is the intensification of that suffering, as he is led to betray more and more. The pattern here is classic, but the timing and the astonishing climax are new, and genuinely from Mr. Warren's own hand.

The squalor which Mr. Warren reports is given literally and straight with the modest look of mere journalism, but it is saturated with a kind of Greek religious sense. His pivot is the tragic choice between not-knowing and knowing: not-knowing leaves us only the emptiness of the life lived under "the godhead of the Great Twitch"; knowing brings us the anguish of incompleteness in that separation between "idea" and "fact" which is the definition of our age. And between emptiness and doom, Mr. Warren's choice is for doom; it is, in any case, an effort, even if one dies in the effort; it is, at least, a *choice*, and emptiness is not:

> It was like the second when you come home late at night and see the yellow envelope of the telegram sticking out from under the door and you lean and pick it up, but don't open it yet, not for a second. While you stand there in the hall, with the envelope in your hand, you feel there's an eye on you, a great big eye looking straight at you from miles and dark and through houses and through your coat and vest and hide and sees you huddled up way inside, in the dark which is you, inside yourself, like a clammy, sad little foetus you carry around inside yourself. The eye knows what's in the envelope, and it is watching you to see you when you open it and know, too. But the clammy, sad little foetus which is you way down in the dark which is you too lifts up its sad little face and its eyes are blind, and it shivers cold inside you for it doesn't want to know what is in that envelope. It wants to lie in the dark and not know, and be warm in its not-knowing. . . . There's the cold inside your stomach, but you open the envelope, for the end of man is to know.

The explicit knowledge which one fears in the envelope, Mr. Warren described in his verse several years ago under the clearer title of "Original Sin: A Short Story":

Nodding, its great head rattling like a gourd,
And locks like seaweed strung on the stinking stone,
The nightmare stumbles past, and you have heard
It fumble your door before it whimpers and is gone:
It acts like the old hound that used to snuffle your door and moan.

"You thought you had lost it when you left Omaha" and the young Jack Burden, in a beautifully sustained description of the idyllic innocence of summer-love, thought he had never seen it; but that elysium was haunted too, and in the climactic scene of this episode, he suddenly used the word "right": "And I remember the surprise I felt when I heard that word in the air, like the echo of a word spoken by somebody else God knows how many years before. . . ." It was enough to stop him in incoherence for the moment, and for just the moment needed for the older people to descend upon the house like the Eumenides. In another scene, he witnesses a neat, matter-of-fact operation to remove a piece of the frontal lobe of the brain on each side. At one point the surgeons had to do some electrocautery. Jack Burden was "fine" up to that moment. But the smell of the burning brain made him think of some horses that had burned to death in a livery stable when he was a child, and as soon as he realized that brains and horses smell alike when they burn, he "didn't feel good." One's confidence in the very seat of the Great Twitch could be shaken. This is the emptiness which Jack Burden would put behind him at all costs. And when Willie Stark is dead, Burden, who knows the worst about him, knows that he must have faith in what Stark could have done (it is inexcusable to read this passage as a eulogy of Huey Long!), for to turn from the struggle of the "man of fact" and the "man of idea" to join and complete each other—despite the doom which awaits them every time—is to reject the responsibility of our guilt and to choose not to choose. I do not think that Mr. Warren ends just there. He talks about "doom," but he seems to think that there might be a way out, a way of coming back to the innocence of the mimosas and the diving floats in the sun and the pine grove. It will be after knowledge and a painful purgation, in "the convulsion of the world" and "the awful responsibility of Time," and the book ends in the hope of it.

T. S. Eliot once complained that most modern novels are not "written." "All the King's Men" is completely written. The language does all the work. It does all the slowing down, and the speeding up; it controls all the tone and volume; and it controls the reader; you read this book not at your own pace but at Mr. Warren's. It is language that gives us not only the characters (even, in an extraordinary way, the most casual characters) but the internal "selves" within a single character. If Mr. Warren gave us only Willie Stark, we should be grateful for an important contribution to American rhetoric. But there are the accents of all the other characters. And in the thoughts of Jack Burden, one sees how Thomas Wolfe would have written if he had had flair and coherence. There is not a sentence in this book that is free of Mr. Warren's writing. For such completeness we can be doubly grateful and commend both his integrity and his generosity.

"Proustian Exploration"
[*The Circus in the Attic*]

Henry Nash Smith*

The novelties [*sic*] and short stories collected in Mr. Warren's new book, displaying his development over a period of seventeen years, show how his imagination has nourished itself upon Proustian exploration of a remembered world of childhood in Northwestern Tennessee. The chronological line is not neat and simple, but it is nevertheless clear that he has moved from isolated moments of recapturing the past toward a fuller and fuller imaginative grasp of the society within which he grew up. This tendency culminates in the vivid political awareness of "All the King's Men."

The most prominent theme of the earlier stories is the integral relation between a rural folk and the land, and the normal source of conflict or disaster is the violation of this organic pattern by some outside force. The stranger in "Blackberry Winter" is potentially such a force, although the menace he embodies is kept at the edge of a child's consciousness. Luke Goodwood, the hunter and baseball player, is fatally shattered when he is drawn away from the land to attempt a career in professional baseball. Jeff York kills himself when his wife forces him to sell his farm so she may buy a hamburger stand in town. The divisive and tragic impulses at work in the novelette "Prime Leaf" originate in the meaningless fluctuations of tobacco prices in distant markets.

But the outside forces could not affect the society if they did not encounter some answering evil within it. This is often a kind of irrational compulsion, as in the two companion stories about Elsie Barton and her daughter. Benjamin Beaumont the tobacco buyer and Frank Barber the railroad detective and bootlegger, both felt as alien and sinister, are the immediate sources of evil, but here the attention is fixed rather on the dark currents of motivation in the two women. If Mr. Warren finds in his characters compulsions that recall Faulkner, his treatment of them is

*Reprinted from *Saturday Review*, 31 Jan. 1948, pp. 14–15. Copyright © *Saturday Review*, 1948. All rights reserved.

quite different, for he analyzes them with clinical thoroughness and brings to the surface matters that Faulkner ordinarily keeps buried and mysterious.

Despite the occasional triumphs of these earlier pieces, none of them is an entirely satisfactory thing-in-itself. They suggest, in fact, that Mr. Warren is a novelist rather than a short-story writer. The awareness of society as a complex structure of individuals and classes can hardly be rendered in a brief flash. This is even more certainly true of the concern with the relation between past and present which is so central in Mr. Warren's work. The psychological basis of this interest is perhaps the very process of childhood reminiscence, which revives the past within a present from which it is irretrievably separated by time. The Tennessee folk whom Mr. Warren depicts so well and whose vernacular speech he puts to such remarkable use are themselves a product of time, of long residence in a given environment. Indeed, the whole character of Southern society as it appears derives from its traditional quality, which confers upon every aspect of life a ceremonial order. These matters are not adapted to the quick intensity of the short story.

But Mr. Warren needs only a slightly greater space to manage them perfectly. The newly published novelette which is the title piece of "The Circus in the Attic" manages to pack into sixty pages an historical perspective stretching back a century and a half, an accurate diagram of social relationships in a Tennessee town, an analytical biography of the central character, and adequate portraits of half a dozen others. Bolton Lovehart, the hero, is imprisoned by his mother's cannibalistic fixation on him. After several desperate and pathetic efforts to escape, which he himself only dimly understands, he finds in the secret hobby of carving a toy circus from wood compensation for the actual life she has forbidden him to lead. By the time his mother dies at eighty-seven he is past fifty and no longer able to take advantage of his freedom. These themes and various subordinate ones, such as the impact of the Second World War on the community, are managed with an autocratic precision that could hardly have been predicted on the basis of the work preceding "All the King's Men." "The Circus in the Attic" confirms the impression left by that novel, that within the past couple of years Mr. Warren has raised himself to a new command over his materials and by that fact has entered the first rank of American writers.

"Virtue Plundered in Kentucky" [*World Enough and Time*]

A. B. Guthrie, Jr.*

Robert Penn Warren has written a book that is sure to arouse attention, make the best-seller lists, and excite disagreements.

For the stuff of what is presented as "a romantic novel" he has gone to an old and celebrated Kentucky case—the Sharp-Beauchamp case—which writers have turned to before and probably will again, since high tragedy and ludicrous comedy, honorable intention and tortured conclusion, honesty, duplicity, resolution, despair, antique compulsions here are so scrambled as to provoke the imagination and invite constructions.

The facts in so far as we can be sure of them are that in Kentucky in the early years of the last century a young man murdered his benefactor to avenge the betrayal of a young woman who later became his wife. At the time of the seduction she was unknown to him. She was only Virtue Plundered and simply as idea appealed to his overblown sense of honor and justice. According to the long account that the young man wrote while a prisoner, a challenge to a duel had brought from the benefactor only a remorseful admission of guilt and a declared readiness to die but not as the foe of his friend on the field of honor. The offense against virtue might have been forgotten thereafter except that the scandal was aired, with an accurate calculation of results, in a subsequent political campaign. Thus baited, the young man took his vengeance and forfeited his life on the gallows.

It is largely from his account that Mr. Warren appears to have reconstructed the case. He has done some violence to the factual record, however, with the consequence that comparisons are sure to be made, though the departures from actuality seem to me of no great importance. More if not most important are the accuracy of characterization, the capture of motive, the pitch and tone of re-creation. Some special students of the subject, like J. Winston Coleman of Lexington, Ky., author of a nonfiction treatment, would dispute a number of Mr. Warren's interpretations.

Even these are not the foremost questions. The foremost question is the question of a novel as a novel. Is it persuasive? Does it create and maintain illusion? Here I find myself forced to hedge. I believe a work of fiction can be a distinguished book and an undistinguished or even bad novel, by professional standards anyhow. We know, or think we know, the techniques of illusion these days. We say, correctly, I think, that an author must keep himself off the page. He must lose us in the experiences

*Reprinted from *Saturday Review*, 24 June 1950, pp. 11–12. Copyright © *Saturday Review*, 1950. All rights reserved.

of his characters. What he has to say as an individual in and against the world must be implicit in the story itself. Every time he enters the scene it is at the cost of belief in his story.

Mr. Warren, as a teacher and a craftsman, of course is entirely familiar with this method. Yet in this book he has chosen to disregard it. He keeps reminding us that at this distance from the scene we cannot be sure of this point or that one. And by reminding us he keeps pulling us a century and more away from his story; he tells us this is about something over and done with, this is only an attempt at a re-creation; he gives his novel something of the odor of biography. And that isn't all. He editorializes. At the end he adds a page and a half of critical comment about present-day Kentucky. The comment is pointed and good and perhaps is an aid to focus, but it is still difficult to see that it belongs in a story of the early nineteenth century.

The consequence of his approach is that his book lacks immediacy. We see his characters dusty across the long field of time. We aren't caught up and concerned as we were, for example, in "All the King's Men." We are willing to believe that these things happened but we don't feel that they happened to us or anyone we know.

Mr. Warren's choice of method leaves one wondering. Did he think, as he must have, that in this way and only in this way he could retell the ancient story? Did he think we needed the open contrast with today, the open comment, the naked author? Why?

The rewards of "World Enough and Time"—and they are genuine—lie elsewhere than in illusion. Mr. Warren, a native of Kentucky, knows Kentucky, contemporary and historical. He can speak the strong idiom of the frontier. He knows what kind of men peopled the state and what kind of problems they met with what kind of solutions. When he wants to he can set his reader in time, place, situation. In his lines one recognizes his rightness and his talent.

If his is not a distinguished novel, it is a distinguished book, an arresting and provocative book, a wise book, a masculine book, a book of immense and mature disillusion. A keen and stout mind is at work here, telling us things we haven't known till now, telling us things we've known but haven't dared to believe. This is more a philosophical than a romantic work. It has an impact that won't quickly be forgotten.

"On the Underside of the Stone" [*Brother to Dragons*]

Randall Jarrell*

This is Robert Penn Warren's best book. It is the story of a peculiarly atrocious murder that took place in the family of Charles and Lucy Lewis, the brother-in-law and sister of Thomas Jefferson. The murderers were their sons, Lilburn and Isham: the murdered man was their slave. These people, Jefferson, Lilburn's wife Laetitia, Lilburn's Negro mammy Aunt Cat, Lilburn's (and Jefferson's) cousin Meriwether Lewis, Laetitia's brother, and Warren himself speak the poem. They say what people do not say, but would say if they could. When they are through we know them, and what they have done, very thoroughly, and we give a long marveling sigh.

About Laetitia and Ishey-Boy, two of the most touching creations in American literature; about Aunt Cat, whose concluding lullaby Schubert and Mahler and Wolf together couldn't have done justice to; about that brother, about Lilburn, about the moth that lights on Lilburn's hand, even our disbelief is suspended forever. We *were* Laetitia and Isham and Lilburn: so they are clubs we can beat Jefferson and Charles and Lucy and Meriwether Lewis and—but only half the time—Warren over the head with, when these seem to us more rhetorical and moralizing than life.

Warren's florid, massive, rather oratorical rhetoric, with its cold surprises, its accustomed accomplished continuations, its conscious echoes of Milton and Shakespeare, its unconscious echoes of Eliot and Arnold and Warren, is sometimes miraculous, often effective, and sometimes too noticeable to bear. Warren's impressive verbal gifts are less overwhelming than his dramatic gifts, one is tempted to say; but then one remembers Laetitia and the others—and the first speeches of Adam and Eve and the animals were hardly fresher, hardly more natural, hardly more unexpected, than the best of the speeches of these descendants of theirs.

Warren moralizes for effect and out of necessity: man is the animal that moralizes. Man is also the animal that complains about being one, and says that there is an animal, a beast inside him—that he is brother to dragons. (He is certainly a brother to wolves, and to pandas too, but he is father to dragons, not brother: they, like many gods and devils, are inventions of his.) The character in "Brother to Dragons" most loathingly obsessed with man's dragonish heart is a part of Warren which he calls Thomas Jefferson. The live Jefferson spoke and believed that Noble Lie of man's innocence and perfectibility which, Meriwether Lewis is made to say, "was my death."

The live Jefferson had not prepared Lewis for the ignoble truth of man's depravity; the dead Jefferson hammers it home with ignoble avidity. The dead Jefferson looks at the obscene underside of the stone and—he can do no other—licks his lips: he knows, now. Most of us know, now, that Rousseau was wrong: that man, when you knock his chains off, sets up the death camps. Soon we shall know everything the eighteenth century didn't know, and nothing it did, and [it] will be hard to live with us.

"Brother to Dragons" is written out of an awful time, about an awful, a traumatic subject: sin, Original Sin, without any Savior. The time is the subject; but the poem is a net, wide enough, high enough, deep enough, to have caught most of the world inside it—and if happiness, "a butterfly and not a gloomy bird of prey," has flown through its iron interstices as if they weren't there, it wasn't happiness Warren was in pursuit of, but the knowledge of Good and Evil.

Cruel sometimes, crude sometimes, obsessed sometimes, the book is always extraordinary: it does know, and knows sadly and tenderly, even. It is, in short, an event, a great one. There is a wonderful amount of life in it, of living beings who are free of Warren's rhetoric and moralizing, and of ours—are freed by their share in that reality or power or knowledge or glory which, as Warren says contradictorily and very humanly, is the one thing man lives by.

"The Dragon of Guilt"
[*Brother to Dragons*]

Delmore Schwartz*

It is likely enough that some readers may be put off by the mere and deceptive fact that Robert Penn Warren's new book is a narrative poem, "a tale in verse and voices." For it is true enough, in a misleading way, that the modern reader is no longer accustomed to reading books which are presented as narrative poems, however devoted he may be to modern poetry and fiction. Probably no author since Edwin Arlington Robinson has succeeded in winning the attention of the serious reader by efforts which were explicitly narrative poems, and certainly such long poems as *Four Quartets* and *Conquistador* are essentially lyrical and not narrative works. But the prevailing feeling that the narrative poem belongs to the past is entirely false, apart from surface appearance and nominal title. For when we read Faulkner, Joyce, Malraux, and Proust—when we read *Mme. Bovary*, as when we read Djuna Barnes' *Nightwood*—the nature of

*From *The New Republic*, 14 Sept. 1953, pp. 17–18. Reprinted by permission of *The New Republic*. Copyright © 1953, *The New Republic*, Inc.

our attention as readers is and of necessity must be the kind of attention which narrative poetry has always required: an awareness of style, of tone, phrasing, rhythm, metaphor, and symbol, a consciousness of the texture of the writing as such which poetry has always required and narrative fiction in some of its purest forms—in Stendhal and Tolstoy—naturally and triumphantly excluded. Once this is kept in mind, Warren's poem will not seem to be a *tour de force* in an outmoded literary tradition, but a new realization of the dominant tendency of modern literature to be narrative poetry, no matter how often the works in question are entitled novels. It is also important to remember that Warren's previous poetry and fiction often seemed to aspire to the condition of narrative poetry.

The subject of *Brother To Dragons* is the senseless killing of a Negro for the trivial offense of breaking a prized pitcher. Since the murder occurs in 1811, in Kentucky, and since all the characters except the poet himself have returned from the past and from death to agonize about the meaning of the crime, the universality and the modernity of the theme may not be immediately apparent. For the significance of the poem is certainly not limited to the South, nor to the relationship of white man and Negro, nor is it limited to America itself although part of Warren's explicit intention is clearly to fix upon the death of the heart which occurs when violence transforms the American dream into a nightmare.

It is for this reason that Thomas Jefferson is present as a character. The murderer is Lilburn Lewis, his nephew and his sister's son, but the family relationship is less important than the relationship of the crime to Jefferson's image of America and of man. For it is the nature of man which is in question and in doubt, here as throughout Warren's work. The key recurrent word in all his work is *definition*, as the chief recurrent subject is violent brutality. And it is the brutality which leads to an absolute loss of definition and identity. For whether we think of lynchings or concentration camps—and the crime in Warren's poem is a symbol of both—we can hardly escape the state of mind which made Eliot write: "After such knowledge, what forgiveness?" and which made Malraux say: "Man is dead." Which is to say, once one has faced the actuality of human evil, how is it possible to believe truly in any human ideal and aspiration?

The characters of *Brother to Dragons* exist within the disillusion and despair of this question, striving and failing to answer it. But the poem does not depend upon an answer, but upon the courage of various confrontations of the question as something which must be faced and lived through on all levels of experience; the only answer is the courage of consciousness and the acceptance of guilt, the courage to live with the consciousness that we are all guilty.

In some of Warren's previous work, there was a gap between the ideas which concerned him and the experience upon which the ideas were focussed. The experience possessed a rich vividness which gave the ideas the appearance of being superimposed. But here there is perfect proportion throughout, and perhaps because of Warren's mastery of a blank verse style of the utmost flexibility, a style which supports a great variety of reference, tone, and modulation, of colloquial speech, conceptual formulation, and narrative exposition without the least diminution of poetic power. Perhaps the most impressive passage is the sustained cadenza in which Meriwether Lewis suddenly appears to accuse Jefferson of having deceived him. But it is wrong to single out any passage as it would be misleading to quote from a work which is most remarkable as a sustained whole. The work as a whole makes one think of Warren's resemblance to Melville. There is the same natural eloquence, which sometimes becomes nothing but rhetoric; there is a gift for sheer narrative and a gift for passionate poetry, but the poet and the storyteller do not always unite; and there is the same obsession with guilt and innocence, and with nature as an inexhaustible threat to the human condition.

"Souls Lost in a Blind Lobby" [*Band of Angels*]

Carlos Baker*

With his sixth novel, "Band of Angels," it is clear that one central drive in Robert Penn Warren's career as a writer of fiction is the illumination, through people, of the dark backward and abysm of American time. In "John Brown: The Making of a Martyr," his nonfictional biography, he explored the fanatical darkness of a mind that glimpsed light but could not win it, and thus established a consuming interest that has since sustained him in the study of various other forms of fanaticism. There was, for example, the tobacco war between the fanatics and the compromisers in "Night Rider"; the case of Murdock and his rebellious daughter in "At Heaven's Gate"; the memorable portrait of Willie Stark in "All the King's Men"; the fanatical romanticism of Jeremiah Beaumont in "World Enough and Time"; and the story of the brothers Lewis, nephews of Thomas Jefferson, in "Brother to Dragons," Warren's novel in verse and voices of two years ago.

Each man, he said in the verse-novel, and each woman, too, is lost "in some blind lobby, hall, enclave, crank cul-de-sac, or corridor of Time. Of Time. Or Self. And in that dark no thread." The problem, sooner or later, for all his characters is the location of the thread, the following of that thread out towards whatever light there is. That a band of angels will come in thunder from the stars and carry people forth is unlikely in the extreme. The way out is step by step, with many backslidings.

*Reprinted from *Saturday Review*, 20 Aug. 1955, pp. 9–10. Copyright © *Saturday Review*, 1955. All rights reserved.

The blind lobby of self, the Cave of the Ultimate Spleen, is nowhere more apparent in Warren's work than in his latest novel, "Band of Angels," which in its deeper reaches is a parable of slavery and freedom, with a long dark road between the two poles. He tells the highly adventurous life story of Amantha Starr, an orphan of Kentucky, who flourished, if that is the word for it, between 1844 and 1888.

Little Manty spends her motherless childhood on a decaying estate called Starrwood in the country south of Lexington, and her adolescence at a Scripture-reading school in Oberlin, Ohio. Only when her father dies, on the eve of the Civil War, does she discover that her mother was a slave at Starrwood, and that she is therefore a chattel of the estate, to be sold¦ by her father's creditors, down the river to New Orleans. There she begins a life which spans the fall of that city to Farragut, the corrupt administration of "Beast" Butler, the great war to the north, the Emancipation Proclamation, and the passage of the Fourteenth Amendment, the piteous wandering of the displaced colored refugees, the New Orleans race riots of 1866, and twenty years of married life in St. Louis and sundry small towns in Kansas. What begins, one might say, at something like the level of Tara, the O'Hara plantation in "Gone With the Wind," turns into something like George Washington Cable's "The Grandissimes," and concludes on a note that might be drawn from Hamlin Garland's "A Daughter of the Middle Border." For moods, that is. No "influence" is to be inferred.

As often happens in Warren, the life of the central character is defined by the people who environ it, governed by a dialectic of half-realized ideas, and dominated at times of crisis by a consuming desire to discriminate truth from error. Amantha will no doubt strike many readers as too much of a pawn, more sinned against than sinning, but a kind of waif-wife, with the waif's self-pity and half-clinging dependence. The shape of her life is drawn by the men who own her, in the various meanings of ownership—no band of angels, certainly, except in the most ironic sense, yet the means by which her waifism is stiffened and saved until she can discriminate her truth from her error and be born into life. Which is to say, into freedom: the good air at the mouth of the cavern.

Yet each of Amantha's "angels" is enslaved, too, awaiting the moment of egress, the mind-born conviction that one is at liberty to take action for good or ill, for ill or good, but in any case with free choice. Her father, Aaron Starr, to take the first example, conceived the child on the body of the slave Renie. He thinks that by raising Amantha as a lady he can deliver her from the bonds of her origin. But the solace he seeks with Miss Idell, whose name is almost a pun, is the very means by which his impoverishment becomes inevitable so that when he dies his daughter's bonds are riveted the more firmly. Or there is Seth Parton, Amantha's dour and pietistic Oberlin sweetheart, slave to the doctrine of self-sanctification, whose ultimate release, again through Miss Idell, comes in slashing cold-eyed financiering, the making of a fortune in the Chicago grain-market.

The forms human bondage may take are legion. The assumed name of Hamish Bond of New Orleans, Amantha's owner, protector, and lover, might also be a pun. His bondage to the past, which comes out in a horrific, bloody, nightmarish, half-cynical flashback to the days when he traded for slaves in the Congo, is only to be expiated now by a kindness so calmly powerful that it overruns him like a disease. Another disease, a form of social narcissism, besets Tobias Sears, the handsome young Union captain and idealistic disciple of Massachusetts transcendentalism, who marries Amantha Starr in a mixture of noble motives. His bondage is to his own sense of magnanimity. For if Bond had kindness like a disease, Sears had nobility like an epidemic.

If this is not Warren's best novel, a guerdon I would still reserve for "All the King's Men," it is a good book on a serious and important subject, giving another thematic emphasis to his perennial preoccupation: the perils of self-deception in the blind lobby of self. Freedom—from what? For what? These questions are as important as ever in the affairs of men. Warren offers a variety of applicable answers.

"Melodrama With Meaning" [*The Cave*]

Granville Hicks*

Robert Penn Warren's "The Cave" is that rare thing, a continuously exciting novel. Sustained excitement is not the greatest of literary virtues, and it should be said at the outset that the book has other and more important qualities, but what hits the reader first and hardest is the pace of the story, the tempestuous speed of the telling. There is nowhere a point at which one can willingly put the book down.

The pace is the more extraordinary because the story is not told in a straightforward fashion. It opens with a pair of boots and a guitar standing in a glade. Into the glade come a boy and a girl, and they are about to make love when the girl, after a cryptic remark, starts running. One hundred and fifty pages further on we find out for certain why. In the meantime we have met the book's principal characters, and not merely met them but been plunged into their lives.

Warren's narrative skill is such that the reader becomes absorbed in each new character in turn and forgets all the questions that have been left unanswered. In due time the answers are given and the situation is

*Reprinted from *Saturday Review*, 22 Aug. 1959, p. 13. Copyright © 1959, *Saturday Review*. All rights reserved.

defined. The boots and the guitar were left in the glade, near the mouth
of a cave, by Jasper Harrick, and the girl, who is Jo-Lea Bingham, runs
for help because she suddenly realizes that he would not have left them
overnight unless he was trapped in the cave. Monty, the boy with Jo-Lea,
is Jasper's younger brother, and their father is Old Jack Harrick, "old
heller of high coves and hoot-owl hollows," now dying of cancer. Jasper
had been planning to exploit the cave in partnership with Isaac Sumpter,
and we have Isaac's story and the story of his father, the Reverend Mac-
Carland Sumpter. Then there is Mr. Bingham, Jo-Lea's father, who is
Johntown's banker, and there is Nick Pappy, proprietor of a restaurant.
All of these characters are indispensable to the development of the story,
and one realizes on looking back that, while his narrative has been racing
ahead, Warren has been doing a magnificent job of exposition.

Once Jo-Lea has told her piece of news to Old Jack Harrick, attention concentrates on the rescue operations, although Warren continues to
move from one point of view to another. Crowds gather near the cave's
entrance, and Nick Pappy, spurred on by Isaac Sumpter, who has plans of
his own, sells food to the multitude. Isaac's opportunities come by way of
press, radio, and television, and he becomes interpreter to the nation of a
drama in which he has cast himself in the role of hero. Isaac's deceptions
and their consequences carry the reader through complication after complication to the novel's climax.

"The Cave," I am confident, will be popular, and its popularity will
disturb certain students of contemporary literature as the popularity of
Warren's earlier novels has done. Warren's right to be regarded as a
highbrow is indisputable: he is a formidable and influential critic; he has
won general recognition as a poet; he has taught at some of our best in-
stitutions. Moreover, from the point of view of either structure or style,
his novels could serve as texts in writing courses. Yet these same novels
have had large numbers of readers, and not through any of the accidents
that sometimes create best sellers but because they are deliberately designed to seize upon and hold the interest of the general reader. Since
what is intended to interest the general reader is not ordinarily of the
highest quality, Warren has understandably fallen under suspicion.

Even the most skeptical of his critics, I suppose, would agree that
Warren's fundamental intentions as a novelist are completely serious. He
simply tries, as nineteenth-century novelists commonly tried and twen-
tieth-century novelists commonly don't try, to entertain the reader who is
looking merely for entertainment and at the same time to reward one who
is willing to make some effort of intellect and imagination. The question is
whether, in his desire to provide entertainment, he allows himself to fall
short of his highest possibilities.

The careful reader of "The Cave" will answer the question in the
negative but only after he has given it some thought. The pace is so swift,
and one's interest in what is going to happen next—what is going to hap-

pen to Jasper, to Isaac Sumpter, to Jo-Lea, to Nick Pappy, to Monty—is so intense that for many pages the book seems to be no more than an absorbing diversion. But in the end one realizes not only that Warren has something to say but also that he has found the best way of saying it.

It is the ordinarily not very perceptive Mr. Bingham who reflects, almost in the same thought, on "the outrage of life" and "the pathos of life." Warren uses as epigraph a passage from Plato's "The Republic," an allusion to the famous image of the cave in which men are imprisoned so that they see only shadows, never realities. Only one of Warren's characters is literally imprisoned in a cave, and he is the one whose mind we are never allowed to enter. But the others, who work or don't work, who pray or don't pray, for his release, are prisoners in Plato's meaning.

What happens to Jasper Harrick's body, or to any other of the bodies that figure in the story, turns out not to be very important. Behind the melodrama of the flesh goes on a drama of the spirit, and the true climax comes, after the announcement of Jasper's death and after the saturnalia that follows the announcement, in a quiet conversation between the two old men, Mac Sumpter and Jack Harrick. The book finds its center in the relations between these two men and their sons, who are both trapped, one literally and one figuratively, and both doomed. When we understand what Sumpter has done, and done in vain, for his son and what Harrick has not been able to do for his, we realize that the novel's major theme is the problem that has preoccupied Warren from "Night Rider" on, the problem of guilt. A secondary theme is the problem of identity: each of the characters is forced to ask the question that Amantha Starr asks in "Band of Angels": "Who am I?" And even Banker Bingham and Nick Pappy, men not much given to introspection, have a glimmering of an answer.

The truth is that this is the way Warren writes and we had better make the most of it. He tells a story, and the story is fascinating in its own right, but it is not for the story's sake that he tells it. All his skill as a storyteller—his mastery of narrative form, his wonderfully racy style—serves his real purpose. He is concerned with the deepest realities of the human spirit, and if it is true that a thoughtless reader could get a kick out of the book without ever grasping its basic nature, it is also true that Warren rewards the reader who is willing to stretch his mind.

"Crusader in a World of Chance" [*Wilderness*]

Granville Hicks*

Robert Penn Warren's new novel, "Wilderness," bears as subtitle "A Tale of the Civil War." This is enigmatic, for not one of the major characters in the book is a soldier, nor is there any account of military action. The war, to be sure, is always in the background, but there it stays, even to the end.

"Wilderness" is the story of Adam Rosenzweig, a Bavarian Jew with a twisted foot, son of a poet who had been imprisoned for his part in the uprising of 1848. In spite of his handicap, Adam decides to go to the United States to fight for freedom. After misadventures on shipboard, he reaches New York in the midst of the draft riots and nearly loses his life. A wealthy man, to whom his uncle has given him a letter, helps him to reach the Union Army, but in a civilian capacity. Finally he does fire a shot and does kill a man, but it is by no means clear that he has struck a blow for freedom.

Again and again Warren's characters have sought for the meaning of life: Jack Burden in "All the King's Men," Jeremiah Beauchamp in "World Enough and Time," Amantha Starr in "Band of Angels," Isaac Sumpter in "The Cave," and many others. None, however, has sought with such a single mind as Adam Rosenzweig. "I don't understand things," he says near the end of the book. "I don't understand anything. Oh, God, I want to understand."

At the outset he is an innocent idealist; he is thirty years old, but life has taught him little. As soon as he starts for America, however, the lessons rain bitterly upon him. The accidental bad temper of a recruiting agent nearly puts a quick end to his crusade, but he is helped by a whimsical sailor. In the draft riots his life is saved by a Negro, who subsequently insists that he was acting purely out of self-interest. Everything that happens to him, for good and for ill, happens arbitrarily, nor can he find meaning in what happens to other people.

The first word in the book is "If." If conditions had been just a little different, Warren says in an elaborate passage, Adam might not have decided to go to America. A little later the same rhetorical device is used with comic effect to explain why the recruiting agent persecutes Adam. Finally, looking back, Adam reflects that if he had behaved differently, this person and that might have escaped disaster. "He knew," Warren writes, "that, in the end, he would have to think every *if*—every *if* which was life." The world into which he has ventured is a world of chance.

The novel is concerned with what Adam learns. He learns not only

*Reprinted from *Saturday Review*, 18 Nov. 1961, p. 19. Copyright © 1961, *Saturday Review*. All rights reserved.

that the motives of others are unfathomable but also that his own motives are not what he would like to think them. When he resists the temptation to abandon his cause for the sake of a woman, he comes to suspect that he has been moved not by strength of purpose but by fear of his companions' opinions. ("He asked if there was such a thing as virtue in the last private darkness of the soul.") Ultimately he learns that he is capable of violence, capable of hatred, capable of cruelty.

He has teachers of many kinds, the most sophisticated being Aaron Blaustein, the rich man who befriends him because he is looking for a substitute son. "The hardest thing to remember," Aaron tells him, "is that other men are men." And again: "God is tired of taking the blame. He is going to let History take the blame for a while." Coarser men make their contribution to Adam's education. Tough Jed Hawksworth asks, "Do you think I'm free? Do you think I am? Do you think anybody is—is free?" When Adam starts to protest against a peculiarly wanton act of cruelty, saying he cannot bear it, Mose, the Negro who saved his life, tells him, "Bear. Lots of things you better git so you kin bear." And a man who has planned to take Adam's life, and says he doesn't mind much if Adam takes his, remarks, "A man gits tahrd."

Adam's experiences set agonizing questions before him. "Was no man, in his simple humanity, more to any other than a stir or voice, a sloshing in the dark?" Again: "Who cares about anything?" Yet he persists in his search, pushing on into the Virginia wilderness, where fighting is taking place. When at last he strikes a blow, the action seems as much an accident as anything else that happens in the book, but from it Adam learns something of what he needs to know. "He had done only what he had had to do, he decided, good or bad. . . . Yes, he was only human, he thought. Yes, and if necessary, he would do it all again, he decided. . . . But then cried, in his inwardness: *But, oh, with a different heart!*"

The wilderness of the title is surely not simply the scene of a battle; the word sums up what Adam finds in human hearts, including his own. It is perhaps also intended to remind us of the wilderness in which Jesus spent the forty days of his temptation. (Adam, it may be remembered, is thirty, the age of Jesus when he began his mission.) Adam sets forth with his innocence and with his twisted foot, reminder and symbol of human frailty. ("There is always something from birth," Aaron Blaustein tells him. "There is your fate to bear. There is yourself.") He encounters cruelty and indifference and sometimes kindness, always flawed by self-interest. Traditional religion attracts him, as it had attracted his father at the end of his life, but what strength he finds, he finds in himself. He has accepted the human condition and thus has risen above it in the only way that is possible.

Although the minor characters are vividly described and given an air of reality, Adam remains strangely abstract. This, one has no doubt, was

Warren's intention. Our attention is always focused on Adam's search for the meaning of life, and nothing is allowed to distract us. The style is calm and dignified, quite unlike the racy vernacular of "The Cave." There are lively incidents, but they do not interrupt for long the course of Adam's quest. If Warren chooses to call the book "A Tale of the Civil War," it can only be because the author believes that that war—or any war—is an expression of the human condition.

In the process of rigorous abstraction Warren has sacrificed some of the qualities that have made earlier novels exciting. The book does not have the richness of "All the King's Men" nor the vitality of "The Cave." But it is a remarkable book just the same. From the beginning of his career Warren has been one of the more thoughtful of our novelists, always pushing below the surfaces of experience. Here he has tried to sum up what he has learned about the nature of man and the character of life. He has done this, of course, wholly in imaginative terms, offering an experience, not a formula. What the reader makes of it is up to him.

'The Uncorrupted Conciousness" [Flood]

Arthur Mizener*

The initial reception of Mr. Warren's novel was lackluster and uncomprehending. Perhaps the reviewers would not have liked it even if they had seen what it is; the philosophical romance may not really be popular today (if it ever was), despite our academic enthusiasm for safely dead examples of it like *The Scarlet Letter* and *Moby Dick* and *Light in August*. But at least readers would have known what Mr. Warren has been up to, even from unfavorable reviews, if reviewers had made it clear that *Flood* is, as its subtitle plainly says, "A Romance of Our Time," not a Marquand novel that has somehow got buried under a load of philosophical commentary.

It is pointless to get worked up about this misfortune: most reviewers do not write out of personal malice or wilful misunderstanding; but there is no use pretending (as some of us often do) that we do not concur with the all too common reader more than we can rejoice to believe. It is worth reminding ourselves what the cost of such misfortunes may be. Mr. Warren is a gifted writer; he will not cease to be so because one of his major novels has been misunderstood and under-valued. But he may be affected by this experience in ways that are not good. Leon Edel has pointed out the extent to which Henry James was affected, in ways that are at least

*Reprinted with permission from the *Sewanee Review*, 72 (1964), 690–98. Copyright © 1964, The University of the South.

complicating, by the "very big tempest in a very small teapot" stirred up by his *Hawthorne*. It brought James, as Mr. Edel says, "to a strange turning point in his inner development which was reflected immediately in his work"; from then on James used up a great deal of creative energy, both in his life and in his work, hiding from people in elaborately mannered ways. Such turning points in authors' lives, for all our tendency to make the best of them afterwards in histories and biographies, are by no means all gain.

There is no use looking in *Flood* for the virtue of the Marquand novel—the vivid, detailed, representative image of the everyday world; *Flood* has its own kind of vividness and relevance, but it is not the realistic novel's. The title alone, without the subtitle, ought to warn us what kind that is: can anyone think "flood" without thinking of The Flood? Immediately, of course, the title *Flood* refers to the literal events of the book, which is about a Tennessee town called Fiddlersburg that is going to be flooded by the building of a dam—a means of "getting shoes on the swamp rats . . . teaching 'em to read and write and punch a time clock, and pull a switch," as an earnest young engineer puts it. Socially speaking it is all very well meant and, as far as it goes, good. One of the major points about the world Mr. Warren is making is that, however intimate a man becomes with the "black beast with the cold fur like hairy ice that drowse[s] in the deepest inner dark, or [wakes] to snuffle about" in his own nature, he must accept—indeed love—the outer world where time always moves and very ordinary people go about their well-intentioned business of destroying what has become precious to make way for dams and highways and motels; he must "know the *nowness* of God's will."

But if *Flood* has its consistent commentary on society and history, what it is most deeply concerned with is consciousness. Consciousness exists in time; with all its realized accumulations from the past and its active hopes for the future it must live in the actual present. But it is the consciousness, not the world, that counts. It must somehow survive with hope the flood of time, recognizing, as the dying country preacher of Fiddlersburg says, that the life one has lived, whatever it has been, is blessed. The essential story of *Flood* is the story of how Brad Tolliver, trying desperately to avoid this knowledge, struggling to conceal himself in a series of delusions, and in his struggles blundering about destructively among the lives of those he loves as much as he can love anyone, learns gradually to accept "the secret and irrational life of man." "Being you," as the blind Leontine Purtle says, "[is] like being blind," and Brad with all his human pride of intellect cannot endure the thought of it. The country that is being whelmed by Mr. Warren's flood, that is forever being lost under the irresistible flow of time, is the consciousness. But it is not until the last page of the novel that Brad admits to himself "there is no country but the heart."

From the beginning he has sensed that there is not, but since he had as a college boy written his book of short stories about Fiddlersburg, *I'm Telling You Now*, he has been trying to escape knowing it. One way he has done so is by becoming an expert at his trade, and the history of the movie script he tries to write about the flooding of Fiddlersburg shows us the result. First he offers himself a sardonic parody: "[Writer] comes back to Fiddlersburg, sees sister, becomes aware that he admires her legs, discovers she is really his mother in disguise, which explains everything. End: view of healing waters rising over Fiddlersburg in the dawn." Then he admits to his producer that he is stuck, unable to write merely expertly about Fiddlersburg and unable to face going back to the vision of *I'm Telling You Now*. Finally, in an excitement of half-understood irony ("Wheel and deal!" he shouts), he does produce an expert script—not "a bolt out of place or a nut loose." Yasha Jones, his producer, turns it down, and when Brad defends it on the ground that the plot is "exactly the way things have a way of happening," Yasha says, "It doesn't matter. . . . What matters is the feeling. Where in this is the feeling we want? Where is Fiddlersburg?" "You have," as he says elsewhere, "to document things. But if you depend on the documentation, then the real thing—all right, I'll say it—the vision, it may be—" To be overwhelmed with the multiplicity of the world, as he reminds Brad, "is the last sin for people in our business—no, in any business—the sin of the corruption of consciousness."

Brad's struggle with this script is one image of *Flood's* meaning. As with all his other experiences, Brad knows, even as he tries to hide behind his *expertise*, the truth Yasha Jones is insisting on. Only at moments can he take comfort in remembering the reviews of his most recent Hollywood success, *The Dream of Jacob*; "Dear God, it was an awful movie," his sister Maggie says to Yasha. Brad knows that too. "An expert," he says, "is a man who can do something on an artificial leg almost as well as you can do it on a real one . . . practice a lot and learn to do the rhumba with it, and give exhibitions in hospitals to hearten the inmates in their infirmities and he will get his picture in the papers. He will be an expert." This remark is a typical example of the way Brad, the ingenious intellectual, uses his awareness of the real nature of man's consciousness and his world to avoid facing it.

From the novel's cunningly timed beginning square in the middle of Brad's struggle, when he drives from Fiddlersburg to the Nashville airport to meet Yasha's plane, we watch him seeing everything with this double vision. We do not yet know why he does, but we see how he is using irony at once to recognize and to deny the realities of the world and himself. "If everything is fake then nothing matters," he tells himself comfortingly as he passes a horrible new motel called The Seven Dwarfs, where no expense has been spared. But a stream beside the motel bothers him: it is unavoidably real. In this way his attempt to believe that nothing matters is constantly being defeated, but he does his best to use even his awareness of the reality of the world to sustain his hope that it is fake. So, as he watches the stewardess opening the door of Yasha's plane, he thinks, "would she fly off and bring back an olive branch in her beak?" What a marvelously absurd ark a DC-7 is; as long as Brad can hold on to that sense of the world's absurdity, he can avoid admitting the truth. This is a powerful help to him, since the world is ridiculous—tasteless, pretentious, stupid, corrupt in nature. When a guard at Fiddlersburg's penitentiary refuses to shoot a madman who is murdering a guard for fear of hitting an innocent man, Mr. Budd, the Deputy Warden, says, "Jesus Christ, a innocent man! There ain't no innocent man! You are fired." Mr. Budd knows this because in his way he also knows what Fiddlersburg's cultivated lawyer puts more elegantly when he says, "I look out the window and see some pore misguided boogers doing the best they can—according to their dim lights . . . [and] what you might call the pathos of the mundane sort of takes the edge off my grim satisfaction. . . ." It takes the edge off Brad's too (Mr. Budd is too "simple" a man ever to have felt any).

But Brad's most powerful help in maintaining his grim dissatisfaction with himself and the world is the way he has reduced his originally uncorrupted consciousness, the consciousness that went into *I'm Telling You Now*, to romantic idealism. For twenty years he has been turning Fiddlersburg into a sentimental myth that in its more sophisticated way bears the same relation to truth as the pathetic dream of happiness expressed by the Seven Dwarfs Motel. So long as he can define goodness as this unrealizable myth, he is safe from having to believe the actual world is good, can see it as material for romantic irony. He expends a great deal of creative energy on doing so, and the effect is formidable, for Mr. Warren is an impressive wit. Yet there is always a disturbing hum of suggestion behind Brad's ironies, a hint that in the end the joke is on him, that his irony is not a way of dissociating himself from the homely, vulgar, shocking world but a way of acknowledging its blessedness, though he does not consciously take that hint until the end of the book.

So powerful is this romantic irony that it is almost as easy for the reader as for Brad to be lulled by it. When, for example, he observes that "the whores of Nashville, it was officially stated by Federal authorities, did more than the matchless cavalry of Nathan Bedford Forrest to stem the tide of human freedom and hard money" and adds that the United Daughters of the Confederacy ought to put up a monument "to those gallant girls of the VD brigade who gave their all to all," it is hard not to be convinced of the adequacy of this view of history. It is funny and, as far as it goes, right. The same thing is true of his remark that modern Nashville "aspires to be the Kansas City of the upper Buttermilk Belt"; yet he refuses to go on to subject Nashville's absurd replica of the Parthenon to the same irony: something stops him. It is hard not to accept the bitter truth of his assertion about Fiddlersburg's Confederate statue that "he's been standing there a long time now, holding off gunboats and Yankee investors and new ideas" and easy to ignore it when he adds that the statue stands for "the lie that is the truth of the self." Romantic irony is Brad's defense against recognizing that truth; but we ought to recognize it.

The design of *Flood* surrounds Brad with characters who in their various ways have faced that truth—like the intellectuals Yasha Jones (in realistic terms the least plausible of Mr. Warren's characters) and Blanding Cottshill (who has to suffer not only the loss of the Negro mistress he loves but the knowledge that he is to blame for that loss), like Brother Pinckney, the cultivated Negro preacher, and Brother Potts, the uneducated white one who is dying of cancer. In Brother Potts's life Mr. Warren gives us his plainest image of the desperate difficulty of accepting the truth. Brother Potts has seen it as his duty to go to the penitentiary to pray with a condemned murderer, a Negro who "with a claw hammer of the value of six dollars . . . did with malice aforethought and against the peace and good order of the State of Tennessee, beat the pore bleeding be-Jesus out of the head of pore old Mrs. Milt Spiffort. All he could say in court was that she made him do it." As Brother Potts is on his knees in the cell praying, Pretty Boy leans forward and carefully spits in his face. "But I didn't get off my knees," Brother Potts says. "Something held me down and I name it Glory. . . . I did not make a motion to wipe that spit. I let it run. And I was praying again, out loud. . . . I was praying for God to make me know that what happened was right because it was His Holy Will." Brother Potts "is merely a good man, full of suffering and befuddlement, doing his best to walk in the steps of the Master. He has no irony . . . [no] awareness of that doubleness of life that lies far below flowers of rhetoric or pirouettes of mind." He is incapable of the pirouettes by which Brad avoids this knowledge. But even Brad cannot avoid it when his Lady of Shalott from Fiddlersburg, the blind Leontine Purtle, turns out to be real.

The most important human experience for Mr. Warren appears to be sexual experience; it is perhaps a romantic attitude. For all his major characters, especially for Brad and his wife Lettice, it is the testing occasion. Brad and Lettice, the beautiful New York girl, were strongly attracted to each other, and for a while that was enough. But it had gradually gone bad because Brad used it more and more as a momentary release from the knowledge he could not get out of it. At the end of the novel, years after they have parted, Lettice realizes that "we could have had a life together . . . and been happy, even if I got old and slow, for we might have loved one another" (as Yasha Jones does Maggie, despite "the infinitesimally sagging, scheduled failure of her body"). When they are driving to Nashville for the last time, Lettice asks Brad to make love to her one last time; "in a sardonic trance" he takes her into a "grassy glade by a stream under a cedar bluff." That sardonic trance is a major rejection. "Wouldn't you like to remember us really ourselves?" Lettice says; but

Brad says, "God damn it, I don't want to remember a God-damned thing!"

That was twenty years before the present time of the novel (1960), but Brad has never been able to endure the thought of that grassy glade since. He cannot stand it any better now that it is occupied by the Seven Dwarfs Motel, where a bright Fisk student leans against the high-test pump in an Elizabethan fool's costume and pretends to be a "Yassah, boss" Negro—and as Brad drives away from the pump in his white Hollywood Jaguar the Negro says, "Thanks, Mac." This is part of Mortimer Sparlin's revenge, *his* romantic irony (and it is part of Brad's awareness of his self-deception that when Yasha Jones pays him a compliment he grins boyishly and says, "Thanks, Mac"). The other part of Mortimer Sparlin's revenge is to sleep with aging white patrons of the Seven Dwarfs and then have to go "out into the predawn dark, hating the world and himself."

When Brad returns to Fiddlersburg, he focuses his romantic myth on Leontine Purtle; when he was fifteen "there had been a promise in the moonlight that spread all over the world westward without end. Where had that promise gone?" Now he persuades himself he has found it in a pure and innocent blind girl. He has had plenty of warning; Leontine has bothered him badly by showing him she understands what he was saying about Fiddlersburg in *I'm Telling You Now*. She is, like Brother Potts, wholly her limited self and therefore without despair or shame. But she is no Lady of Shalott. So desperately does Brad cling to his illusion about her that he does not even notice the absurdity of lusting for the Lady of Shalott. When he calls her that, Yasha Jones says, "What does that make you? Lancelot?" and Brad says, "It was the Queen he was getting it off." But though he says it, he does not see it. Driven by his incongruous desire to possess what has become for him what it is precisely because it cannot be physically possessed, he takes Leontine to the Seven Dwarfs Motel, to the spot where he had once before rejected himself by rejecting Lettice. He is now sure that what he thinks was the promise of his boyhood, the promise of a simple, happy, innocent life, is about to be fulfilled—until he feels the diaphragm Leontine is wearing and she is saying, "Oh, slower, slower, oh, slow." With practiced ease, Brad slides back into his protective irony. "Who the hell is running this show, girlie?" he says. When they leave, Mortimer Sparlin, "grinning at him, not idiotically now," whispers, "Tell me, Mac, how do you like blind tail?" "You bastard," Brad says, "You bla—" and Mortimer, a Golden Gloves boxer, knocks him down. "Sure," he says, "everybody knows Miss Purtle. Lots of boys, it would seem, like blind tail. And you, Mr. Tolliver. . . ." A man like the rest, Brad has fooled himself so badly that not even finding himself with Leontine in the Candy Cottage of the Seven Dwarfs Motel could awaken him from his dream of her as the Lady of Shalott. It is not Leontine's fault; "shy and hesitant like a child asking for praise," she says afterwards, "Brad—I sort of fooled you didn't I?" She is, without false shame, herself. It is Brad who is not, who has been asking something both impossible and inferior of life in order to avoid being himself.

For Mr. Warren, uncorrupted consciousness is the "awareness of evanescence," a grasp of the precious "human moment" when one has "the past and the future in a present vision." To live in this knowledge is to live so that the incommensurables of the imagination with its tempting promises and of history with its recalcitrant actualities become commensurable. The novelist who tries to realize this consciousness must recognize "the story of someone who had no story," not try to create and enact a story. Good fiction documents a vision; it does not lose itself in the way things happen, in documenting the multiplicity of the world. That is why *Flood* is not a realistic novel with a carefully articulated plot, minutely lifelike characters, and a deadly serious system of motives. You have to document the vision, and therefore Mr. Warren provides the necessary amount of facts but he does not "depend on the documentation." *Flood* is a complex metaphor with the vision I have been crudely paraphrasing as its tenor. "Life," as Yasha Jones says, "is so logical—superficially, that is—therefore so plotty. . . . But . . . don't we [writers] have to violate life? To stylize life?"

Instead, then, of being a "realistic" picture of life, *Flood* is an image; instead of appealing to our interest in "what happens next," it appeals to us as a poem does. It is an action, arranged, "stylized," with wonderful skill to bring a very large number of events into the best possible order for documenting a vision—"like those long strands of lights for Christmas trees you take out on Christmas Eve and can't for hell's sake untangle." One may or may not share Mr. Warren's vision, but one ought to recognize its depth and inclusiveness. Nearly every important American way-station of the spirit is here with all its self-deception—complacent or suffering—and all its human pathos: our nostalgia for the imagined past; our earnest dreams of a sensible, school-lunch future; our longings for the nirvanas of manly lust and pastoral love and romantic disillusion; our delight in gadgetry and mere skillfulness; our desire for the release of war's respectable violence or of political dogma's solemn irresponsibility. The vision projected in *Flood* is large and relevant, and the form Mr. Warren uses for it—whether, again, one approves of its kind or not—is used with a sureness of control that gives the documentation of his vision a marvelous, eloquent coherence.

"Down the Line" [*Who Speaks for the Negro?*]

Joseph Epstein*

In *Segregation*, one of his earlier works on "The Problem," Robert Penn Warren attempted to uncover the various philosophies of social change prevalent in the South after the 1954 Supreme Court decision. Consisting mainly of interviews with Southerners about their plans for dealing with integration, the book, published in 1956, anticipated what we now know to be yet another failure of a large segment of the white South to come to reasonable terms with history. Reading it today as a historical document, however, one is more struck by the changes—in emotional climate, if not in material conditions—that have taken place in nine years. In 1956, for example, a Southern Negro lawyer told Warren: "A Negro, he doesn't really know some things, but he just goes walking pregnant with worries, not knowing their name. It's he lost his purpose, somewhere. He goes wandering and wondering, and no purpose."

There are very few pages in *Who Speaks for the Negro?* which do not serve to invalidate that remark; moreover, the very conception of the book shows how much things have changed. As in *Segregation*, Warren continues to be interested in philosophies of social change, but now he puts his questions exclusively to Negroes: to civil-rights leaders and rank-and-filers, to writers and artists, civil servants and businessmen, college presidents and students—to a variety of people who, as the saying goes, have been down the line. And rightly has Warren chosen to do this, for the fact is that for the first time Negroes are now in a position to exert a major influence on decisions concerning their future in this country. Indeed, for the moment it appears that the initiative for any radical realignment of American society has passed into Negro hands. As Warren suggests, it is almost as if the helots had been called in to rewrite the Constitution of Athens.

In this long and valuable inquiry, Warren seeks to determine precisely what the helots have in mind. Although a large part of *Who Speaks for the Negro?* is made up of interviews caught on that most impersonal of modern instruments, the tape recorder, it is in many ways a very personal book: interspersed with the interviews are editorials, long analytical essays, and fragments of autobiography. The interviews themselves are conducted with an utter lack of condescension—no matter whether Warren is talking with Carl Rowan, formerly head of the United States Information Agency, or a freshman girl at Tougaloo College in Mississippi. They are introduced by short, often quite brilliant, biographical and physical sketches, and are occasionally interrupted by a personal aside, a

*Reprinted from *Commentary*, Oct. 1965, pp. 101–05, by permission of Georges Borchardt, Inc. Copyright © 1965 by Joseph Epstein.

reminiscence from Warren's own past, or a simple notice that "here there was a change of tape."

It would be rather more than naive to assume that anyone as interested in social change as Warren doesn't have some firm ideas of his own on the subject; nor does he try to hide them in any way. In the course of his interview with Dr. Kenneth Clark, for instance, the name of the abolitionist John Brown comes up, and Warren tells us that a French critic, in writing an introduction to one of his novels, once remarked "that the mythic Brown figure recurs again and again in my fiction, in various disguises, the man who at any cost would strike out for absolute solutions—a type toward whom, I suppose, I am deeply ambivalent." As a novelist, Warren may well feel ambivalent toward men like Brown, but as a student of social change he clearly views the type as an abomination; in the latter capacity, in fact, he is the least apocalyptic of men.

Such a disposition is frequently of considerable advantage for the task at hand, as when it enables Warren to pick his way through a goodly portion of the rhetoric of the civil-rights movement. Consider, for instance, the slogan "Freedom Now!"; Warren is always asking his subjects what is meant by "Now." Many of them are hung up dreadfully by this simple question, and the closest thing to an authentic answer is supplied by SNCC's Robert Moses (now known as Robert Parris), who confesses that the slogan is really a poetic statement.

His own distaste for absolute solutions leads Warren to react less than favorably to those who cry out for them: Adam Clayton Powell, the late Malcolm X, James Forman, and, on a much more sophisticated level, James Baldwin, who is felt by many to be something like the civil-rights movement's Trotsky. Baldwin's writing has always been rife with contradictions, and Warren is devastatingly thorough in pointing them out. On any given day, for instance, Baldwin will accuse the white man of inflating the Negro's sexual prowess and then turn around and speak of the "poverty of the white cat's bed." And when he is not contradictory, he is likely to be excessively bitter. Thus he told Warren that no matter what the white worker for SNCC or CORE does—and presumably he includes Michael Schwerner and Andrew Goodman in this category—"his work has no resonance." Something other than mere rhetoric or foggy thinking is at work here, and I think Warren puts his finger on it better than anyone else who has written about Baldwin:

> [It] is not that what Baldwin has to say in any one instance is not interesting and significant; it is that he instinctively makes this shift of the center of gravity of a discussion, toward an undercut, toward the more general and more charged, toward the absolute. He is, in fact, impatient of the nagging problems of ordinary situations, of half-measures and compromises, of the slow grind of adjustment and improvisation. He must turn toward that "interior life" which is real, turn inward to be

refreshed at the foundation of his own being. But some people—including many Negroes—must deal with the nag and slow grind. They must try to discipline their interior life to some sad facts of the exterior world in order to change those facts.

Perhaps Baldwin is not the Movement's Trotsky after all, but rather, in an informal and rather elegant way, the head of what might be called its Agitprop Section. Agitprop certainly has its uses, and not only the eloquent brand dispensed by James Baldwin. Some of the young SNCC workers in Pine Bluff, Arkansas, for example, have told me that the late Malcolm X was of inestimable value in arousing the teenage Negro community in that city. There had been copies of the Muslim newspaper *Muhammad Speaks* around the SNCC office, and some of the local kids read them and were greatly impressed by Malcolm's articles and speeches—not so much by their content as by the sheer (and to them unique) fact that here was a Negro telling the white man straight out to go to hell. It was a new and not altogether unhealthy experience for them. But at some point one must do more than tell the white man to go to hell; at some point, agitprop must yield to genuine thought. A particularly poignant moment occurs in the course of Warren's interview—by far the most candid in the book—with Ralph Ellison, when the author of *Invisible Man*, whose remarks are free of all agitprop, says: "Perhaps I can talk this way because I'm not a leader."

As for the leaders, Warren writes of them: "In general, the Negro leadership has given the public little reason to be appalled, for in a situation as complicated as this it would not be easy to imagine a higher level of idealism, dedication, and realistic intelligence." By and large, one can agree. The civil-rights leaders' commission is awesome and terrifying in its dimensions, and it is unfortunate for Warren's book that, as Ellison suggests, candor is not—not yet, anyway—part of that commission. Warren hangs in there all right, trying to draw the Big Brass out, trying to pry them loose from the images so carefully cultivated over the years. But in the pages of *Who Speaks for the Negro?* they are the old familiar gang: Roy Wilkins, reasonable yet reasonably militant; Whitney Young, solid and aggressive, coming on like a pro tackle with a doctorate in sociology; James Forman, a combat officer, slightly contemptuous of anyone not serving with a line outfit; the rugged and austere James Farmer; the saintly Martin Luther King, Jr.

Along with a high level of idealism, dedication, and intelligence, these men share one other characteristic: an unrelenting need for victories. According to Whitney Young, victories are needed to contain the danger of "overreach" and to forestall violence. But they are also needed to perpetuate the present leadership. Even now SNCC, the most revisionist-minded of the civil-rights organizations, is questioning the necessity for any national leadership whatsoever.

Clearly, then, positions of leadership in the civil-rights movement are not strong on tenure or other security benefits normally accruing to those who serve long and faithfully in high places. One explanation for such a state of affairs has it that this is perfectly natural, that the civil-rights leader's precarious position is very much part of something called "the revolution of rising expectations," by which is meant that each victory only makes one's following hungrier for bigger victories. But the trouble goes deeper and is, I think, peculiar to the movement at this particular point in its history. The main problem, as the slum organizer Saul Alinsky among others has pointed out, is that the movement has largely remained a single-issue movement, attracting people who are interested in one thing and one thing only—the Negro.

As a single-issue movement, it has definite limitations. One cannot, for example, very well demand jobs for undereducated, unskilled Negroes if in fact there are few jobs for anyone who is undereducated or unskilled. The point is that discrimination can no longer be solely blamed for the situation in which many Negroes now find themselves; for if the remaining barriers of race were instantly to be dropped, there would still be a large number of people generally unequipped to make out in modern America—a goodly proportion of them being Negroes.

Thus far the civil-rights movement, as a movement, has not in any definite or serious way addressed itself to the question of what is to be done once discrimination will no longer be the major issue. True, Bayard Rustin feels that the time has come for the movement to switch from protest to politics, and tells Warren: "I reject the idea of working for the Negro as being impractical as well as immoral if one does that alone." True, James Farmer defines integration as the "maximum opportunity for significant choices"—and by this he means maximum opportunity for the maximum number of people. True, Martin Luther King, Jr. now speaks of a "Bill of Rights for the Disadvantaged," much as for years Whitney Young has been speaking for a domestic Marshall Plan. Yet little has thus far been done to turn the civil-rights movement in this direction. But until the movement comes to terms with such larger problems, its leaders can be expected to remain on the spot, caught up in tactics and forced to supply rhetoric because victories become ever harder to achieve.

Up to now the biggest single victory the Negro has won, as Warren's book makes amply clear, is the moral strength to speak for himself. It is an important beginning—but it is only a beginning.

The Enormous Spider Web of Warren's World [*Meet Me in the Green Glen*]

John W. Aldridge*

Robert Penn Warren's *Meet Me in the Green Glen* seems certain to be recognized as one of his most distinguished novels since *All the King's Men*. The new work is far more tightly structured than its immediate predecessors, *Wilderness* and *Flood*; the rhetorical fattiness that has always been characteristic of Warren's fiction has been replaced by a hard texture of language very like his poetry. Yet the book is complex enough to sustain the illusion that there are several kinds of narrative form through which the action is simultaneously developed, each providing a view of the action both complete in itself and indispensable to the completion of the whole. As in most of Warren's novels, the central dramatic situation is that of the murder mystery, although this work can also be seen as a romantic parable existing with perfect rightness on the levels of melodrama and moral philosophy; a love story that, contrary to current fashions, is finally neither sentimental nor narcissistic; a prose poem remarkable for its lyric intensity; a Southern novel in which the characters are both realistically depicted cultural types and personifications of forces so violent and destructive that they seem almost more Elizabethan than contemporary.

The literary qualities of the book are considerable enough to assure it an important place among serious novels of the last several years. But of perhaps equal interest to admirers of Warren is the fact that he offers here a distillation of themes and materials which have preoccupied him throughout his career but have never before been made visible in quite this concentrated a form. As a result, this novel may help to clarify Warren's position at a time when, in spite of his years of sustained achievement, the size of his critical reputation, and his wide popularity with the reading public, he still projects a rather anomalous image, is still somehow more admired as a writer than accepted as a shaper of consciousness.

Since 1939, in addition to his many books of nonfiction and poetry, Warren has published eight novels, nearly all of them vital and original works which have been respectfully received and, in some cases, commercially very successful. Yet only *All the King's Men* can be said to have made a real impact upon the imagination of our time, and to have appealed equally to literary intellectuals and to the general public. A possible explanation is that *All the King's Men* was the sole instance in Warren's fiction when he dealt with contemporary life in terms that were

*Reprinted from *Saturday Review*, 9 Oct. 1971, pp. 31–32, 35–37. Copyright © *Saturday Review*, 1971. All rights reserved.

familiar and fashionable to both classes of readers. Although the setting and many of the central materials of the book were specifically Southern, it was as a whole less regional than generally American.

The work also dramatized the dilemma of the narrator-protagonist, Jack Burden, within a philosophical framework that, on the face of it, seemed modishly existential—the tough-talking young cynic confronting the meaninglessness of his life, the empty relativism of his moral attitudes, at a moment when he is forced to define his responsibility for a series of tragedies that overtake almost all the people he has admired and loved. Jack Burden was the quintessential anti-hero of the Age of Anxiety, a textbook case of contemporary alienation with whom intellectuals could easily identify. The popular audience, on the other hand, undoubtedly responded almost altogether to the thriller aspects of the novel, and as usual their instincts for separating the glitter from the gold were infallible. There were murders and suicides by the dozen, just enough sex to titillate without really arousing, and the whole story was beautifully cast in the Hollywood mold. Not only were most of the characters stock movie types, but the seemingly effortless and quite successful translation of the novel into film made it clear that the meretricious values of that medium were highly compatible with certain, but by no means all, of the values implicit in Warren's materials.

His other novels have, for the most part, lacked these qualities of box office theatrics combined with high philosophical chic, and they have suffered from the additional difficulty of depending for their significance much more directly upon the Southern experience. This in itself would scarcely seem crippling when one considers that for a great many people the Southern experience is no less valid and real—and may even be considerably more dramatically complex—than the experience of New York or the Midwest, that it has enjoyed for a good many years the distinction of being a chief source of literary materials for the American novel, and that Warren's treatment of the South is imaginative enough to endow it with a dynamic life and a generality of meaning far larger than that of a merely regional subject-matter. But two factors have operated to cause the Southernness of his novels to be construed as a limitation. The first is that during the period of Warren's greatest productivity as a novelist, Faulkner had already established himself so securely as the official literary imagination of the South that it soon became almost impossible to think of the South except as a mythical Yoknapatawpha County or to believe that any other writer could possibly have anything new or important to say about it.

Also, over the same period, as a result partly of Faulkner's apparent exhaustion of the Southern material and partly of a radical shift of cultural interests, we began to take it for granted that the really central experience of our time is that of the Northern urban intellectual, of characters like Augie March, Herzog, and Portnoy, who personify the experience not of Wasp intellectuals of the Thirties and Forties—many of whom, significantly, have been both native Southerners and Faulkner's and Warren's most vigorous supporters—but of the New York literary establishment. Since urban intellectuals are now the principal shapers of literary opinion in this country, it is only natural that they would promote into celebrity such writers as Bellow, Mailer, and Roth with whom they can identify most closely, and that Warren, writing out of a background they find alien, would seem to them a peripheral and rather parochial figure. This attitude is itself of course extremely parochial, but because it is also extremely influential, it has created the impression that only certain forms of American experience are suitable for literature, only certain writers are qualified to tell the real truth about American life.

Yet the problem is not merely that one kind of regional experience has been accepted as more authoritative than another kind. It is also that, perhaps as a result of this development, we have grown accustomed to a particular metaphysical approach to experience in fiction. We now seem to believe that the only really tenable view for the novelist is the nihilistic view, in which events without meaning are seen to occur in a world without standards, and neither author nor characters presume to suggest what standards there may once have been or ought to be. The fictional situation we tend to find most artistically serious and relevant to life is one involving the continuous search for identity among people who have no realization of either the presence of the past or the possibility of the future, and so exist in a state of paralysis or dreary preoccupation with the merely sensational, with violence enacted without motive, sex enacted without passion or love—hence, from which all human meaning has disappeared. The fictional characters who speak to us most convincingly are usually those who become deranged by the anarchy of life to the point where they perhaps retreat, like Portnoy, into compulsive masturbation or, like Augie March, seek in the provisional structures of belief fabricated by others some means of understanding and controlling the anarchy in themselves. The experience depicted in our most respected novels again and again poses the problem described so well by Gide's Michel in *The Immoralist*: "To know how to free oneself is nothing; the arduous thing is to know what to do with one's freedom."

As his novels make clear and *All the King's Men* demonstrates in perhaps too programmatic a form, Warren is fully aware of this problem in its connection with contemporary nihilism. But he differs from most of our novelists in realizing that the question of what to do with one's freedom is unanswerable unless and until the limits of our freedom are defined by the beginnings of our responsibility. This is to suggest that Warren brings a morally conservative—albeit politically liberal—vision to the problems of nihilism and reveals a clear understanding of just how men should behave, how they may find, or search for and never find, their salvation through self-knowledge, what standards should be used to measure our fall from standards, in exactly what way we should relate to our history and confront what he calls "the awful responsibility of Time."

If such a view is unfashionable at this time, it probably is so because the urban liberal mind is unfamiliar with, or finds politically reprehensible, the premises on which it is based. Yet in a nihilistic and dehumanizing society there is a massive, if seldom articulated need, of the kind confessed to by Nick Carraway in *The Great Gatsby* for "the world to be in uniform and at a sort of moral attention forever," and Warren gives concrete dramatic expression to this need. For him no contradiction exists between liberal politics and moral conservatism. Both are implicit in his broadly humanistic philosophy, and both are inextricably joined to his subject matter, which is always derived from the Southern experience. It is most unlikely that he would be able to dramatize the philosophy without the subject matter, for the South is uniquely a region in which the issues that most profoundly engage his imagination have a living and dynamic basis in social fact.

Warren once wrote that in Faulkner's view "the old order [of the South] . . . allowed the traditional man to define himself as human by setting up codes, concepts of virtue, obligations, and by accepting the risks of his humanity. Within the traditional order was a notion of truth, even if man in the flow of things did not succeed in realizing that truth." The same view might, with minor alterations, be attributed to Warren himself. For him as for Faulkner, the literary value of the South is that it provides cultural and mythic structures against which, since they rest upon an idealistic "notion of truth," human character and conduct can be morally—therefore, dramatically—evaluated amid conditions that are the exact opposite of those prevailing in the urban North. In fact, one of the central themes of the Southern novel is the conflict between an established humanistic tradition, with its inherited "concepts of virtue," and the forces of materialism, relativism, and opportunism that typify the modern South and the modern world. This is the sort of conflict which is exemplified in Faulkner by the opposition between his Compson-Sartoris and Sutpen-Snopes families. Historically, if not at the present time, the South has existed, or sought to exist, as the metaphysical antithesis of scientific rationalism. Warren has spoken of the tendency of science to create a division between intellect and emotion, between head and heart knowledge, which he calls "the terrible division of the age." Jack Burden's problem is that he cannot reconcile the teachings of his head and heart. By temperament a romantic and an idealist, he wants to love, have faith in, and give his assent to life. But his cynical intelligence causes him to see people as stereotypes—The Boss, The Brass-Bound Idealist, The Scholarly Attorney—and the process of existence as simply biological function, "the dark heave of the blood," "The Great Twitch." This divided view results in Burden's nearly fatal separation from those he loves and from himself. Only through discovering and affirming his identity with the past and accepting responsibility for having helped to shape it can he bring together the disparate sides of his nature.

The Southern mind has traditionally aspired to this kind of autonomy and relationship, this state of being harmonious with nature, history, and the flow of life, and it has attempted to exist by concepts of fidelity and responsibility intended to preserve both individual and communal order. The cavalier code of manly honor and feminine virtue is one such concept. As an ideal, it has had forces at work against it in Southern society that have always been of the strongest potential violence, self-destructiveness, and racial and sexual guilt. Unlike New England and the Midwest, where a long puritan history has led to the repression of so much of the demonic in human nature, the South has existed in a state of constant dialectical tension between a romantic urge for absolute purity and the most sensuous appetite for corruption. Hence, it provides a moral situation in which the issue of guilt and responsibility can be dramatized because both the decorums of virtue and the potential for their violent overthrow are concretely present in the social scene.

In addition, the South has provided and continues in many areas to provide factual verification of the idea that past and present are closely interrelated, that there is an observable connection between past actions and present conditions. It is still quite common in the South for people to be born and spend their whole lives in the same community, to know the histories of their own and one another's families in intimate detail, and to live every day with the results of the deeds and misdeeds of their ancestors. Thus, experience confirms the truth of Warren's belief that "the world is like an enormous spider web," and, as Amantha Starr says in *Band of Angels*, "You live through time, that little piece of time . . . is yours, but that piece of time is not only your own life, it is the summing-up of all the other lives . . . It is, in other words, History, and what you are is an expression of History, and you do not live your life, but somehow your life lives you, and you are, therefore, only what History does to you."

The need to confront one's true nature within history, to live by an ideal of responsibility while learning to accept the facts of human existence, both past and present, these are ideas that can be used in fiction only when the writer has available social materials that embody them. As the examples of Warren and Faulkner make clear, the materials of the Southern experience do embody them in great abundance. Hence, it is not surprising that their novels represent the most vital alternative we have to the urban novel of anarchy. Warren's Southern contemporary, Allen Tate, once observed that "in ages which suffer the decay of manners, religion, morals, codes, our indestructible vitality demands expression in violence and chaos . . . men who have lost both the higher myth of religion and the lower myth of historical dramatization have lost the forms of human action . . . they capitulate from their human role to a series of pragmatic conquests which, taken alone, are true only in some other world than that inhabited by men." That other world is the one most commonly reflected in novels of our time.

"A man that is born," said Joseph Conrad, "falls into a dream," and he may remain in a dream for the rest of his life unless some physical or psychic accident, some signal of destiny, forces him awake. The knowledge that he is in fact alive may come with overwhelming force and be destructive. But an acceptance of that knowledge is the only chance he has to confront himself and recognize his fate. For as Warren believes—and the idea is very Conradian—"The end of man is to know." Jack Burden's awakening to life occurs when he hears his mother's scream of anguish over the suicide of Judge Irwin, his real father, and discovers in that scream not only the identity of his father but a mother he can for the first time honor and love.

Nearly all the characters in *Meet Me in the Green Glen* have fallen into a dream, find life unreal and themselves unreal in life, and there are those who exist permanently in the dream state. Others are awakened, some brutally, some with a great and exhilarating sense of liberation. But each is changed and given significance by the manner of his awakening and the truth or lie he awakens to. The catalyzing agent for them all is a young Sicilian, Angelo Passetto, who comes out of nowhere down a road one day in the Tennessee hill country, enters by chance the life of a woman named Cassie Spottwood, who can never be quite sure he is real but falls in love with him and, like Faulkner's Joanna Burden after becoming the lover of Joe Christmas, is awakened into sexuality and self-recognition. Angelo, however, remains locked in his narcissistic dream. Cassie is unreal to him. He sleepwalks through her life, taking from her, even in his way loving her, but is untransformed. Finally, he leaves her, and she, understanding his need, helps him to leave. Then, realizing for the first time her own need, Cassie murders her husband who has been paralyzed and in a coma for many years. Angelo is inevitably accused of the crime and although he is convicted, Cassie rises in the courtroom and proclaims her guilt. But she is taken in charge by her husband's old friend, Murray Guilfort, who manages to convince the authorities that she is insane.

In a sense the novel is really about Guilfort, the familiar figure in Warren's fiction of the man who has never found release from the prison of himself and so has lived his whole life in envy and fear of those who, like Cassie's husband, are or once were in vital possession of themselves and their freedom. Guilfort's recognition of his failure compels him in the end to suicide but not before he realizes that: *"The dream* [of life] *is a lie, but the dreaming is truth* . . . not knowing what it meant, but thinking that, if so many people moved across the world as though they knew what it meant, it must mean something."

Taken in terms of the events themselves nothing could conceivably be

more melodramatic and sentimental. Cassie's last-minute courtroom confession is pure Perry Mason, while the story of her affair with Angelo, his
conviction for a murder she committed and the closing image of her huddled semiconscious against the stone wall of the prison after he is elec-
trocuted might have come straight from the tear-stained pages of a
nineteenth-century ladies' magazine. Yet Warren contrives by some
magic to make these bathetic materials not only acceptable but entirely
convincing. The melodrama is given appropriateness by the fact that the
characters belong to a pastoral milieu in which emotions are felt with an
almost aboriginal nakedness and intensity, and as Warren has repeatedly
demonstrated in his novels, it is in the extremities of violence and passion
that the moral issues of human conduct may be most sharply defined. But
he is also vindicated by his choice of form, the parabolic romance, where
the characters are meant to be less true to life than crystallizations of
elemental and extravagant attitudes.

In this respect, *Meet Me in the Green Glen* is, as I have said, a
remarkably pure poetic distillation of Warren's typical themes and
materials. As such, the novel possesses a coherence at the levels of idea and
action which makes it impossible to separate one from the other. There is
no conflict here between head and heart knowledge, between philosophical truth and feeling. Warren, if not his characters, has been able to
transcend "the terrible division of the age" and to achieve an autonomy
that is at once metaphysical and esthetic. He has done so undoubtedly
because he is committed to a holistic vision of human experience and to a
kind of literary material peculiarly suited to its dramatic expression.
There is reassurance at just this time in seeing him affirm with continued
power his belief that a possibility exists for us beyond the prevailing anarchy. But Warren finally offers no program for the rehabilitation of the
moral environment. He is fully aware of the fact that life is a dialectical
process and that, as he says, "in so far as [man] is to achieve redemption
he must do so through an awareness of his condition that identifies him
with the general human communion . . . The victory is never won, the
redemption must be continually re-earned." He might have added what
his novels seem always to suggest: that the victory is not in the redemption, but in the process of earning and re-earning. That is the process
which creates such meaning as we have in history.

"A Technician's Romance"
[*A Place to Come To*]

Richard Howard *

Near the end of Robert Penn Warren's tenth novel, the narrator and central figure explains his boredom yet again: "But now my research and writing, like women, became valuable to me as a way to fill up time, and as I had more time to fill I had more fame. I tried to be kind to my students, but to bear down on them. I still had one belief, held with some passion, that good technicians—and you notice my choice of the term, for what it is worth—are better than bad ones."

It is difficult not to believe the novelist (and difficult not to believe he is speaking for himself, the obsessed professional) when he turns to us this way, addressing his readers directly from the center of his story. Here is a narrative of one man's self-recovery, believed in by its narrator and made believable to us only insofar as it is the product of a good technician. Of course, a good technician, in matters of fiction, is not necessarily a writer who avoids mistakes. Rather, I think he is a writer who can turn his mistakes, his crudities, and even his fatigue to his own advantage. He can perceive in a sentence about lovemaking—"I am sure that, in the occasion at my house, we both had expected to recapture something of the old magic"—both the corny shorthand that is unacceptable even to his hero *and* the necessary refinement of it, nearly a hundred pages later on: "I have never had the slightest notion of what happiness is—what I thought of all my life as happiness was only excitement." A good technician, then, is the storyteller who trusts his talent, if not his tale; his words, if not the world.

And it is hard for the reader to trust the tale told in *A Place to Come To*. So extreme are the terms of it, so sensational the world whose ways are grinningly recounted here, that we need a lot of slow convincing if we are to be brought round. We do get what we need, and Robert Penn Warren's novel is a success, but you would never believe it in any words but his.

Jediah Tewksbury, age nine, begins the telling of his story with the death of his father, at the end of World War I, in an accident that spreads a pall of penis envy over the boy's entire life. Not even in Hemingway has the central male figure been such a successful (and determined) lover as this affectless Alabama outsider, spurred by his iron-maiden mother to escape the South. With the assistance of the kind old maid Latin teacher that one assumes had been patented by Faulkner, Jed does escape the South, even though—once the University of Chicago, marriage, widowerhood, and even fighting with Italian partisans behind Nazi lines

* Reprinted from *Saturday Review*, 19 March, 1977, pp. 30, 34. Copyright © *Saturday Review*, 1977. All rights reserved.

have intervened—the South is not to escape Jed. For the native returns—to Tennessee, and to a sybaritic set of high-living profligates, including, of course, the Pretty Girl from back home in Alabama, who is now up in the world and down on her luck. Jed makes terrible depredations, as an earlier generation of southern novelists used to say, among the ladies and must again escape—to Paris, Chicago, another marriage, fatherhood, fame, and fortune. "Hating the South I had fled it," he says, "and ever afterwards blamed my solitude on that fact. I had fled but had found nowhere to flee to. I told how I had tried to buy my way out of solitude by supporting the causes of virtue, but I felt isolated even from that virtue, an interloper, one might say, into Yankee virtue."

In that passage, surely, the difference between my graceless summary and Warren's "good technique" is apparent. Whenever one is tempted to put aside this romance—for that is what it is, this account of spiritual withdrawal—Warren is there at one's elbow, murmuring slyly that yes, the characters, even if they are only effigies, are incredible; and that yes, the plot is manipulated entirely by the appearance, at seasonable intervals, of letters, phone calls, and behind-the-scenes shenanigans; but that there is more to this romance of the Recovered Comrade than that. There are words here in which all things are said to happen, even made to happen, and these words are worth hearing out: "With the willing suspension of disbelief, life is thus the richer, even if you are fed, and know it, on a meat of shadows."

Of course, the Pretty Girl from back home turns up again—in Italy, where Jed is being given yet another honorary degree (he hates the things). She has married again (a false swami but a real Negro, as she insists), has learned Italian, French, and "Do you want me to tell you about Lévi-Strauss and structuralism?" Jed lets us off that last one, but treats us to others. Returning from the fool's gold of the European educational establishment, Jed takes Ephraim, his son by that odd, off-stage second marriage of his, on a canoe trip, where we hear "Ephraim's voice by the fire while we drank whisky and he quoted Baudelaire, Rimbaud, Vigny, Valéry and Villon (which seemed to stuff infinitely his head, tucked away among his formulae)." Such an excursion would, I maintain, destroy any other novel by any other novelist. But Robert Penn Warren can permit himself these sensational effects of bathos, which seem to stuff infinitely his head, tucked away among his formulae: "The woman had thrust a being forth from her body into the blaze and strangeness of the world, and now, half a century later and half a hemisphere away, a heavy, swarthy man, running to belly and getting a little bald on the top of his head, lay naked in a strange room in a strange country, and the voices rising from the street below, as the afternoon shadow lengthened, were in a tongue that, all at once, was strange to him." That is Jed, on hearing in Italy of his mother's death back in Alabama.

These are the lapses, though, which the good technician so warily, so wickedly, takes up like dropped stitches. If we do not believe the Pretty Girl from back home could really tell us about structuralism, and if we do not for a moment credit the catalog of French poets recited over the campfire by the unimaginable son, we discover that the novelist, too, has had his little joke, and that if we submit to Jed and his sentimentalities ("Anything can become a way of life. Even death. Even the question why death should become a way of life could itself become a way of life. That question was there continuously and inevitably . . . but in its inevitability it had long since ceased to demand an answer. It had become . . . purely rhetorical"), we can gain something else.

What we gain is precisely the product of the good technician, the man upon whom nothing in the visible, tangible world is lost. This man is present in *A Place to Come To* (the "place" is the grave), as is the fabulous artificer of effigies obliged to articulate so shadowily the narrator's preposterous quest for authenticity. It is why I should like to call the book not a failed novel but a successful romance, for its theme is the gallantry of human experience, the high heroism of an effort—in this case Jed Tewksbury's—to give the realia of life a shape and a texture that risk just the sort of solecisms I have instanced. The mistake would be to assume that Jed Tewksbury is Robert Penn Warren. And of course sometimes Jed speaks so wittily, so eloquently, and so idiosyncratically that one could easily make that mistake, as when he learns Latin: "If you found a new name for a thing, it became real. That was the magic of the name. And if you found the names of all the things of a world, you could create a world that was real and different. The crazy word on the page was like a little hole in a great wall. You could peek through the hole and see a world where everthing was different and bright. That world, I realized with a strange numbness of awe, was not far away. It was just on the other side of a wall."

But by the end of the book we know better. We know that the fabulous artificer and the good technician have concocted an uneasy alliance, not a coincidence, and that the novel they have made together is a splendid hoax. Or as the technician says: "Until you can understand that these things are different but are the same, you know nothing about the nature of life, I proclaim this."

[*Now and Then: Poems 1976-1978*]

Harold Bloom*

Warren's epigraph, from Second Isaiah, is "let the inhabitants of the rock sing. . . ." Warren, himself past 70, heeds two other admonitions of the same text: "Sing unto the Lord a new song" and "Let them shout from the top of the mountains." I can think of no other living poet writing in English who has the authority to sustain so consciously Sublime a stance, but the author of *Selected Poems: 1923–1975* has earned his solitary eminence.

The three dozen new poems of *Now and Then* add at least the following to the Warren canon: "Evening Hour," which is Warren's version of Wordsworth's "Boy of Winander"; "Red-tail Hawk and Pyre of Youth," which is a deliberate and overwhelming self-interpretation of this poet's obsessive hawk-imagery; and several lyrics memorializing moments of vision—"Mountain Plateau," "Heat Wave Breaks," and most remarkably "Heart of Autumn," which ends the book. But the quality of achievement is consistent almost throughout these poems. Like Hardy, Yeats and Stevens, Warren is at his strongest past 70. He is now achieving the height in verse that Faulkner did in prose, though we are slow to recognize this.

Warren's early verse stemmed from Eliot's, and not at all from Frost's or from Stevens's, and I cannot recall that Warren ever has written or said a favorable sentence about Emerson. But more than Eliot or Tate among the anti-Emersonians, Warren battles the Emersonian prophecies about the American poet with the sad and formidable inner knowledge that Emerson, like Wordsworth, is inescapable. *Now and Then* is a book of American Romantic Poetry, as Romantic as Hart Crane. Warren is hardly seeking to adjust his individual talent to tradition. He is taking his stance, not as an ironist or as a reductionist of any kind but as a seer whose synecdoches mount through controlled hyperbole to an ever-early vision. Only 10 of the new poems are grouped as the nostalgic "Then"; all the rest are part of a speculative and so prophetic "Now," the admonition to turn now, as at the close of "Heat Wave Breaks":

Will you wake when clouds roll and the roil and lightning make
Again wet leaves twirl on their stems in the green-flaming glare,
And blasphemy of thunder makes the mountain quake?
For what should we pray to our God in the rumble and flare?
That the world stab anew to our hearts in the lightning-stricken air?

The burden of Warren's prophecy is morally very harsh, because his vision of God, though personal and undogmatic, in uniquely devoted to

* From *The New Republic*, 30 Sept. 1978, pp. 34–35. Reprinted by permission of *The New Republic*, Copyright © 1978, The New Republic, Inc.

an unforgiving spirit, who sees and knows all and is incapable of pity or pardon. An immanent and temporal godhead, exalting its own history, is thus opposed to the transcendental, atemporal Gnosis of Emerson, who denied that history even existed. Ideologically the clash is straightforward and very fierce, and I vote for Emerson, but the poetic mode that helps give Warren his force is uneasily indebted to Emerson's tradition. Part of the fascination of Warren's late phase, for a Romantic critic, is to watch the struggle within the poetry between its purposes and its rhetoric, for the rhetoric increasingly is High Romantic. Not that Warren, who seems to know everything a poet can know, does not know all this. A strong, firm poem in tercets, "Rather Like a Dream," which I admire intensely but reluctantly, without affection, seeks to demystify Wordsworth at his uncanniest. Remembering Wordsworth's own remarks upon the "Intimations of Immortality" Ode, Warren acknowledges the same felt impulse, reaching out "To touch stone or tree to confirm/His own reality." But the impulse in Warren becomes the dialectical reverse, a knowledge of mortality. The Romantic intuition is acknowledged, but the interpretation is usurped, almost convincingly.

I find it disconcertingly impressive that in "Evening Hour," an even more eloquent poem, Warren should have written what may be the most Wordsworthian lyric of our century, which would have adorned the *Lyrical Ballads*. Recalling a graveyard in which he played as a boy, Warren muses back until the epiphany of his own poetic incarnation is made manifest to him, as surprising now as it was when he was a child:

> Not morbid, nor putting two and two together
> To make any mystic, or fumblingly philosophical,
> Four, he sometimes kept waiting, if decent the weather,
> In a lonely way, arrowheads forgotten, till all
>
> The lights of the town had come on. He did not know
> Why the lights, so familiar, now seemed so far away,
> And more than once felt the crazy impulse grow
> To lay ear to earth for what voices beneath might say.

The language partly disowns the remembered experience, which is the intuition of poetic power, yet Warren affirms more than he feels easy at affirming. He has attained a kind of poignance that I think has to be called noble, as when in "Mountain Plateau" he contrasts his poetic voice to the capable cry and up-thrust gleam of a solitary crow:

> I can make no answer
> To the cry from the immense distance,
>
> My eyes fill with tears, I have lived
> Long without being able
> To make adequate communication.

If Warren's obsessive bird imagery is contrasted with Yeats's, the particular achievement of the later poet is clarified. He lacks the full power of the Yeatsian identification with the brute blood of the air, and he lacks also Yeats's Gnostic sense of freedom from time's tyranny. Warren cannot exhilarate us with the conviction of an occult knowledge. But his more vulnerable Sublime can persuade us, in ways that Yeats cannot. Watching the wild geese go over, in the marvelous "Heart of Autumn," Warren feels his estrangement from their "imperial utterance," but gives us a final vision of an even more deeply moving Sublime:

I have known time and distance, but not why I am here.

Path of logic, path of folly, all
The same—and I stand, my face lifted now skyward.
Hearing the high beat, my arms outstretched in the tingling.
Process of transformation, and soon tough legs,

With folded feet, trail in the sounding vacuum of passage,
And my heart is impacted with a fierce impulse
To unwordable utterance—
Toward sunset, at a great height.

That last line is Warren's achieved stance, the signature of our wounded and still vital poetic tradition.

[*Brother to Dragons: A New Version*]

Harold Bloom*

Warren's *Brother to Dragons: A Tale in Verse and Voices* was published in 1953. A quarter century later, he gives us a new version that is, as he says, "a new work." His poetic style changed radically with *Incarnations: Poems 1966–1968*, a change that continues in his increasingly distinguished canon of poems. He stands now, at almost 75, as our most impressive living poet because of his work since 1966. Reading *Brother to Dragons* in this new version, side by side with the 1953 text, is an instructive experience, particularly in regard to the vexed problem of poetic revisionism. The famous dictum of Valéry, that a poem is never finished but is abandoned, is severely tested by Warren's rigorous reworking of his longest poem.

I myself was one of the readers, previously cold to Warren's verse,

* From *The New Republic*, 1 & 8 Sept. 1979, pp. 30–31. Reprinted by permission of *The New Republic*. Copyright © 1979, The New Republic, Inc.

who converted to him on the basis of *Incarnations* and the subsequent long poem *Audubon: A Vision*. Reading *Brother to Dragons* in 1953, I was made uneasy, acknowledged the poem's vigor, disliked its ideological tendentiousness, and gloomily admired the Jacobean intensity of its more violent passages. The poem seemed then a good enough extension of the tradition of T. S. Eliot, sounding at times the way Eliot sounded when he was deliberately closest to Webster and Tourneur. Warren's quite explicit argument seemed to be another churchwardenly admonition that original sin was indeed the proper moral burden for *our* poetry. Thus, poor Jefferson received a massive drubbing, for being an Enlightened rationalist, and the drubber, a tough interlocutor named R.P.W., prodded the author of the Declaration of Independence into saying: ". . . I once tried to contrive/a form I thought fit to hold the purity of man's hope./But I did not understand the nature of things." The nature of things was that Jefferson's nephew, wielding a meat-axe, had butchered a 16-year-old black slave, in December 1811, for having broken a pitcher belonging to his deceased mother, Jefferson's sister. In his "Foreword" Warren dismissed with polemical gusto the evident fact that Jefferson never referred to this family debacle:

> If the moral shock to Jefferson caused by the discovery of what his own blood was capable of should turn out to be somewhat short of what is here represented, subsequent events in the history of America, of which Jefferson is the spiritual father, might still do the job.

A reader more Jeffersonian and Emersonian than Warren was could be forgiven for muttering, back in 1953, that if there was something nasty in the meat-house, there was something pretty nasty in the "Foreword" also. But I too am a quarter century older now, the age indeed that Warren was when he first published the poem. I am not any happier with the implicit theology and overt morality of *Brother to Dragons* than I was, but subsequent events have done the job all right, to the degree that I am not tempted to mutter my protest anymore. Warren does seem to me the best poet we have now, and the enormous improvement in the poem's rhetorical force is evident upon almost every page. I am never going to love this poem, but I certainly respect it now, and a poem that can overcome one's spiritual distaste probably has its particular value for other readers in my generation besides myself.

The difference in the tale comes in both verse and voices, especially in the voice of R.P.W., which has an authority and resonance that little in the 1953 text prophesied. I could argue back [then?] at what seemed only another Eliotician, but I just want to listen to this sublime sunset hawk of 1979:

>   . . . and lift our eyes up
> To whatever liberating perspective,

> Icy and pure, the wild heart may command,
> And so the glimmering night scene under
> The incalculable starlight serves
> As an image of lethal purity—
> Infatuate glitter of a land of Platonic ice.

In the 1953 version those six and a half lines appeared as eight and a half and between the "lethal purity" and "Infatuate glitter" came, most tendentiously, "the incessant/And whirling dream of desperate innocence." Warren now trusts his reader to interpret the trope of the passage's final line on his own, and a poem of 216 pages has been reduced to 133. In the central poem of *Incarnations*, "The Leaf," Warren had celebrated being blessed by a new voice "for the only/Gift I have been given: *teeth set on edge.*" This grim Biblical trope epitomizes the ethos and the style of Warren in his major phase, and is realized in the new *Brother to Dragons*. Our teeth are set on edge by the harsh power of this verse.

Warren, in his revised "Foreword," asserts that the dramatic effects of his poem have been sharpened, which is true, particularly in the exchanges between Jefferson and R.P.W., where the poet no longer maintains a rhetorical advantage over the president. That Warren is still dreadfully unjust to Jefferson could go unsaid, except that I fear no one else is going to say it. If presidents were morally responsible for their nephews, then our twice-born incumbent would have to confront a parody of Warren's dramatic situation, since I believe a son of one of President Carter's sisters is currently serving an extended term for armed robbery.

Warren might argue that his sense of Jefferson's greatness is dialectically demonstrated throughout the poem, in much the same way as there is a projection of Emerson's adversary power in the ironic sequence "Homage to Emerson, on Night Flight to New York," which preceded the *Incarnations* volume. Still uneasy with his ideological ferocity, I content myself here with expressing admiration for the revisionary skill and intellectual persistence he has shown in this new *Brother to Dragons*. There is a greater Warren, the poet of "Evening Hawk," "Sunset Walk in Thaw-Time in Vermont," "Red-Tail Hawk and Pyre of Youth," and scores of other visions of an authentic American sublime, including *Audubon* and the work in progress, a volume intended for his 75th birthday. That greater Warren compels homage, and has transcended his polemics against Jefferson and Emerson.

INTERVIEW

"An Interview in New Haven with Robert Penn Warren"

Richard B. Sale *

SALE: We might start with your notion of place. I'm interested in your concept of place, especially since you've been here in Connecticut so long. So much of the fiction is involved with a feeling for place. How is it, for example, that you picked this area for a permanent residence rather than, say, the Tennessee-Kentucky "back home" country?

WARREN: That's accident, pure accident. There was a time— twenty years ago—when I considered going back to Tennessee to live. I even got far enough to try to locate a place. I discovered the world had changed; it would have been artificial. That is, the world I'd be going back to would not be the one I was remembering. And then I settled up here. Again it's accident. I married up here. That's not the decisive factor but is *a* factor: I married a Connecticut girl. The other thing was that I began to do a little teaching at Yale.

SALE: Your children feel, for example, that this is home?

WARREN: This is home. Of course it's home for them. It's the only home they know. One can't rewrite the script, you know, even if one wanted to. And one should be grateful I think for the favors one gets out of life without trying to rewrite the script arbitrarily. But as far as writing is concerned, the basic images that every man has, I suppose, go back to those of his childhood. He has to live on that capital all his life. There are grave defects if you *are* out of touch with your world, no doubt. It also has some advantages, I flatter myself to think—or encourage myself to think.

SALE: I was thinking of the novel *Flood* and its central character. Much of his dilemma is the business of going back.

WARREN: Yes, that's a part of the novel. Clearly that novel has in it a kind of tangential, peripheral reference, an issue of coming back and trying to pick up a world arbitrarily. That was not the germ of the novel; that was something at the end of the novel, later on.

SALE: Or that entered it.

WARREN: Almost inevitably entered the novel. But I didn't start

*Reprinted with permission from *Studies in the Novel*, 2 (1970), 325–54. Copyright © 1970, North Texas State University. The editor has incorporated several corrections suggested by Mr. Warren and Mr. Sale. The interview took place on March 4, 1969.

with that notion. As far as that theme is concerned, the novel begins to deal with the question, "What is home?" Ultimately home is not a place, it's a state of spirit, it's a state of feeling, a state of mind, a proper relationship to a world. It represents a—I don't want to use a big word; it can sound too ambitious, too grand—but the world view is your home. Your world view in one sense is your home. At least that's what I was trying to say in that novel, one of the things I was trying to say. That you're no more at home; you go back to the place and the place may not be your home anymore. It may stand for whatever you don't like, for instance, or that place where you're not at home. I would not interpret that as being my case if I went back to Tennessee or Kentucky; that certainly would not be the case. But there would be something artificial in doing it by an act of will. It would be an attempt to reenact sentimentally a piece of the past, which I think is always false.

SALE: Was your imagery of "washing it away," the flooding of the country, saying this same thing?

WARREN: That is a part, but it was not planned into it. That was just happen-so, as it were; it was a given. The novel itself started simply from—I can tell you how the novel started.

SALE: I'd like to hear it.

WARREN: If you think it might be of some psychological interest. In April, 1931, the anniversary of the Battle of Shiloh, I passed through southwest Tennessee. I saw the old house, hanging over the bluff of the river, which I think was Grant's headquarters during the battle—the second day of the battle, I think it was. Anyway, I forget the name of the house. I didn't go in; I just saw it, drove past it, and the village was the germ of Fiddlersburg and that house was the germ of the Fiddler house. I just caught a glimpse of it in passing, about a ninety-second glimpse. It stuck somehow. I couldn't describe the town now, only the impression I carried away from it. The—now, my God, what is it?—thirty or thirty-two years I've been writing that novel.

And another thing, I've seen one or two flooded-out places in the TVA system in Tennessee. For years and years, I thought maybe somehow this was an image, this kind of doomsday to a community. Then, arbitrarily, BANG, the community is gone. What happens to human relations in that context? This was something vaguely in the back of my mind, a speculation, no reference to fiction.

SALE: No reference to fiction in the original idea?

WARREN: No such idea then. As I began to move into the book the question arose of people who come back. I have friends who have arbitrarily attempted to come back and pick up a world by an act of will, and it's never worked for them, the ones I've seen—never worked for any of them. The sentimental reenactment without some practical justification—

SALE: —is somehow false?

WARREN: Those three things flowed in. Then the penitentiary, another germ from another place. I've seen a couple of prisons at different times. In fact, I started to write this novel, I toyed with it, twenty-odd years ago. And Elsa Moranti, the wife of Alberto Moravia, wrote a novel which had to do with a very similar situation: the prison inside and out in a small place, an island prison. And this novel, in a way, was so close to the novel I was then meditating that it killed mine off. I put it aside. Her novel came out in the mid-fifties. I've forgotten the title, but it's a very powerful, very beautiful novel. So I laid my book aside for some years before I began again. I thought I'd better let that one cook, get the other one out of my mind. I wrote two novels in between before I finally came around to my *Flood* novel.

This is rather funny. The name of the family of mine in *Flood* is Tolliver. And I was vaguely modeling the character who became Maggie on a woman I used to know, who I thought was a terribly nice woman, terribly attractive and bright—vaguely this woman was in the back of my mind in making that character. I was casting around for names. I called her a dozen different things. I'd always liked the name Maggie, and I'd known some nice people named Maggie; so, you know, it sort of seemed all right. And so I gave her the name Maggie. The next thing I knew I saw a review or an essay saying the book was clearly derived from *The Mill on the Floss*, a rewriting of *The Mill on the Floss*, because there's a Maggie Tolliver in there. I haven't read *The Mill on the Floss* since I was twelve years old, and I don't intend to, furthermore. A big construction of interpretation of some kind around Maggie Tolliver and other characters who have equivalents in *The Mill on the Floss*. Well, you better watch it, boys!

SALE: The critic made a concrete set of parallels.

WARREN: Criticism is a dangerous trade. So is fiction writing, for that matter. Well, there it is. All right. Fiddler. Fiddler came from a movie columnist. I just happened to see the name on the column he had written. I said that's a good one. Put it down as Fiddler and Fiddlersburg.

There we are. That's the novel I think I'd have to rest my case on, though, for better or worse. That's one of the two or three best I think I ever did.

SALE: I was going to ask if you had preferences or favorites among your novels. You say that's one of them. Do you have a similar feeling about *Wilderness?*

WARREN: No, no.

SALE: What reservations about that one?

WARREN: I don't think it's the same. That's really a novelette. It was conceived to be about 30,000 words long; it's now about 65,000 words long. It began to exfoliate and develop, and the incidental characters began to be more important to me than they had been in the beginning. The ratio of the main character's interest to the incidental characters shifted along the way.

SALE: They took up more space.

WARREN: More space, and they become more interesting in many ways than the central character. The wealthy Jew, or the old North Carolina sutler, whom I was rather fond of. Of course, Southern abolitionists are a very complicated sect. I've known a lot of them, and maybe I'm even called one of them sometimes. But they're very complicated people. Anyway, the ratio of interest changed between Rosenzweig and incidental characters like the sutler or the Negro, or the rich Jew in New York, or the girl on the Pennsylvania farm. They became more demanding to me in a way than the central character did. So you have two kinds of books going on at the same time.

SALE: But you knew where you were going to take the main character.

WARREN: Yes, yes, I knew roughly where I was going to take him, you see. But, oh, let's talk about something: now here's a question. The Wilderness was called "The Pizen Woods," you know. Literally, historically. When you put the Pizen Woods in there, which is what history gives you, this is called symbolism, arbitrary symbolism.

SALE: But you had it to start with.

WARREN: History gave it. It *was* called that. (Unless I read the wrong memoirs.) This is arbitrary symbolism, says somebody. But it's what it was called. Pizen Woods. But there you see you can't win. I mean, you're historically straight, factual, and it becomes symbolism.

SALE: Are you saying you've been damned for it or praised for it?

WARREN: I was damned in this case. For using "arbitrary symbolism." It may have seemed so, but you shouldn't be too sure until you've checked it.

SALE: Back to *Flood* for just a moment, I was curious about your use of water and flood images. After the first three or four pages, the airline stewardess peeked out of the airplane like a bird with a sprig of olive branches.

WARREN: Did I say that? I've forgotten it.

SALE: Yes. Was it just an incidental image? You didn't refer to the flooding for the next fifth of the book.

WARREN: I hadn't remembered that. It may have been a slip.

SALE: I was really asking this: do you use the technique of consciously tying imagery together throughout a long piece, with incidental image branches running off the main lines?

WARREN: Well, I can tell you in my case those things are almost always—accidental is the wrong word—spontaneous. They're not planned, and I throw them out or keep them as I choose. But sometimes I don't notice them; they'll be there and I won't notice that they're there.

SALE: Then the choice is going to be at the revision stage?

WARREN: It may or may not be. I may throw them out at the moment, but planning is a strange thing in these matters, anyway. How can you say that you plan a thing that happens in a flash? The word pops into your head. The whole notion of intention and planning in these matters is a very, very peculiar thing, it seems to me. And the planning and the intention are primarily negations in so far as they're conscious. You're throwing out something rather than saying, "Now I want something." Because you can't know what you want until it comes. You have no way. You can do only one thing, it seems to me. You can describe to yourself the kind of problem you have. And hope that by describing to yourself the problem that you're up against at the particular moment, that somehow this will help your unconscious, your guts, deliver you the right thing. But you can't plan the thing itself. It has to come completely fulfilled. Or have the germ of fulfillment.

A friend of mine, who is now quite an extraordinarily good Elizabethan scholar, Arnold Stein, used to be an undergraduate here at Yale. As an undergraduate, he said to me, he was mad for Housman's poetry and he wrote Housman. He was a sophomore at Yale then—it was a long time ago now: "Dear Mr. Housman, I am devoted to your poetry. Can you tell me please, sir, how you always manage to choose the right word? Thank you very much, etc. Arnold Stein." Well, the old curmudgeon up at Cambridge answered the letter, strangely enough. And I've seen the letter. "Dear Mr. Stein, I do not choose the right word. I get rid of the wrong one. Period. Sincerely yours, A. E. Housman."

SALE: That's the only answer.

WARREN: The only answer. Yes, about the planning. When it comes to the actual thing, it has to be more a matter of saying, "that thing is wrong," kick it out, and hope that God will help me make it better the next five minutes or five days or five months or five years. It has to be a negative, a veto. It's where you can be conscious and argue with yourself. Or you can describe the nature of the problem. You can envision the kind of book, but the envisioning is unplanned again. The envisioning is a thing that has to come out of something as a happen-so. Now here's a kind of planning I use that makes sense. You can plan to be the kind of person that might write a certain kind of book. Put it that way. If you want to write poetry, you can study poetry, you can memorize poetry, you can live with poetry. This is your planning. You can plan by immersing yourself in poetry in as many ways as possible. Your planning can be done at this level. After that, the planning is a very, *very* strange process. It's primarily a negative. Or a process of envisionments which themselves must be spontaneous. And I don't know how to put it differently than that. But the cold-blooded planning I think is utterly a matter of basics. It's a matter of willingness to soak yourself in the world of the thing you're dealing with, both in a literary sense of, say, soaking yourself in poetry, memorizing it, reading it, thinking about it, studying with your own poems—all these things. And on the other hand realizing in planning what for *you* can be the life that you can write poetry. That is, trying to find the way in which you can have the right kind of privacy of spirit to write the poem or the novel. And this is different for different people. I have to have some other activity going on to gain a kind of privacy. I have to have a thing to flee from, pull away from, the right ratio of that. That is, I like some kind of job now and then, objective and simple.

SALE: That's one kind.

WARREN: One plan. The other kind of plan goes right with it. It's trying to—by experiment, I guess is the sort of way—figure out the kind of life you could live that allows your mind this kind of privacy that is necessary for writing. It's different from person to person. You can never be sure you're quite right about *yourself* either, of course.

SALE: The kind of planning you were talking about rejecting is that sort of cold-blooded, cold-headed planning—

WARREN: That's immediate. That's right.

SALE: —that would plot out patterns. This is what you said you do not do or cannot do.

WARREN: I quit that. I did one novel by a carefully worked-out synopsis. I had about an eighty-page synopsis—almost paragraph by paragraph—of what I wanted to get accomplished in that novel. I had it all worked out. Practically a book by itself. I spent a year or two in the planning, trying to live the novel in the planning level. Put it that way. In other words, I was trying to compose the novel in my head without breaking fully into language. I was separating language totally from mechanics, from plot and characterization. I had a bitter struggle with that novel because I had done the one thing I found I couldn't do in my work. I was violating what I conceive to be, for me at least, a basic necessity: the thing of character, the thing of action—idea—must be in terms of the *language* of the novel.

SALE: What was the book?

WARREN: Oh, *Heaven's Gate*. I had a bitter time trying to feel fresh on the things that I had already planned out so carefully, that looked so beautiful in the plan. I was only saved by the mountain man because he got me free-wheeling again. I dreamed of that in a fever dream. So I was home free on that.

SALE: So it came together finally?

WARREN: Typhus. While suffering from typhus in Rome, I dreamed the whole part of the thing in a sort of long fever fit. And I was free then. It released me to think of the novel as really happening then, rather than as a novel to work out, executing the plan from a blueprint. I know that there are people, I know some of them, who can plan in the way I said I can't plan. I know them, and history would give us many cases of that kind of planning. I can't. I can only plan in two ways. I can only plan by seeing the action of a book or of a poem. By seeing the big basic movements of it I will know ahead of time, and I'll say Roman one,

Roman two, Roman three, Roman five, or whatever it is. Those are the basic movements of the novel, and there'll be certain key scenes I will have—germ scenes.

The germinal scenes that are to be there will be in my mind ahead with the various movements of the novel or the feeling of what each movement means emotionally for the novel. And the knowledge of how I want the novel to *feel* at the end. What the actual events are at the end may be very dim in my mind until I'm very close to the end. I have a very clear notion of how I want the novel to feel and what I have in the germ scenes will have been very carefully worked, probably written, sometimes long before I get to them. That much planning I do do. I just finished a long poem, "Audubon: A Vision." It's about Audubon's life as a kind of focus for a lot of things about humans. I hope it's the way life is. It's about his heroic solution of his problems and the problem of being a man. Well, after I'd written about one third of the poem, probably 150 lines, suddenly, in the middle of something else, I began to write like fury. Wrote the last two little sections of the poem just like that! I didn't know where they would fit, but those two sections of the poem are now the end, section eight or ten of the poem. The poem is about 440 lines long, quite a long poem. I've been working at it for many, many months, started it twenty years ago. But then this section came in a flash when I was about one-third through the poem. But having settled the end, I knew exactly what the poem was going to be, what I was shooting for. Actually I wrote that passage totally formed, almost like dictation. And I hope I remain as pleased with it as I was then and am now. I may be quite wrong.

SALE: So there's gestation in everything you've mentioned, a lengthy gestation period somewhere either before or during the composition.

WARREN: That's right. It may be years. Sometimes twenty years, twenty-five years.

SALE: And you keep several things in that work stage?

WARREN: Have to. I let nature take its course. That's unplanned. Only one kind of rule I make: if the poem comes, the poem gets the right-of-way. Stay with the poem as long as it feels hot. That's why I have got a novel now I've worked on five years that I've not finished.

SALE: That's what I was going to ask. It seems like you've given more attention to poetry in recent years.

WARREN: Yes. I've had a long run of it. I'm not complaining.

SALE: No, I shouldn't think so.

WARREN: But there has to be some rule about this, and I have one more chapter to go on the novel. Then rewrite. But the last three summers—no, the last two summers in France in '66 and '67—I sat down and said I'm going to finish the novel this summer. And in three days I was writing poems. In a year and a half I had written a book of poems. Then the fall came and I had to revise the poems. Not much of the novel got done. But you have to take some kind of a vow about priorities, and the start of a poem is more precarious than the start of a novel. So therefore I think you ought to give it more priority.

Usually the poem gets started, a few lines or a few passages, and then it's laid aside and finished later. And I try never to crowd them. Let them rest. I don't believe in crowding things.

SALE: Can you feel it when you're pushing one project too long and too strong and it's not functioning properly?

WARREN: When I don't want to do it, I don't do it. If I don't feel like doing it, I don't do it. If I don't feel hot, I leave it alone. Fiction has certain craft elements, for me anyway, that are more obvious than in poetry. I mean there are certain things, like having to do a certain amount of typing to begin with. You have to sit there with the fiction. You do have the problem of writing the expository paragraph. There are many things that are matters of intelligence and craft and, in a crude way, "know how."

SALE: And not in any sense inspiration or flash.

WARREN: That's right. But it must be done in terms of an inspiration, with some reference to inspiration. But these matters are not inspiration. Now the ratio of that material, that kind of material, to the whole, to inspiration, is much greater than it is in poetry. Certainly greater than in short or lyric poetry where you depend on heat to keep it going. So you do, you can live through slack periods.

SALE: And produce fiction.

WARREN: By intelligence and will in a novel in a way that you can't do it in poetry.

SALE: And keep the thing growing.

WARREN: And keep it growing. And in other words, the ratio of a mechanical and critical intelligence to a novel is a little different, I think.

SALE: This is what I was asking. I think the writing of long prose demands a certain dogged stamina.

WARREN: I think so. I think so, too. But it doesn't mean that fiction doesn't depend equally on the inspiration element or the other element. I think it *does* depend equally. But other things flow into it in different proportions, different relations; a portion of it may sound mechanical. You can because more hours go into the mechanics of it.

SALE: Well, it soaks up more energy, more will, to get a lengthy work finished.

WARREN: More energy and more will. But to poetry. You have to be willing to waste time. When you start a poem, stay with it and suffer through it and just think about nothing, not even the poem. Just *be* there. It's more of a prayerful state than writing the novel is. A lot of the novel is in doing good works, as it were, not praying. And the prayerful state is just being passive with it, mumbling, being around there, lying on the grass, going swimming, you see. Even getting drunk. Get drunk prayerfully, though.

SALE: Then you had the kind of life in recent years where you could do this, when you chose. Is that correct? Or is there always limited time?

WARREN: Well, if you can't do it that way, you'd better not try. If something seems to be there to rob, always rob Peter to pay Paul. If anybody's going to be a writer he's got to be able to say, "this has to come first, to write has to come first." That is, if you have a job, you have to scant your job a little bit. You can't be an industrious apprentice if you're going to be a poet. You've got to pretend to be an industrious apprentice but really steal time from the boss. Or from your wife, or somebody, you see. The time's got to come from somewhere. And also this passivity, this "waitingness," has to be achieved someway. It can't be treated as a job. It's got to be treated as a non-job or an anti-job.

SALE: And you have to block out those other responsibilities completely.

WARREN: Block out the other obligations and responsibilities. And if you can have a job where you can fudge a little bit, so much the better. But I have known people that got up at five o'clock in the morning and wrote from five until eight before they went to the job. Five days a week. That's herioc. I've known people who've done this, done this for years.

SALE: They're novelists in the dark hours of the mornings.

WARREN: That's right. Or at night. Shut the door late at night and get at it. I know many people who have done that.

SALE: After a day of reporting or whatever they were doing.

WARREN: Whatever they were doing. It just has to be done. One thing about this—I don't want to sound nasty—but I think that everybody who means to be a writer should go through a short period anyway where he does not have everything done for him, by a foundation or something else. Where he actually has to suffer a *little* bit, just a *little bit*, mind you, just enough to know what it's like to steal the time to give up something, in some way. And to offend wife or child or mother or father or best friend. Just to do what he wants to do. Just to know this: that he is able to make this reservation in life. To know how to achieve his inner privacy. If he doesn't make a try at it once in his life, he doesn't know anything about whether he wants to write or not, really, unless he's paid a price for it, a little price for it.

But I think there is some sense in the matter that I think a person should find out some place, somewhere fairly early along the way: How much effort he is willing to put in there to gain this inner privacy, this blankness, this right relationship to what he is doing, by giving up something? So he knows then exactly how much the process of writing is worth to him. Something of that. It doesn't have to be the financial thing. That was sort of half kidding. But that's putting it on the line, though; it is a matter of that.

SALE: With many people, that sacrifice comes in the business of making a living.

WARREN: It does in making a much better living, getting a better job. Getting promoted in the university or getting a better job or pleasing the boss—all these things, you know, enter into it. Also, it's the problem of what *kind* of life you can subject other people to. I know a young man—he's not young any more—who shall be nameless. An extraordinary talented writer, he married the wrong girl. Well, he's had a great success at life. But I know him well, and he sat there and told me, "I just can't do it. It's killing her. She's gonna leave me. I know it. It's gonna happen. She can't take it." She married a man when he was in a military uniform and was a heroic young man. And suddenly he put on those old clothes and locked the door to write. It was different, and she couldn't take it. So he quit writing and has made a great success of another kind of life.

SALE: That satisfied her?

WARREN: That satisfied her—and now they're divorced. Just recently, after twenty years.

SALE: There are all kinds of ways not to win.

WARREN: Lots of ways not to win. You can't win by losing, it's a cinch.

SALE: There has constantly been, there still is, a sense of history in your fiction. Now, I don't know how to phrase the question around it other than this way: Has there been any change in the part that historical reality plays in your writing of fiction?

WARREN: Well, the time, you mean?

SALE: The time, perhaps. I was thinking of such comments as Woodward makes about the soul of the South. What the Southerner is, what his milieu is. Have your attitudes changed over a period of decades?

WARREN: Well, my attitudes on a particular question have changed very greatly and I hope they will continue to do some changing. I'd hate to think I was frozen. But on the question of historical relevance of history to my way of thinking or feeling, I don't think there's been much change. You know the habits, how things were in the South. If you lived, say, in my generation, you still live in two kinds of time. The element of the past, the tale told. The things that happened before were told by older people, particularly if the older people were big in the Great War of '61–'65. A different feeling toward the present event and the past event somehow overlap in what was like a double exposure photograph almost.

SALE: And the real world was one picture?

WARREN: The real world was there and the old world was there, one photograph superimposed on the other. Their relationship was of constant curiosity and interest.

SALE: Which did they consider the more real? The old or the current?

WARREN: It would vary, I think. But the relations are the same, the two things.

SALE: Oh, but both were there constantly?

WARREN: Both are there. Both are there making a world of unfulfilled chances and unfulfilled options. This was always very important. The boyish imagination was always supposing: suppose, you know, suppose that Abner Sidney Johnston hadn't been killed at Shiloh the first day. Always supposing like that. Suppose that Jeb Stuart hadn't been on that city raid at Gettysburg? All these things the boy supposes. This is his sacred boyhood we're thinking about.

SALE: But adults use this pattern, too.

WARREN: They do! They do it all their lives. They continue their boyhood. The sense of the past and the sense of the present are somehow intertwined constantly. This was a cultural factor in the South; the telling of tales was part of it. And the analyzing of other people's character, from malicious gossip on to high discourse about moral values, was involved in this thing, too. And the fascination with heredity: "You couldn't expect anything better from a son of Mr. Jones," or "Why do you suspect Mr. Jones' son is trying to be so good?"

SALE: You still see it in popular biographies: "His Welsh blood proved itself when . . ."

WARREN: Right. "Mr. Jones' Welsh blood came through." And there was the sense of a community being composed of individual people, on one hand graybeards, on the other hand, babes. So the time sense was ingrained. You saw the object of time around you, the gray hair and the mewling baby. They were both there before you.

SALE: Where did the young man growing into awareness fit into that pattern of those people you were talking about?

WARREN: In between them; he looks both ways, toward age and toward childhood, to the past and the present, and to his own dream of the future. This sense of time is a very important part of that. The time sense has changed, is changing. There's a very interesting passage in Alfred North Whitehead's *Adventures in Ideas* on the question of time, the change of the time-sense. This was written a long time ago now; it was written forty-five to fifty years ago, this passage. But the passage is something like this. He said that before the industrial revolution men had one time sense; after it, quite a different one. Before 1800, say, there were disasters but no changes. No one man could recognize a change in the nature of life. Disasters could be war, famine, plague—they could happen like that. But the world began again roughly the same, at roughly the same point, the same techniques. The changes weren't demonstrable. They weren't obvious. They were so slow no man could notice them in his own lifetime, really. Disasters, yes; acts of God; but not acts of history. And after the industrial revolution we're going to have another world of change. Acceleration was constant change so that no man from 1800 on had the same world in his fifties as when he was one year old. Think what's happening more lately in the last fifty years since Whitehead wrote that. There's a real change, it seems to me, in the gut-time-sense of people. This means for many people disorientation profound.

SALE: Oh, I think so.

WARREN: Profound disorientation. Don't you think so?

SALE: And I think it stretches down to just what you were talking about a moment ago. In that sense we're not a poetic age.

WARREN: We don't know yet. The human being is capable of great flexibility, and since we're the watershed, we don't know what's going to happen to the young. That's always the option. We have adapted to this. We can always see what we were like. What we are like, even!

SALE: And I know I'm not what the young are like. I was not in my childhood what they are like now.

WARREN: I am more like my father than my son is like me.

SALE: Yes, but there's a big jump between my son and my father.

WARREN: Yes. Between my son and my father there's a jump so great I don't know what it is. I'm much closer to my father, or even my grandfather, than I am to my son. Let me add that my son and I are very close in terms of affection and relationship. We are.

SALE: Oh, yes, I know. I know what you're saying.

WARREN: But the world he's come into is so different from the one I came into. So different. My father could vote when the last Indian battles were fought. That is, he was a young man of twenty-one when the battle of Wounded-Knee was fought. Three regiments and a battery against the Sioux. And my grandfather, whom I knew well, fought the Civil War. And now my son reads in the morning paper about the astronauts. That's no relation between those worlds.

SALE: Let me jump to a new idea, about prose style. Because I was coming to see you, I read most of the novels again and was amazed to see the difference between the styles of the novels. Of course, the stories and their characters set the tone of the telling, but I'm speaking of the expository passages, the descriptive parts. I wanted to describe some of the prose in *World Enough and Time* as having a "brilliant" style as compared to, say, the "stark" style of the last book, *Flood*. Is there a conscious picking of the style in your work?

WARREN: Well, consciousness is negative again. The *World Enough and Time* book is based on a counterpoint of style, a counterpoint that has to do with the theme of the book. There is the modern man writing the book, the "I" of the book. Then there's the Jeremiah narrative which is a period piece, and a period piece in more ways than style. It's a period piece in psychology and other things. It's in a way a set historical piece, the whole thing. But the interplay of the two things offered me the reality, the interest of the novel. I'm speaking of the stance toward the novel rather than the content of the novel, if you can make that distinction. And the stance was a given; the material gave it. There was a document written by a man. The prototype of my character and the me who read that document were the germ of the novel. So me, a modern man, reading that historical document, was the germ of the novel itself. Katherine Anne Porter put that document on my desk and said, "Read it, Red. This is for you." I read it as a man of a certain period and a certain age, a certain education, a certain world. That was the middle of the Second World War when I read it, a strange time to be reading that document. So just that contrast caused the contrast of styles in the book. It was a given, in other words; the situation of writing the book gave the contrast.

SALE: I was asking because in the "I," the modern-man portion of the book, there was a sort of flash and irony throughout that I didn't find in the two more recently published books.

WARREN: Well, I see what you mean.

SALE: What I was asking for were your comments on the style rather than the intent of the whole novel. It's artificial to do that, I know, to completely separate them.

WARREN: No, it's a perfectly legitimate question, and I think I can answer it. I say I can try and answer, put it that way. I was about to say this: there was an interpenetration of the two styles in *World Enough and Time*, the historical style and, some would say almost a parody of that, the modern-man style. Now that is a kind of mirror-facing-mirror thing.

SALE: That's what I was calling irony in the modern-man style.

WARREN: The technique was conscious, but it was conscious only after a time. It happened originally by accident, by impulse. Then it became, to a degree, conscious and methodical.

SALE: And continued throughout.

WARREN: Continued throughout. But at what point I became aware of it as a possibility I couldn't remember.

SALE: Well, I caught it on the early pages, even. It was there.

WARREN: It probably was. It's somewhat similar to that in *All the King's Men*.

SALE: Yes, it is. As far as the general writing style, I would put the two close together.

WARREN: Well, Jack Burden and Cass Mastern have the same relationship as the "I" narrator and the Jereboam Beauchamp-Beaumont fellow in *World Enough and Time*.

SALE: Well then, further, Jack Burden's ironic worship of Willie—

WARREN: Yeah, that doubleness—

SALE: —causes his misery.

WARREN: Yes, that's right. The method of treating the two groups is not too far apart.

SALE: I wonder if you sometimes found yourself writing in a style that didn't fit either your temper or the book you were working on.

WARREN: I do indeed, I do indeed. Of course, I try to spot that and do something about it. This is where the negative comes in again, the veto.

SALE: When you find yourself practicing "fine writing" or whatever?

WARREN: Well, fine or any kind of writing that is wrong for you. Poetry is even more disastrous, and I've made some very bad slips, such as in the volume of poems called *You, Emperors, and Others*. When I came to do my *Selected Poems* a few years later, I discarded many of those poems entirely. I was on the wrong track; I was writing poems that were not on my line, my basic impulse. I got stuck with a lot of sidetrack poems. I hadn't caught them early enough. Now you can write—it isn't a question of being good or bad, you see—you can write a *bad* poem, by some kind of standard, you know, off the mainline. But the good poem off the mainline is the poem you ought to get rid of.

SALE: When it's out there by itself.

WARREN: A little bit of that's all right, but you can't do it too much, I've found. Several years later, now, I found myself throwing away most of that book. At least, quite a lot of it. The poems didn't belong to the mainline; this is something that happens. With poems, you see, you have a particular object you can spot. Now if you were writing along in a novel, you see, a part here and a part there, and maybe you throw this out and that out. But of course you can't be throwing out pieces of the novel like you can throw out individual poems, unless you throw the whole novel away. You can throw it out if you're still writing it. But it's more obvious in poetry; you've smaller units. The whole poem is involved, and sometimes you can see one sentence or one line in a poem that is right, but the whole poem may somehow feel wrong. You can't neatly save that phrase, put it up in a notebook to use if the occasion comes up again. Oh, it stays back in your guts somewhere. The constant problem is to keep on the mainline. It's a real problem, now.

SALE: Do you have a feeling that some ideas simply suggest themselves as short pieces or poems rather than material for novels?

WARREN: A poem or a big thing, fiction? Well, short stories are out for me. I haven't written a short story in, now, let's see, since '46. That's twenty-three years. The last two I wrote were my best ones, and I may never do another one. But I discovered that the overlap between the short story and the poem was very bad for me. I didn't finish a single short poem for ten years, from '45—God, it must have been '44 or '45, along in there—until '54. I didn't finish a single short poem, not one. I was working on a long poem during that time, *Brother to Dragons*, but I didn't finish it then. I must have started fifty short poems. Not one panned out. I threw them all away, and some of them were going OK. I couldn't finish them; they died on me. For ten years, every one of them died. Which is all to the good! During that period I reassessed my whole feeling about the question you were asking me. I began to see that I had, in a way, too abstract a view of what constituted the germ of a poem *for me*. I mean that when I went back to writing short poems, the poems were more directly tied to a realistic base of facts. They're more tied up with an event, an anecdote, an observation, you see. They were closer to me, closer to my observed and felt life. They had literal germs. That doesn't mean they were autobiographical in the rigid sense of the word. But they were tied more directly to the sort of thing that might become a short story. And once this sense of using such material for poems became clear, I said, "I don't want to write another short story." It was killed just like that. I'd never write short stories again. I just didn't want to have any more to do with them. They felt cramping to me, and I just didn't want to fool with them any more. Happy I was to quit. But this decision somehow seemed to be related to the notion of a poem that is tied closer to the texture of casual life, incidental life, incidental observation, direct experience. There's that. They moved into that world, poetry did. So most of the short poems—that is, many, many, many since then—could very easily have turned at one point into a short story.

SALE: But now poetry has come to take the place of the short story.

WARREN: That's it, that's right. When I wrote the last two short stories, I really liked them. I've only liked three or so that I've written—maybe four at the most. I was thinking the best at the very end, and I suddenly got nauseated with the whole idea of doing short stories or novelettes. And there it was. The poems and a complete change of attitude toward what constituted the germ of a short poem happened in that period.

SALE: But writing the short poem continues to give you considerable pleasure?

WARREN: Oh, sure. That's central to me. I love it; I love working with that. That's a central fact of life for me. Writing poetry to me is bread and meat.

SALE: And the novels as long as they come. Is that what you're saying?

WARREN: I've got a novel going right now. I'll write novels as long as they'll come; I love writing novels, but there's no pleasure writing short stories any more. I wouldn't touch them. There's none, and therefore I won't do it. And I have a positive feeling, no pleasure—anti-pleasure—for writing critical prose.

SALE: Do you still get trapped into writing it sometimes?

WARREN: I trap myself into it, in a sense. Because there are things you want to say. It's like conversation, you see, where it has cultivated, "made" pain. You have to write and you have to struggle. You have to work so hard at it for such small pleasure in the doing. Occasionally I've had great interest in prose; I wrote a long piece on John Ransom for his eightieth birthday. I wanted to do it, and I wanted to say certain things about him to clarify my own mind about certain things as best I could. I wanted to do the piece, but I hated the process. You see what I mean?

SALE: Yes. You wanted to get the piece done.

WARREN: I wanted to *have done* the piece. I don't feel the "had done" about a poem. I want the doing. I want the process.

SALE: Otherwise, you wouldn't keep producing them.

WARREN: Or the novel. I like the process of doing it. I want to be in with the novel, you see. But I don't feel that way about the stuff that's one dimension of drudgery.

SALE: Well, you obviously did have a period where it was pretty exciting at one time. The textbooks.

WARREN: I didn't really enjoy it that way. The textbooks were sociable. That is, they came out of collaborations and arguments and teaching in the classroom. There is the dimension of social life to it. It wasn't the other, the creative thing. It had a lot of drudgery.

SALE: Well, the texts continue to have a life of their own very nicely. I was thinking of *Understanding Poetry* and *Understanding Fiction*. Don't your publishers ever push you into revisions, forcing you back to these things?

WARREN: I do revisions, but that's still sociable. We've done *Understanding Poetry* three times; it's been out thirty-odd years. But the point is, again, that it's a social event. We work together.

It's a world of argument, a world of discussion, a world of—the chore aspect is reduced. It's a matter of one's social life in the deepest way.

SALE: And it's separate from your creative activities.

WARREN: Totally separate because the creative side isn't in the conversations. In having this person you like to argue with, you disagree enough so that you're not just saying yes to each other. You are arguing back and forth, trying to explore something in terms of friendship and old association and differences of intellectual attitude and emotional attitude. So you come out with a text. This is fruitful; this is social life; that keeps it alive. If I were sitting off in a room alone, it could get pretty dreary. The actual drawing it out would be pretty horrible to me.

Let me shift to another subject. Put it this way about writing: If it isn't a kind of way of life, it's not fun. I'm not talking about textbooks now. I'm talking about the poems or a novel. If you can't feel this is the way of your living and feeling, a way of finding your own feeling, doing your own living, I don't see why else anybody does it.

SALE: Part of it is a romantic glamour that the beginner may expect.

WARREN: Oh, people start for all kinds of reasons. But once you're into it, the need is there. If it isn't there, to hell with it. Or as a friend of mine—my publisher, in fact—said, "The trouble with most writers is that most of them want to *have* written, not to write."

SALE: That's what I mean about the glamour surrounding the trade.

WARREN: And some of it is the rewards. But if the process itself is not your process of trying to find your way into your own life and life in general, to learn respect for your own feelings and your own values, then to hell with it. A writer's real nightmare is a fear of being trapped in repetition without that vital experience connected with it. That would be a terrible experience. It's the panic I think all writers get when they get to middle life.

SALE: The feeling they've done this before?

WARREN: That's right.

SALE: And they're just repeating themselves.

WARREN: They can't change. Now, John Ransom told me something astonishing years ago—and I think he was wrong. He's rarely wrong, but I think he was that time. John and I were just carrying on a conversation, and he said, "I'm gonna quit writing poetry." I said. "What do you mean, quit?" He was at the height of his powers, maybe thirty-six he was. I was appalled. He said, "Well, I want to quit while I'm still enjoying it." He said, "I don't want to be a pro, a professional." He said, "I want to be an amateur. To me poetry is something I love." He said, "I can go on writing poems, better than any I've written. I know more about it all the time. They'd be better. But I wouldn't have any fun with them. I'd have no fun with them." He said, "So I'm gonna quit." Now he has a very tidy mind and a very tidy life. He controls himself consciously and thoughtfully. His methodical, philosophical mind makes him say to himself, "I'm gonna quit." He did quit. He did quit indeed. Now I think he was wrong. I think he was a better philosopher than a psychologist; put it that way. He said, "When I get a new way in, I may start again. A new way in, and I may start again." Here's where I think his psychology was defective. The way you gotta do is be there when the rain hits you, Randall Jarrell said.

SALE: Yes, I would think so, too.

WARREN: That, or else writing poetry sitting in the rain. Lightning hits you once, you're good; hits you six times, you're great. You have to be in the rain to be hit by lightning. Well, John was going to come in out of the rain, so an inspiration couldn't hit him. If he were with the medium out there he might be hit. Stay in the rain, as Randall would put it.

SALE: Even if it was just a long, dreary drizzle.

WARREN: Just being out there in the rain and hoping for the best.

SALE: It's the old boxer analogy, isn't it: He's going to quit before he gets punchy.

WARREN: Yes, that's right. Everybody's afraid of himself. Every writer's afraid of being a writer. Some people want to quit. Some people don't quit in time. But it's a pattern.

SALE: Who's to know when it's time to quit?

WARREN: Well, you don't. You don't know when to quit. There's a poet whom I'm very close to, a very good friend of mine, one of the very best poets in the country. I'd say one of the most appreciated. In a letter he wrote to me last spring, he said, "I still feel it when it comes on. I like my new poems." He's right, the book with those has come out since then and the book has three or four beautiful poems in it, at his very best level. And so he's right.

SALE: And how long has he been practicing his trade?

WARREN: Well, he's in his sixties. He's my generation.

SALE: So there are many poems before this last batch.

WARREN: Oh, absolutely. He's sold quite a few volumes. But he's in his sixties, and he's thinking about it, too, you see.

SALE: Yes, "Is it time now?"

WARREN: Makes you nervous. It's bound to be a nightmare.

SALE: When a man decides he's found his stopping point, does this resolution necessarily mean levelling off? Couldn't it mean a continuing exploration?

WARREN: I don't think it means necessarily levelling off. I think you have to find out, reassess and regroup. In its simplest terms, young poets have a great way of coming together. They should. Young people feel the necessity of a passionate friendship, association. They have the willingness to think each is great. They give roles for everybody to play. This is fine; they're getting into real life. There is a drama of youth, and that dims, has to dim. Deeper commitments take place in individuals, about individuals. But this sense of shared experience is gone, in a way. The fragmenting of life is happening. The deepening of individual affections takes the place of it, in a way. Family things come in, too. Love in the family is something quite different again; it's another form of privacy really. But excepting individual affections and family, there's something else that people need. They need some rational sense of a general communion. But the drama's gone.

SALE: But it can still be a world of action and realization.

WARREN: Yes, that's right, the sense of your relation to society. The sense of obligation, of patterns of values, which is more abstract, more rational than this sense of solidarity in the young. As an aside, the old have another kind of clubbiness: "Ain't they awful now." That's the worst thing they can do. That's using this attitude as a substitute; the old coming together and berating the young is a substitute for what they had when they were young, when they had this sense of a communal drama.

SALE: That's a very poor substitute.

WARREN: It's a poor substitute, a great temptation but a poor substitute, I think. But the need to find a rational set of values which enables you to keep some contact with the general world is the important thing.

SALE: That idea was working in two novels, *Wilderness* and *Flood*. It wasn't their main theme, but the new awareness of pain made the characters able to continue.

WARREN: That's the idea. Yes. I hope that's visible in the novels.

SALE: I also thought it was Wordsworthian that a new, more philosophical awareness took the place of the "animal spirits" of the young.

WARREN: Well, *The Cave* was the book where it was most explicit in my mind. The old man who is the old hellion, who is really jealous of his son and can't die because of his jealousy, can't take his role as a dying man. He can't accept himself being the age to die. He is the enemy of his son and the son knows it.

SALE: He can't give up the juices of youth.

WARREN: All of this is the father-son business; the old man can't, will not be a father and take his biological role. He's playing another role all the time. He has to learn to—well—take a sedative for his pain. He has to learn how to give his box to the boy. All these things he has to do. But that was quite the very center of the book. That notion of how this man is to learn his painful role. And I'll tell you this. I was working on that book when I wrote the essay, "Knowledge and the Image of Man." Towards the end of the book, I wrote the piece. It came out of the book.

SALE: They worked very nicely.

WARREN: The piece came out of *The Cave*. Well, let me just say this on the side about these people who are finding allegories everywhere. *The Cave* goes back to the Floyd Collins case which happened around my home, that part of Kentucky. When it happened I was so deep in John Donne and the Elizabethans, I didn't bother to go up there. Only several years later, after I'd been away from Tennessee for a little while, I began to discover Tennessee. The working title of *The Cave* was originally *The Man Below*, and the man below is the man inside, of course, inside you. The submerged man in you and the man in the ground. Somewhere along the way this became the point. When the novel was finished and going to press, it had to be settled, titled. Albert Erskine, the editor, said, "This is a terrible title. You can't use this title. It's terrible. Find a title." The last day, the last afternoon in his office, closing date, no title still, I said, "Oh hell, call it *The Cave* and be done with it."

SALE: You said this?

WARREN: Well, I think I did. Maybe he said it. It was just like that. Get rid of the goddamn thing.

SALE: That sounds pretty satisfactory.

WARREN: Then I said or he said again, "What about Plato's Cave?" We can have a little epigraph here to stick on it. So we went to Hiram Haines' office next door to Albert's at Random House, got Plato down, and hunted the passage. Stuck it on like that. Impulse. Last minute.

SALE: That's fun.

WARREN: That's the story of the notion of this deeply plotted allegory from the start.

SALE: Someone has said that your book on John Brown was a step toward fiction. Do you think he's right, or do you know of any further explanation of that? Was it, in your mind, a move in that direction?

WARREN: No. I hadn't. It may have been true, but it wasn't in my mind. At that time fiction was beneath contempt in my scale of values. I had written, when I was a freshman, a story or two. They were terrible. I didn't begin writing fiction until after *John Brown*. But poetry was all, and I was a reader of history. I read a lot of history, and I have continued to read a lot of history. But *Brown*, I guess, was an approach to fiction because it presented a psychological problem to deal with and the question of narrative. It worked out that way but it was not programmatic. It just happened so. Well, once you sit down and write a long book all the way through, you're different. You know you're just different. You know you can do it. You know you can suffer through it, I mean. You can type that many words. Period. The kind of narrative in there became the stock in trade of my fiction. Issues that book raised remain in the fiction.

SALE: And, maybe even the character.

WARREN: And sometimes the character, yes.

SALE: The passionate man—

WARREN: I think that a Frenchman first pointed that out. It hadn't occurred to me till later, long years after. But in reviewing *Night Rider* a Frenchman said it was the John Brown story over again. But it's true the world of rural violence which that novel had always remains in my work. It was part of my generation, caught in my imagination. It was there. My God, I saw it myself with my own eyes. With my own eyes, as they say, early image. This is an aside, too: Someone will say, "Why do you write historical novels." I say, "I don't. I write very few." They say, "*All the King's Men*." Well, historical, my foot! I was a grown man. I don't think they're historical novels. What I'm trying to find is what happened, something that has the distance of the past but has the image of an issue. It must be an image, a sort of simplified and distant framed image, of an immediate and contemporary issue, a sort of interplay between that image and the contemporary world. That's the only historical novel of interest to me. It must have this personal reference, a feeling of something, whatever that strange thing is that's making that story relevant for you, that involves something that is in you.

SALE: What about the problem of getting into a character who has some fanatic dream or commits great acts of violence?

WARREN: I don't know. I suppose you do it because you have that potentiality, I guess.

SALE: And you can depict it because you have it.

WARREN: I think you have to assume that there are no psychic accidents. You have to assume that in ordinary life I wouldn't want to be fanatical and force that to the point of mania. But there's something that makes an issue interesting to you; otherwise you couldn't live through the writing of the book. There's some issue there, concealed or not concealed, that involves you deeply enough to make you stay with it. I don't mean identification in any simpleminded way with you and the protagonist. In fact, every man is many men. And he's always splitting himself up anyway in his social life. Social life, ordinary life, no man is the same man to everybody unless he's a saint.

SALE: And you don't manifest all these possibilities to other people.

WARREN: No, and you'd better not or you'd be in jail, you'd be crazy. I'm not talking about some simple sublimation; I just mean that every man has only one story. He doesn't know what his story is so he keeps on fiddling with the possibilities of that story. Every writer, no matter how trivial, and every writer, no matter how great, has only one tale; and the great writers have more versions of it. Shakespeare has more versions of it than Milton does. And Dickens has more versions than F. Scott Fitzgerald. And Faulkner has more than Hemingway. But you have to assume the central story.

SALE: Well, you've answered one of my other questions, about your intentions of writing poems and novels rather than criticism.

WARREN: It's not a matter of choice. I just don't think of myself as a critic. Like I said, criticism is a kind of conversation or speculation that gets into writing. I have no critical sense. I've never had a critical sense, never had the ambition. By ambition I mean desire to force a thing through to the last ditch, as far as I can. Such critical pieces I've done were one way of thinking about issues that concerned me. Now, I'm not denigrating criticism. The critics are systematic, want to force the thing through to its ultimates. I. A. Richards, Cleanth Brooks, or Ransom, they are people who must try to drive the thing through, you know, and whose way of study and effort is in that direction. Now for me it's a very different thing, whether it's reading criticism or an essay I'd written. Because it's usually *ad hoc*, usually came out of the classroom, or it's come out of my interests. Such work has been side efforts, excursions looking back on what my main interest was, rather than things in themselves. I have no professional commitment to it. It was subsidiary to the other, creative process for me.

SALE: An interested man's comments.

WARREN: That's right. That's good to put it that way. Oh, I'm sure that criticism has modified my writing, which is a way of thinking about writing. It's the way I think about my reading.

SALE: It's played a good auxiliary role.

WARREN: I'm the same way with drama. I started too late to make a career out of it. But I was interested in it. I think it had a very definite effect on my poetry. The interest in theater, which was always limited with me, had a tremendous effect on the poetry and on the novels. *All the King's Men* was a play first, and this is a sort of submerged interest that I fool with in experimenting, felt my way into. These are probings into the nature of things and the nature of yourself. Even now if you stumble on something, well, all right. But there's no sort of the abiding commitment there.

I had a play on last fall. *Brother to Dragons* was done extremely well at the Providence Repertory Theater, Trinity Theater at Providence, an extraordinary production of it. Well, I worked on it a little bit; I sold it, and I was delighted with what they did with it. I have a big stake in it, a particular stake in it, but this doesn't mean I'm going to write another one. It was a special thing, I just feel it's a way of whetting your tools for something else, for fiction, for the novel, or for poetry. No, what I'd like to do is just write some more novels and write some more poems and nicer ones.

SALE: You mentioned several writers just in passing at different times. What of your early interest in other writers, in Faulkner, say. When did you first come across Faulkner's works, do you recall?

WARREN: Exactly. Every detail of it. When I was a student at Oxford I knew John Gould Fletcher in London, and John Gould Fletcher came up to Oxford for a weekend visit with me and brought me several books as presents. One was Hart Crane's *The Bridge* in the Black Paris edition, and one was MacLeish's *New Found Land* in the Black Paris edition and one was *Soldier's Pay*, just out in England. He gave me this book and said, "You want to read *Soldier's Pay*. It's wonderful writing. You'd better read it right quick." I read it and I remember on the back it had a blurb by Arnold Bennett which said, "An American who writes like an angel."

SALE: That's one of those generation bridges you were talking about before.

WARREN: That certainly is one of them and how ironical that one is. And I read the book and I thought it was just great. Of course it's not great but it set well. What was wonderful about it was the scene in that book—a certain shock of recognition to see a certain aspect of the South that you were aware of but never formulated. I'm not a Mississippian, but somehow there's enough generalized South for this to be interesting and important to me, and I read it at a time when I was starting to write. I'd already started my first novel, and my first piece of fiction was being published: "Prime Leaf." I was writing it at the request of Paul Rosenfeld for *The American Caravan*. He'd asked me to do a piece of fiction along the line of the tales we've been taking about. I was living back into my South, and here comes a novel about the South bringing a real shock of recognition. This hit me at the moment when I was puzzling with the question of what to do with Southern tales. And Katherine Anne Porter's tales about the South had been very important to me and so had Caroline Gordon's and some others. I got to know some fiction writers, you see. They talked about fiction the way I'd always heard poetry talked about.

SALE: With the same excitement.

WARREN: Same excitement, same sense of being a complicated,

rich thing inside. You know about it. That's the excitement they brought to it.

SALE: When you were at L.S.U. in 1934, was Faulkner a popular author there?

WARREN: Well, again, I read him. I read the short stories when they came out and was mad for them. I read all the books when they came out. Yes—I, and all of my friends were this way, my historian friends were. Yes, the people who were interested in history had a passionate devotion to his work. I don't mean uncritical devotion, but a passionate interest in it. People had read him there. I felt I'd discovered him, but everybody I know practically had discovered him.

SALE: I guess a lot of people had privately discovered him.

WARREN: A lot, yes. Well, you know a few years later you couldn't find one of his books. I've recently read all, practically all, the reviews of Faulkner from 1929 to 1941,

SALE: And it didn't take too long.

WARREN: Incredibly, to the whole Marxist school, he was the Southern fascist. They polished him off.

SALE: Not to be read.

WARREN: It's incredible. It's one of the saddest, most humbling and distressing pieces of intellectual history I know. About then *Strange Fruit* came out. You had a pack and chorus, even being led by the Roosevelt administration, of praise for that book. And what a cocky book. *Go Down, Moses* came out then, too. "The Bear" was in it. Nobody mentioned it. That book died a-borning. And *Strange Fruit* was a great big thing.

SALE: Yes, it was.

WARREN: Now, after that you couldn't buy a work of Faulkner's. They were all out of print. There were a few paperbacks floating around, but you couldn't get one through a regular channel.

SALE: You could in England, but you couldn't in the United States.

WARREN: You could in Italy.

SALE: You mean they believed the critics, too? They thought he was a Southern Fascist also?

WARREN: No, Faulkner was published there by the Fascist government because it showed the bad side of America. An Italian friend of mine, who is a publisher now, said that the American novel drove him to desert the Italian army and go to the partisans. He was a literary young man and he said he and his friends read those books like Dreiser and Faulkner that they were allowed to read and were enraptured by them. "We at first thought, well, a country that allows those books to be written must be a great country," he said. "So we deserted, went to the mountains."

SALE: That's funny.

WARREN: He wasn't kidding; he was a partisan leader. But it backfired on Mussolini.

SALE: It kept Faulkner hungry, though, for a long time.

WARREN: It kept Faulkner hungry for a long time.

SALE: Oh, about Katherine Anne Porter. Have you got any comment to make about where *Ship of Fools* fits into the total work.

WARREN: I don't—let's see. *Ship of Fools* is a big, important book, but I think its powers are powers of a series of novelettes imbedded in it. I couldn't put the book down when I read it. I read it straight through in two solid days of reading. Didn't get out of my chair except to eat and go to bed. It is faulty, but I was expecting it; the end is not the end of a novel. You've had some wonderful novelettes on the way, I think. This is nothing against it. I say it's nothing against her. She's a terrific writer. Of the world's best twenty novelettes she might probably have two of them. They're really great. I mean they're at the world level you know. I would think "Old Mortality" and "Noon Wine" or maybe "Pale Horse" would be at the top level, you know, in that collection of the world's short novels. She would have one or two. She's bound to have one. She may have two in there. And several short stories are absolutely first rate. I'm not talking about wonderful; I'm talking about really the first-rate ones, you know. She's a terrific writer. She's natural for it. She has a genius for short fiction. The amount of density, of philosophical density, the human weight that she can get into things like "Old Mortality"! It's as big as a big novel. Or what she could get into "Noon Wine."

SALE: Or—what's the phrase—to *get away with* having that much in it.

WARREN: That's right, that's right.

SALE: To get away with it, not just packing it in.

WARREN: Having it there, having it totally absorbed in its own scale. The resonance and the drama and the echoes of it. This is terrific. Now I don't think about her personally. She's one of my oldest and dearest friends, and I don't think this is just friendship making me say this. But, she has this power of getting these ranges of meaning into the short form. I think these same powers are in *Ship of Fools* but not as a *novel*, not in *Ship of Fools* as novel, but in elements of *Ship of Fools*. They're not digested in the novel, they're not digested. But the novel, the novel thing does not hold all that's in that novel.

SALE: Would you put Eudora Welty in her category?

WARREN: I think Eudora is a terrific writer. I'll say that, yes, I think Eudora's best stories are in the top level. There are not many first-rate short story writers, not many natural short fiction writers. Eudora's one of them. In this country, how many do we have really? We've had—Faulkner. He's had several short stories and "The Bear" which are top level. Katherine Anne, Eudora Welty, Hemingway. Fitzgerald has a couple of them, I think, that are real beauties. The rather long one called "Winter Dreams" is a beauty and "Rich Boy" is gratifying. And then you begin to thin out fast, you know. You begin to grope around. Now you will find many fine stories, men of two or three stories.

SALE: Single stories.

WARREN: A single story or maybe two by somebody who's a novelist. There's a wonderful story by John Peale Bishop, quite a wonderful story. Caroline Gordon has two beautiful stories. Let's see—John O'Hara, now he is a short story writer. The same kind Moravia is or that Pirandello was. The same kind that Chekhov was or de Maupassant. He pours them out. Just pours them out automatically. And the problem is reading him. I've come lately to this view, but I got to reading a lot of them in a great run when I was in France last year just because they were available there in paperback. I was detached from them so far I began to see that some of these are quite wonderful. But you have to read ten to find the good one. This is the way with de Maupassant. He's a very great writer, I think. He's much out of fashion now. He also was a fine novelist. And Pirandello or Moravia, but you have to read through so many to find that one because the good ones look like the bad ones. And the bad ones are so well turned out. They are so close to the good ones, don't you see. You have to take three or four looks to see the difference. And I've come to think that John O'Hara is really a superlative short story writer. I think you have to look, try to see the bad from the good, the almost good from the really good, but there's some quite powerful things he's done. He's a natural. He's a natural-born story writer; anyway, I think he's underrated. There are two or three novels that really matter, but he's also a real short story writer.

Oh, I also wanted to record my admiration for Flannery O'Connor. I would put her name in that same group of the best short fiction writers. She's written some beauties, much better than her novels.

SALE: Did you know her?

WARREN: I knew her slightly. I spent one weekend as a guest in the same house with her. That's the only time I ever saw her, in Nashville. She was a fascinating woman, wonderful writer. The short story psychology is a strange, strange thing. It's as different from a novel in a way as poetry is. Well, not quite, but there's a real difference. She was a wonderful writer. She's going to be permanent, I think.

SALE: Yes.

WARREN: Well, Peter Taylor's done some excellent short stories.

SALE: OK, one more writer. How does Hemingway wear on you, looking back?

WARREN: Very well indeed, I think. In my fiction class here I use Hemingway, and now nobody's read him. The students haven't read him. Five years ago everybody read him. Now, they have not and they don't even want to because he's dead.

SALE: As far as being one of the in-vogue writers, he's out?

WARREN: Right, but they haven't even read him. You see that even when his books are required. Hardy's out. Nobody's read Hardy. Year after year, I've asked the students in my classes, and these are bright-to-the-roof boys, especially bright and very literary, who have never read a

106 Critical Essays on Robert Penn Warren

single poem of Hardy's. But the real virtues of Hemingway become more apparent, now that the gulf between his good and bad work becomes more apparent, too.

SALE: But they are separating now.

WARREN: They're separating now. I think the real power is there and the real qualities are more impressive than they were before.

SALE: So you wouldn't change any of your earlier estimates?

WARREN: No, no, I would change emphases here and there about a particular work, yes, but I would still think of *A Farewell to Arms* as a very, very powerful book of the same kind I thought it was twenty years ago. Same order of book, I haven't changed my mind about that. I find certain clichés of it more offensive than I found then, or I find Catherine even less of a character than I thought she was then. She's a sort of onanistic dream, in a way, more so than I thought then.

SALE: You've mentioned that Hemingway, for example, is not in vogue with your students. Are there others on the blacklist?

WARREN: I've started taking my census every year, my poll, my questionnaire, by which I've discovered that not one of this class of twelve, the finest flower of Yale literarydom, had read a single novel by de Maupassant or by Dreiser, by Balzac, by Zola. They don't know anything about Zola. The total realistic-naturalistic tradition, including Dickens, is out, totally out. Stendhal, yes, Gide, Kafka, in. Proust is going out. Gide and Kafka are hot; market firm. They are holding steady, and Faulkner's in but he won't last long. The whole tradition of the realistic-naturalistic tradition, the whole meat-and-potatoes school is out in favor of Kafka, Camus, and Gide.

SALE: Maybe Hermann Hesse.

WARREN: Hesse's coming in steady, God help us, and then Salinger, you see—

SALE: Is gone, is long gone.

WARREN: He's long gone, and five years ago he was taking the place of Balzac or Zola. Isn't it funny, but the fancy-fancy, arty-arty fiction with the psychological complication has driven out this other type almost entirely in colleges as far as I know. Now it may be changing back a bit. They only read *An American Tragedy* or Zola at gun point.

Zola's a wonderful writer. In '61 I was in France and I read a novel by Zola every week. I could buy him in the Livres des Poche edition at thirty cents, and I read one every week. In the middle of that summer of Zola, I read Camus's *La Chute*, a fine book; but reading it in the middle of Zola made me feel very strange.

SALE: I can imagine.

WARREN: It was just like coming out from a guillotining and seeing somebody tatting baby socks or something. It just seems so trivial—all that totally created world of Zola, the populated world. Then to come down to *La Chute*. I went back to Zola with an air of relief.

SALE: Back into the world.

WARREN: Back into the real world, all kidding aside.

SALE: Thank you very much—

WARREN: Not at all. I feel I've been yelling my head off. Let's go to the Beinecke and take a peek there.

ARTICLES AND ESSAYS

"The Mariner and Robert Penn Warren"

James H. Justus*

Robert Penn Warren's virtuoso piece of criticism, his analysis of *The Rime of the Ancient Mariner*, is well known. That poem, Warren says, posits as its primary theme man's necessity for repentance and reconciliation after crime and punishment:

> The Mariner shoots the bird; suffers various pains, the greatest of which is loneliness and spiritual anguish; upon recognizing the beauty of the foul sea snakes, experiences a gush of love for them and is able to pray; is returned miraculously to his home port, where he discovers the joy of human communion in God, . . . [and the meaning of] the notion of a universal charity, . . . the sense of the "One Life" in which all creation participates.[1]

Warren further claims that the "unmotivated" killing of the albatross is "exactly the significant thing about the Mariner's act" because it "reenacts the Fall . . ." (p. 227). Warren stresses the Mariner's willing perversity—his individual, not inherited, responsibility for the act—and the crew's willing complicity. Having then submitted himself to "the great discipline of sympathy," the Mariner can walk again, in Coleridge's words, "with a goodly company." In Warren's interpretation, the terms which the Mariner accepts for his reintroduction into human society are resonant of the traditional, mythic punishment of Cain or the Wandering Jew and the dark verbal gift of the *poète maudit* (pp. 256–257).

Whether or not Coleridge's Mariner encompasses those typal figures is probably academic, since the part of the story to which most readers have always responded dramatically is the Mariner's need to communicate his experience to as many wedding guests as he can find. In our time we have come to regard that need as a psychological—and even moral—commonplace. Warren's view of Coleridge's Mariner has been questioned, and it may or may not satisfy students of *The Rime of the Ancient Mariner*, but there is no doubt that Warren's interpretation of that

* Reprinted by permission from *Texas Studies in Literature and Language*, 7(1966), 117–28. Copyright © 1966 by the University of Texas Press.

111

famous figure in his critical essay is anticipated and corroborated in his fiction.[2]

Warren's Mariner is characterized by a need, sometimes compulsive, to recite his story. But Warren's Mariner is not Coleridge's. In novel after novel, Warren rings his own changes on Coleridge's pattern. In the episodes involving this recurring character, who invariably proclaims his guilt for the past acts, his storytelling itself is usually an attempt to justify the teller to others *and* to himself. In such novels as *Night Rider* and *Band of Angels*, Warren's Mariner can more often define his crime and punishment than he can his repentance and reconciliation. In some instances even part of his punishment, the self-flagellating need to tell someone about it, suffers from lack of focus; he is unable to see his true role in his own act, and often the very recital of his story is halting, convoluted, imprecise, even incorrect.

When minor characters act out the Mariner role, their stories become the interpolated tales which readers have come to expect in many of Warren's novels. Sometimes the protagonist, who impatiently or reluctantly listens to the story, becomes in turn another Mariner, a wedding guest who comes to acknowledge the truth of what he has been told and acts upon it. The recurrence of this figure and his checkered fortunes in the Warren universe, in a variety of refinements and developments, indicates two aspects of the author's concern in his fiction.

Morally, that concern is the burden of man's salvation and the adequate verbalizing of it, which is to say, the resolution of guilt and responsibility requires confession (Coleridge's Mariner must explain, cajole, and persuade others of both his sin and his salvation). Aesthetically, that concern is providing statement with a necessary and appropriate vehicle (Coleridge's Mariner can begin his return journey after he composes a poem of blessing). These two related interests Warren writes of elsewhere in various ways—

Morally:

[Conrad's work] is about the cost of awareness and the difficulty of virtue, and his characteristic story is the story of struggle and, sometimes, of redemption.[3]

Man must make his life somehow in the dialectical process . . . , and in so far as he is to acieve redemption he must do so through an awareness of his condition that identifies him with the general human communion, not in abstraction, not in mere doctrine, but immediately. The victory is never won, the redemption must be continually re-earned.[4]

Aesthetically:

We must sometimes force ourselves to remember that the act of creation is not simply a projection of temperament, but a criticism and purging of temperament.[5]

[W]hat good fiction gives us is the stimulation of a powerful image of human nature trying to fulfill itself.[6]

The poet [creates] . . . a self as well as a poem—but neither except in so far as he creates a structure, a form. . . . The poem is, then, a little myth of man's capacity for making life meaningful. And in the end, the poem is not a thing we see—it is, rather, a light by which we may see—and what we see is life.[7]

In this respect certainly Warren's criticism and his fiction are of a piece. Warren's Mariners morally relive the ceremony of confession and aesthetically re-enact the process of the artist. They do not always succeed in transforming themselves into artifacts, examples of the "little myth of man's capacity for making life meaningful." Some fall short of redemption, but many reach at least a point in their spiritual development where they can accept the high cost of knowledge. Since that acceptance, however, demands a strenuous self-examination, most of Warren's fictional Mariners pay dearly for their final peace.

I

Warren's first Mariner is Willie Proudfit of *Night Rider* (1939). Because we meet him after he has achieved regeneration, his story is told impersonally: "He would tell it, not exactly for them [his listeners], it seemed, but for the telling, speaking slowly and tentatively." The act of speaking about his experiences on the western plains becomes a personal reminder of past complicity in crime—that he is still a human creature in constant need of grace. Proudfit verbalizes in order to "name [that] passel of things" he is now ashamed of, to identify them, to be certain that his past definition of them still remains true. Proudfit recounts his buffalo-skinning days in terms of a crime against nature; he emphasizes the hot rifle barrel, the crumpling of the shot animal, the sympathetic gathering of the rest of the herd around the fallen member, and finally, his own estimate of man's irrational impulse to kill the animals: " 'A man lays thar, the sun a-bearen down, and keeps on a-pullen on the trigger. He ain't lak his-self. Naw, he ain't. Lak he wasn't no man, nor nuthen'.' "[8] By implication Proudfit also now accepts the shared guilt of scalping an Indian, even though the act had been committed by a partner. Proudfit tells how he begins his expiation by living with the Indians, sharing their rituals and accepting their remedies for fever. Only when he has a vision of green grass, houses in a valley, a "white church with a bell" hanging near a spring, does he end his exile of penance to begin his journey to Kentucky. That homecoming, when he falls "face down to the water" near his old home, becomes his final gesture, and Warren sees it as a self-ennobling and necessary act.

This story has only a subliminal effect on Perse Munn, the protagonist of *Night Rider*, whose vision is too limited to see that Proudfit's past parallels his own present. But when Munn finally decides to sacrifice the protection offered by Proudfit—to leave the sparse land for Monclair estate to kill Tolliver—the journey is an ironic reversal of Proudfit's journey from the plains to Kentucky. Munn the lawyer at last is a Mariner who has not yet learned what his crime was and who never fully understands the definition of his punishment. His first act, permitting an innocent old Negro to hang for a murder committed by a client, is an unconscious crime (he believes his client, Harris Trevelyan, to be innocent). But his belief is wholly intuitive, and according to all previous indications Munn should have known that his intuition was flawed. He vacillates between liberty and fraternity, between cherishing his definition in his own terms and in submitting his definition to the cause of the Free Farmers Association. Even after he has become a member of the Board he lives on through one fall and winter, alternately exultant and depressed, "as though poised on the brink of revelation." Whenever he is convinced that he can successfully define himself through others, he rides through the countryside persuading farmers to join the Association. After each success he experiences the sharp throb of exaltation; whenever he fails, he cultivates his isolation, seeking the "true and unmoved" center of his being.

His murky idea of self is reflected in his compulsion to explain himself to others. His feelings, because they are ambivalent and ambiguous, can never find adequate expression. He gropes for words that will give shape to his most precious experiences, but his speeches trail off until they have only a remote relevance to his desires. First to his wife, then to young Benton Todd, he tries to explain his motives. After he kills Trevelyan, the compounding of his guilt strikes him even more speechless and he more and more cherishes his isolation.

While hunting, he shoots a dove; the old spurt of exaltation revives, only to be quenched by revulsion. In contrast to Proudfit, who begins the process of regeneration after the buffalo hunts, Munn degenerates rapidly after the symbolic shooting of the dove. The difference lies in the quality of the impulse toward self-definition. Munn's is always contradictory and hazy, and, near the end, when he could make the most of Proudfit's successful impulse, he hardly hears the words.

A similar structuring of the Mariner theme is evident in Warren's second novel, *At Heaven's Gate* (1943). The Mariner here is Ashby Wyndham, whose handwritten "Statement" alternates with chapters dealing with Sue Murdock and Jerry Calhoun. Wyndham's Statement should serve as a kind of self-purgation, but it does not. It is merely another trial, part of a larger punishment. Unlike Proudfit, who finds peace, Wyndham finds only more pain. His theme is "the pore human man," whose dilemma is that he "wants to know, but it is his weakness."[9] Wyndham's albatross is, literally, Marie's mule which he drives into a gatepost and kills during one of his drunken rampages, and, symbolically, his guilt for striking his brother Jacob in anger. This latter act causes Jacob to sell their farm: he turns over the scanty proceeds to Ashby, and each brother, permanently estranged from the other, sets out alone in the world.

Leaving the farm of his ancestors takes Ashby into another sin—to Massey Mountain, where he joins a timber crew stripping the mountain of its trees. His tree-chopping parallels the earlier mule-killing; both are crimes against nature. And when he strikes Sweetwater, the unionist who heckles Private Porsum as he pleads with the men to halt the strike, Ashby repeats his earlier crime against his brother. Ashby says, "I ought never lifted up my hand agin him in no way. If I had helt my hand, may be nuthin would happened" (p. 193). Disasters multiply: he is fired and his child dies. While waking in anguish at night, he hears the voice of his dead child admonishing him to "walk in the world" and tell of his sin against his brother. This moment of illumination confirms Ashby's Mariner role. From this moment on, his expiation is "telling" the Word: "I stood in the street and I told folks how it was. How the Lord had laid it on me to tell folks. I told them my wickedness and how the wicked man will come down low. I met folks in the big road and I told them" (p. 233).

But even in this mission Ashby despairs as he gradually sees himself being enveloped in spiritual pride: "A man can be proud and high in the Lord lak he can in pore human pride and it is a sin. It is a worse sin" (p. 262). (Here the alternating chapters stop, the plots mesh, and Ashby sits in his cell, convinced that God—in all justness—has turned away His face.) Although Ashby never achieves his regeneration, his adamant compulsion toward expiation has at least one positive effect—his role stimulates the public confession of Private Porsum, his cousin who is involved in Murdock's shady financial deals.

Like Munn of *Night Rider*, Jerry Calhoun is inflicted with a Mariner impulse but is denied the concomitant gift for words that can give release, and therefore meaning, to that impulse. Unlike Murdock's other ex-hero, Porsum, Jerry does not have a "silver tongue" to soothe the mobs; instead he becomes an echo of Murdock in his assertive, confidential, cliché-studded rhetoric that persuades business associates of Murdock's honesty. Porsum manages to repudiate his lackey role because he can still define himself; Jerry crumbles passively, without the will to resist or admit defeat, because he never successfully defines himself.

At one time he is afraid of what Murdock will say to him, and when his fears seem unjustified, he calls himself a fool, "patronizing the self he had been and all guilts and fears and confusions" (p. 225). After his merely temporary sexual reunion with Sue, he thinks of himself as two people: "[T]he Jerry Calhoun to whom it had happened kept trying scrupulously to explain it all to the Jerry Calhoun to whom nothing had happened at all" (p. 232). Only after being rescued by Duckfoot Blake and returned to the care of his father is Jerry able to begin the careful definition of self that has so long eluded him.

II

In *Night Rider* and *At Heaven's Gate* a subordinate figure plays the role of chief Mariner, and the protagonist becomes the secondary, almost paradoxically speechless Mariner. In *All the King's Men* (1946) the Mariner dominates both structure and texture. Jack Burden's entire story is an I-narration, a reliving and relieving of a burden—the protagonist's impulse toward self-definition. His easy cynicism, his almost automatic rejection of family (and therefore tradition and the past), his cautious but loyal acceptance of Willie Stark, his profession ("Student of History, and newspaperman), and a talent which makes the maximum use of words— all these give him obvious advantages over Perse Munn and Jerry Calhoun. Whereas those earlier protagonists had only the impulse to tell their stories, Jack Burden has both the impulse and the talent.

His task, for all that, is no easier. His very gift involves him in a compulsion toward completeness, a need to investigate all motives, to speculate if not to conclude on actions. He is not haunted; he is merely nagged by his failure to achieve a fuller self-definition. His mental and moral bent encourages him to verbalize without fear of definitiveness; his philosophic stance, for example, moves from Idealism to a scientistic Naturalism before coming even to a tentative rest. After his trip West he can say, with a touch of dogmatism, that he had learned "two very great truths. First, that you cannot lose what you have never had. Second, that you are never guilty of a crime which you did not commit."[10] He finds, however, in the thrust of events—the mutual destruction of Adam Stanton and Willie Stark—that these "very great truths" are not true, at least for him. And when the time comes to change his mind, his words also change. The verbalizing of his final position is less dogmatic and smug, but it is just as thorough, just as freewheeling. In short, he is not paralyzed by an inability to "tell" at any stage in his development. This ambivalent gift of Jack Burden is an updating of the central tactic used by the Mariner to release his burden and to reclaim his place in nature: the "telling" is important in itself.

The yardstick by which Jack Burden measures his growing moral position is the diary of Cass Mastern, itself a "telling" of guilt and punishment, which lies always in the background waiting for Jack Burden's maturity. His first attempt to understand Cass Mastern (when he is a doctoral candidate) ends in failure. The project is still waiting at the end of the novel when Jack Burden, who has completed his own "telling," can now edit the document. And that which Cass Mastern learned in the

1860's is finally what Jack Burden learns in the 1930's, that "the world is all of one piece . . . like an enormous spider web and if you touch it, however lightly, at any point, the vibration ripples to the remotest perimeter . . ."(p. 200).

In the end, he must accept his own involvement in sending Anne Stanton to Stark's bed and in causing the death of his two friends, Stanton and Stark, whose lives were perhaps doomed but who themselves "lived in the agony of will." Responsibility for past events leads Jack Burden to find the Scholarly Attorney ("for each of us is the son of a million fathers"). Moreover, Jack Burden can see no easy reconciliation in his future: the magnanimous act may come, but "a long time from now." Whatever victory he may achieve will be hard-won, for it must exist in the "convulsion of the world" and the "awful responsibility of Time."

As with Jack Burden's story, *World Enough and Time* (1950) is the long, anguished "telling" of a Mariner figure. It is a more ambitious presentation than Burden's because of Warren's more complex manipulation of perspective. A nameless "effaced" narrator (another Student of History) slips into the background, as Jack Burden does not do, to permit full play to *his* Cass Mastern. His editing of Jeremiah Beaumont's journal and the assembling of related objective reports about Beaumont are sometimes accurate, sometimes not. But for all his flaws, the narrator's energies are devoted not primarily to his own self-knowledge, as was true of Jack Burden's concern with Cass Mastern, but to the unfolding of his subject's terrible progress toward self-knowledge.

If it is true that Warren is exploring one modern version of the old romance genre, then Jeremiah Beaumont becomes a version of the most sophisticated hero of the romance—the knight in search of the Grail. Despite the antireligious position of both Beaumont and Rachel and despite the substitution of the Ruined Maid for the Virgin, the intensity and ardor of Beaumont's rather wormy courtly love are religious. Throughout his life Beaumont's underlying motive—as well as his determining pattern of action—is a personal search for his own identity, not the disinterested search for justice, which he affirms so loudly and so often that even his historian accepts it. Self, rather than Justice, is his Grail, though its winning proves to be just as hard. Jeremiah Beaumont, the serious man of idea who pursues his dream of self to its logical conclusion, upholds an idealism that is itself flawed; he cannot bear the thought of corrupting compromise. Beaumont is a more subtle and complex version of Ashby Wyndham: spiritual pride, because of its status in the hierarchy, carries with it a proportionate risk and punishment.

In the motionless stupor of a backwoods swamp (with sufficient time and enough of an independent world) the lovers reorient their relationship. It is appropriate that Rachel, who throughout their fitful lives serves as her husband's excuse for his acts, should be the agent who permits him his long sought-for knowledge. Rachel both indicts and forgives Beaumont, charging him with doing all for himself, with using her for his own dark needs, but, as she lies dying by her own hand, she tells him that he could not have done otherwise. Only at this moment does he come to the point where he can define his sin (and therefore his elusive self): "It is unpardonable. It is the crime of self, the crime of life. The crime is I."[11] And in his last desperate days he seeks another act to restore a balance that had been scarcely there anyway, the symbolic moment when he can "shake the hangman's hand and call him brother."

Beaumont writes his journal with a tenacious need to justify himself as if his definition lay in justification. Because he is complex, and because his motives are buried beneath layers of surrogate motives, the explanations are involved and tortuous. His style is courtly, learned, graceful. His rhetoric, which reflects his technique of doing, surrounds, surmounts, and underpins the motive and the act so that the sheer enveloping defines the motive and the act in their ideal existence, and, in that process, the self Beaumont hopefully seeks.

As Beaumont gradually sheds all tokens of his former self, his civilizing symbols, he retains his manuscript. Even when doing nothing more than wenching with a syphilitic or drinking with louts, he is compelled to note these facts. Even when his exposed rationalizations grow thinner, he must still scramble for spare leaves of paper on which to record even them. In short, his compulsion to "tell" falls short only of his primary compulsion to act. And when he undertakes to return to Frankfort for his punishment, the well-wrapped parcel of manuscript is the most important item he carries. Even after his unceremonious death, when he is cheated of the dignity of the gallows, the confession remains important for Wilkie Barron, who prefers to keep it in a locked case despite the fact that its existence, if made public, would ruin him.

Beaumont suffers sin, punishment, expiation, and hovers about the brink of reconciliation. And if the desire to shake the hangman's hand is somehow equal to that act, perhaps the last phase of the Mariner process is completed in Beaumont. But for Beaumont, more than for any other of Warren's Mariners, the "telling" itself becomes the major instrument for the final, successful definition, the purgation of self to locate self.

III

In *Night Rider* and *At Heaven's Gate* Warren's adaptations of this figure are Mariners who, though untutored, are highly sensitive to the fact of their own guilt. One speaks out of his recent "peace," the reconciliation after long punishment; the other speaks out in the anguish of his perpetual punishment and his belief that reconciliation is impossible. Both are "primitives," past middle age, who are repositories of folk wisdom. In *All the King's Men* and *World Enough and Time*, Warren turns to Mariners who are both learned and sensitive. In the first the historical situation of a youthful figure acts not only as an *exemplum* for the protagonist but also, because of his youth, as a relevant parallel to him. In *World Enough and Time* the modification of the "ancient" Mariner is projected out of a subordinate role into the role of the protagonist himself; the diary of one whose guilt and punishment assert a paradigm of a severe, almost simple, conscience is expanded and elevated into a journal of one whose conscience is complicated and involuted, and whose very confession reveals a self-deception so radical that it constantly baffles and misleads the shadowy historian who is trying to interpret it.

When Warren returns to a more conventional form in *Band of Angels* (1955), the theme and technique of the Mariner device are substantially modified. The Mariner figure, again with an interpolated confession, for the first time bears a functional relationship to the character who is the listener and to the organic structure of the novel; and for the first time the anguished search of the protagonist, though lengthy, leads finally to a full reconciliation "in joy."

The Mariner figure in *Band of Angels* is Hamish Bond, the man who buys Amantha. The statement which triggers the story of Bond's life is his remark: " 'You don't even know who I am' " and, a moment later, " 'Maybe I don't even know who I am'."[12] The name is important for them both, because the formation of the name or the shaping of the mask is accepted as a necessary step in self-definition. Amantha at least holds passionately to this view, for it is she who insists on knowing Bond's real name, a curious request that gradually grows to desperation. When he finally tells her, his story follows.

The pattern here is much the same as that of previous Mariners such as Willie Proudfit and Ashby Wyndham, whose crimes have been obvious, explicit ones. Bond's crime as slave trader is, like those others, a crime against nature, but is more heinously directed against other humans. Even the obscurely motivated rescue of the African child, nominally an act of conscience, is accompanied by killing the wounded, maternally furious mother. But the child, who comes to be his *k'la*, Rau-Ru, is Bond's one constant reminder of his crime. He serves a special function—"like a brother or son or something"—and finally comes to hate Bond with an intensified fury.

Unlike most of the other interpolated confessions, Bond's comes at a point in the Mariner cycle when his punishment is not yet over and his repentance only nebulously grasped. He can still say, "I did wrong," but his governing position is still the easy appeal to the "we're just what we are" argument. Characteristically, Bond's story suggests little to Amantha except how she has been hurt by his ambiguous profession. She confesses that she stops listening to him even in the process of the telling and describes how she forges her self-pity into a weapon: "[E]ven in that disorientation, some excitement of power had suddenly grown in me" (p. 201).

It is a familiar feeling with Amantha. As her relations with Bond grow stronger, she perfects her technique for using him, for assigning to herself the role of punisher of Bond—not for Bond's own crimes, which certainly require punishment, but because he had, without articulation and conscious art, complicated Amantha's growing need to define correctly *freedom* and *slavery*. It is Amantha's defining trait that she can use her triviality of mind as an instrument of power over the male at the same time she must depend on it as an instrument for solving her more pressing problems.

As for her own story, the reader plays the role of unenthusiastic wedding guest not because her *story* is a mediocre one (rather, it proclaims its historical, even philosophical magnitude at the same time its central concern is with an individual protagonist), but because *she* is mediocre. Unlike Jack Burden's story, hers far outweighs her intellectual and forensic equipment to tell it. Instead of holding us by a glittering eye, she fascinates us because she is so remarkably tiresome when she plays the vain and hurt young lady, a type who can barely discriminate between being snubbed at a ball and being raped by a slave. Much as she communicates her anxieties, ambivalences, self-justifications, and confessions, rarely are there moments when the reader feels that Amantha knows and understands what has happened to her even while she tells all. She gives the impression of an inept raconteur, short on art but long on ego, who expects the audience to share the work. But if we are patient the irritations are mitigated. Her story—every scrap and shred of it, every fragmented musing on it—falls into shape from the weight of its own pieces almost in spite of her storytelling technique or the quality of her mind. It is not accidental that what finally helps to define and answer her primary question ("Oh, who am I?") is not Amantha's overexercised sensibilities, or, as a wedding guest, her ability to learn from Bond's story, but merely time itself. Spiritually, she is an old woman when she achieves her reconciliation.

Warren's concern in his fiction for the theme of self-identity has been consistent and cumulative: for more than twenty years of work in the novel form, the Warren protagonist searches for self-definition despite the fact that the search inevitably requires a difficult, thoroughgoing, and massive outlay of energy and commitment. Those who achieve a viable identity (Jack Burden, Amantha Starr) do so because they accept a personal responsibility for their public acts. Those who fail (Jerry Calhoun, Jeremiah Beaumont) come to understand that necessity too late, when the damage is too great for putting the pieces of self back together again. Moreover, in his novels from *Night Rider* through *Band of Angels* Warren's technique for presenting the search in action is to use a figure who duplicates the shape of experience which Warren sees embodied in and dramatized by Coleridge's Ancient Mariner.[13]

It would be less than just to insist that most of Warren's memorable characters are merely variations on a single literary type; for all their similar patterns of behavior, each is too complex to fit simply the outlines of a received convention. Certainly Coleridge's Mariner is a pertinent typal figure for most of us; so also is it for Warren, who sees him in a special way—a view explicated at length in his essay on *The Rime of the Ancient Mariner* and corroborated in the creation of his own fictional characters. They, like the Coleridge–Warren figure, most commonly must survive the shock of their perception of evil both in the world at large and in themselves. From the older primitive folk types whose message is heard impatiently or not at all, to the younger, more sophisticated sufferers whose tortured fluency sometimes obscures a desire to learn the secrets of self-knowledge, the Mariner stalks the by-ways of Warren's world. As a figure, the Mariner knits up favorite Warren themes in explicit patterns and supplies a consistent artistic strategy to give those patterns tactical unity.

Notes

1. "A Poem of Pure Imagination: An Experiment in Reading," *Selected Essays* (New York: Random House, 1958), p. 222. Subsequent references to this essay are incorporated in the text.

2. The essay appeared originally in 1946; when it was revised for the *Selected Essays* in 1958, Warren recognized and replied to some of the voices raised in objection to his interpretation. The most important demurrer that I have seen since 1958 is Edward E. Bostetter, "The Nightmare World of *The Ancient Mariner*," *Studies in Romanticism*, 1 (1962), 241–54.

3. " 'The Great Mirage': Conrad and *Nostromo*," *Selected Essays*, p. 48.

4. *Selected Essays*, p. 54.

5. *Selected Essays*, p. 48.

6. "Ernest Hemingway," *Selected Essays*, p. 116.

7. "Formula for a Poem," *Saturday Review*, 22 March 1958, p. 23.

8. *Night Rider* (Boston: Houghton Mifflin, 1939), p. 408.

9. *At Heaven's Gate* (New York: Harcourt, Brace and Co., 1943), pp. 35–36.

10. *All the King's Men* (New York: Harcourt, Brace and Co., 1946), p. 330.

11. *World Enough and Time* (New York: Random House, 1950), p. 505.

12. *Band of Angels* (New York: Random House, 1955), p. 176.

13. Even in his experimental verse novel, *Brother to Dragons: A Tale in Verse and Voices* (1953), Warren gives much of the same function of his Mariner figure to his own persona—"R.P.W." Beginning with *The Cave* (1959), Warren's narrative strategy for dramatizing his great theme alters radically. In that work and his two subsequent novels, *Wilderness* (1961) and *Flood* (1964), Warren drops the interpolated tale—often a vehicle for accentuating the speeches and actions of the Mariner figure—and, indeed, much of the solid circumstantiality of the actual world that has sometimes masked his penchant for melodrama. The later novels are marked by bold, if not always successful, manipulations of caricature and stereotype, artifice and rhetoric, of episodes that are more ceremonial and ritualistic than functional, and of the author's own voice as authority.

"Warren's Osmosis"

Victor Strandberg*

To thread forth a central theme out of a writer's whole corpus can be risky business: Ernest Hemingway's resentment of the "psychic wound" interpretation of his novels is a case in point. To isolate such a theme in a writer like Robert Penn Warren is even riskier. Author of eight novels, four major volumes of poetry, four non-fiction books, and innumerable other writings, Warren is more complex and variegated than most writers, both in form and theme. Nevertheless, running through that wide scope of fiction and poetry, and even through the non-fiction studies, a central vision does stand forth. In a phrase, Warren's theme is the osmosis of being.

The phrase is Warren's own, articulated most elaborately in his essay, "Knowledge and the Image of Man": "[Man is] in the world with continual and intimate interpenetration, an inevitable osmosis of being, which in the end does not deny, but affirms, his identity." It is also articulated in most of Warren's creative writing, usually implicitly, as when a character in *Promises* is awakened to the book's highest promise, "You fool, poor fool, all Time is a dream, and we're all one Flesh, at last," but sometimes explicitly, as when Blanding Cottshill tells Bradwell Tolliver (in *Flood*), "Things are tied together. . . . There's some spooky interpenetration of things, a mystic osmosis of being, you might say."

The central importance of osmosis of being in Warren's work is seen in connection with his predominant theme of identity or self-definition. For such osmosis is the final answer to the problem of identity, and is indeed the only answer in the world, as Warren sees it. An awakening to this truth is what normally provides the structure for Warren's fiction and poetry. For example, it is this osmosis of being that finally requires Jack Burden in *All the King's Men* to accept responsibility for history; that causes Thomas Jefferson in *Brother to Dragons* to accept complicity in murder; that leads a long series of Warren characters in all his novels towards acceptance of a father figure, however shabby or tainted; and that draws forth the theme of a reconciliation within the self, between

*Reprinted, with editorial alterations approved by the author, from *Criticism*, 10 (1968), 23–40, by permission of the Wayne State University Press. Copyright © 1968, Wayne State University Press.

conscious and unconscious zones of the psyche, in much of Warren's poetry. And ultimately, it is this osmosis of being that imparts whatever meaning the self may have in the light of eternity; that absorbs the self into the totality of time and nature with the consoling promise, often repeated in Warren's work, that "nothing is ever lost."

Hence, Warren's osmosis has moral, metaphysical, and psychological ramifications; it is his contribution to modern religious thought, having an ethic and a mystical dimension. Looking back over Warren's career with hindsight, moreover, we may find that osmosis was there all the time, much like T. S. Eliot's Christianity, implicit in the early works and explicit later on. Like Eliot's Christianity, again, Warren's osmosis is evoked in the early work by negative implication: the naturalistic fragmentation of the world is intolerable and cries out for some sense of oneness. In "Mexico Is a Foreign Country: Five Studies in Naturalism," a poem written about 1943, a narrator watches some soldiers marching—"And I am I, and they are they,/And this is this, and that is that"—with a vain wish that "everything/Take hands with us and pace the music in a ring." And in the fiction, likewise, osmosis of being is what Warren's characters should be seeking, relating themselves to the totality of time and nature and society, whereas they characteristically are observed bent towards opposite ends, narrowing their identity to a basis of fame, sexual prowess, success in business, or membership in a philosophical, religious, or political sect.

To define the meaning and importance of osmosis in Warren's work, then, I should like to examine in turn its three major dimensions: psychological, social, and metaphysical. Let us begin with the workings of osmosis within the individual psyche, where, Warren feels, something is badly wrong in the way of self-definition. What is wrong, precisely, is that the Freudian id, or Jungian shadow—which is mainly what Warren is getting at in his recurrent motif of "original sin"—this darker, more bestial part of the psyche has been denied its place in reality. An innocent, idealistic figure like Thomas Jefferson (in Brother to Dragons), seriously undertaking to remake the human project from scratch and to do it right this time; or Tobias Sears, the utopian Transcendentalist in Band of Angels; or Adam (the name is deliberately chosen) Stanton, the physician to the poor in All the King's Men—such high-minded humanists are not about to think themselves a brother to dragons or indeed to concede any reality to a monster-self within.

But the reality of evil, though denied for a time, will finally make its presence known. As Carl Gustav Jung says, in The Undiscovered Self: "The evil that comes to light in man and that undoubtedly dwells within him is of gigantic proportions. . . . We are always, thanks to our human nature, potential criminals. . . . None of us stands outside humanity's black collective shadow." In Warren's narratives, humanity's black collective shadow is bodied forth in some of his most memorable characters and episodes: in the two hatchet-wielders, Lilburn Lewis (*Brother to Dragons*) and Big Billie Potts of "The Ballad of Billie Potts"; in the gradually escalating violence of "The Free Farmers' Brotherhood of Protection and Control" in *Night Rider*; in the degrading trip to Big Hump's island in *World Enough and Time*; in the horrific episode of the slave raid into Africa in *Band of Angels*; in the frenzied sexual orgy following Brother Sumpter's preaching in *The Cave*; in the callous butchery of Negroes by whites during the New York draft riots of 1863 as portrayed in *Wilderness*; in the swamprat animalism of Frog-Eye in *Flood*. And actual history, as discussed in Warren's books, adds confirming evidence. Warren's first book, *John Brown: The Making of a Martyr* (1929), shows the famous abolitionist to be a murderous fanatic, an obvious forebear of Warren's recurring fictional killers who lift rifle or meat-axe in an elation of justice, while *Who Speaks for the Negro?* (1965) identifies Malcolm X as the monster self in the inner dark: "Malcolm X can evoke, in the Negro, even in Martin Luther King, that self with which he, too, must deal, in shock and fright, or in manic elation. . . . Malcolm X is many things. He is the face not seen in the mirror. . . . He is the nightmare self. He is the secret sharer." (In saying this, shortly before Malcolm X's assassination, Warren was thinking particularly of the Negro leader's statement at a Harlem rally, "We need a Mau Mau to win freedom!")

From the beginning, Warren saw this discovery of a beast within the self as a basic structure in his work. Away back in his first novel, *Night Rider*, a piously Bible-quoting Professor Ball is heard to say, "Yes, sir, I'm a man of peace. But it's surprising to a man what he'll find in himself sometimes." What Professor Ball comes to find in himself is murder, cowardice, and betrayal, causing the death of the book's main character, Percy Munn. And in the next novel, the masterful *At Heaven's Gate*, Slim Sarrett likewise traces out the melancholy curve of self-discovery. Early in the book, Slim is the artist-intellectual writing of literature and self-knowledge ("Bacon wrote: Knowledge is power. . . . Shakespeare wrote: Self-knowledge is power"), but when his own self-knowledge comes to include the murder-cowardice-betrayal syndrome, Slim writes ruefully not of power but of a dark unbanishable being within the self:

> It came from your mother's womb, and she screamed at the
>   moment of egress.
> The family doctor slapped breath in, relighted his bitten
>   cigar
> While the old nurse washed it and washed it, without complete
>   success.

And in Warren's *Flood*, the main character feels a beast within himself quite literally: "Then, in the inner darkness of himself . . . the black beast heaved at him . . . that black beast with cold fur like hairy ice that drowsed in the deepest inner dark, or woke to snuffle about, or even, as now, might heave unexpectedly at him and breathe upon him."

And if Warren's fiction hints at a beast—a darker being or pollution of "original sin" within the self—Warren's poetry describes it much more explicitly. "And our innocence needs, perhaps, new definition," Warren said at the end of "Billie Potts," and it is pretty clear that this new definition of innocence must embrace, like osmosis, the guilt that "always and forever [will] rise and coil like miasma/From the fat sump and cess of common consciousness," as R. P. W. describes it in *Brother to Dragons*. In all his major volumes of poetry, Warren refers to this guilt in the common consciousness, which Jung calls "humanity's black collective shadow," in terms of animal imagery. *Eleven Poems on the Same Theme* (1942) takes the acknowledgment of this shadow self as its major structure. The conscious ego, sanctimonious and sure of an innocent identity, locks the shadow self out of the house of the psyche in a poem called "Original Sin: A Short Story," where the darker self acts like a loyal though rejected animal: "you have heard/It fumble your door before it whimpers and is gone:/It acts like the old hound that used to snuffle your door and moan," and later, "it goes to the backyard and stands like an old horse cold in the pasture." In "Crime," the conscious ego, finding that the shadow self simply won't go away, murders and buries it in the cellar, only to have it rise again: ". . . memory drips, a pipe in the cellar-dark/And in its hutch and hole . . ./The cold heart heaves like a toad." And so the *Eleven Poems* ends with "Terror," a poem in which the shadow self that had seemed so docile and easily repudiated earlier now assumes, genie-like, terrifying dimensions in the reality of actual history (circa 1940), where "the face . . ./Bends to the bomb-sight over bitter Helsingfors" and "the brute crowd roars . . . in the Wilhelmplatz," while "you now, guiltless, sink/To rest in lobbies."

In Warren's next major poetic work, *Brother to Dragons*, Thomas Jefferson also thinks himself "guiltless" until his sister and R. P. W. finally get him to clasp his murderous nephew's hand and so accept oneness with Lilburn, the emblem (together with minotaur, catfish, and serpent) of man's darker self within. The key embodiment of the shadow self in *Brother to Dragons* is borne by the serpent that scares R. P. W. in his summer visit to what's left of the Lewis house. And though R. P. W. calls it "just a snake," it turns out to have suspiciously human characteristics linking it to the "old hound" and "old horse" metaphors (noted above) of *Eleven Poems on the Same Theme*:

> . . . he reared
> Up high, and scared me, for a fact. But then
> The bloat head sagged an inch, the tongue withdrew,
> And on the top of that strong stalk the head
> Wagged slow, benevolent and sad and sage,
> As though it understood our human pitifulness
> And forgave all, and asked forgiveness, too.

That last line states what the relationship between the conscious ego and the shadow self should be, but isn't (until the very end) in Jefferson's case: "I still reject, cast out, repudiate,/And squeeze from my blood the blood of Lilburn." In *Promises*, too, man's natural revulsion towards the shadow self is implicit in the slaying of a snake by some men getting hay:

> . . . a black snake rears big in his ruined room.
> . . . .
> Men shout, ring around. He can't get away.
> Yes, they are men, and a stone is there.
>
> Snagged high on a pitchfork tine, he will make
> Slow arabesques till the bullbats wake.
> An old man, standing stooped, detached,
> Spits once, says, "Hell, just another snake."
> ("The Snake")

But of course the beast within the self is not exorcised by such impulsive destruction of other creatures, though men are prone to locate evil anywhere outside the self and then move ahead with the destruction, whether of snake, octopus (similarly slain elsewhere in *Promises*), or human enemies.

Warren's collection of poems, *You, Emperors, and Others* (1960), speaks of a beast in the psyche in many places. The emperors Warren writes of are Domitian and Tiberius, whom the Roman historian Suetonius considered monstrous criminals for using their imperial power in the service of greed, murder, incest, and unlimited orgiastic pleasures. The "You" in Warren's title, however, is not greatly superior to the emperors, having a tainted ancestry ("Your mother preferred the more baroque positions./Your father's legerdemain marks the vestry accounts.") and a criminal character of troublesome if not imperial proportions, as is illustrated in "The Letter About Money, Love, or Other Comfort, If Any," in which the narrator pursues a beastly alter ego from place to place ("you had blown, the rent in arrears, your bathroom a sty") and from crime to crime ("your Llewellin setter/was found in the wood-shed, starved to death" and "you fooled with the female Fulbrights/at the Deux Magots and the Flore,/until the police caught you dead to rights—"). The reality of evil within the self, then, is set forth in a long and vividly memorable series of vile characters, violent episodes, and beast images throughout Warren's work, and the acceptance of that reality is the first step toward psychic wholeness—an internal osmosis of being, as it were.

II

Proceeding from the inner caverns of self to the outer world of other people, we find an equally long series of technical devices—plot, character, imagery, allusion, irony, and so forth—sustaining the idea of osmosis on a family and social level. The repeated summons towards a father figure—felt by Sukie Christian in *Night Rider* (1939), Jerry Calhoun in *At Heaven's Gate* (1943), Billie Potts in the "Ballad" (1943), Jack Burden in *All the King's Men* (1946), Jeremiah Beaumont in *World Enough and Time* (1950), R. P. W. in *Brother to Dragons* (1953), Rau-Ru (alias Oliver Cromwell Jones) and Amantha Starr in *Band of Angels* (1955), Ikey Sumpter in *The Cave* (1959), Adam Rosenzweig in *Wilderness* (1961), and Bradwell Tolliver in *Flood* (1964)—this call to acceptance of a father is especially fundamental to Warren's work because it grounds the osmosis of being in physiological fact. As Jack Burden puts it in *All the King's Men*: "The child comes home and the parent puts the hooks in him. The old man, or the woman, as the case may be, hasn't got anything to say to the child. All he wants is to have that child sit in a chair for a couple of hours and then go off to bed under the same roof. . . . This thing in itself is not love. It is just something in the blood. It is a kind of blood greed, and it is the fate of a man. It is the thing which man has which distinguishes him from the happy brute creation. When you got born your father and mother lost something out of themselves, and they are going to bust a hame trying to get it back, and you are it. They know they can't get it all back but they will get as big a chunk out of you as they can."

It follows, then, that the true villains in Warren's work are not the hatchet-murderers like Big Billie Potts and Lilburn Lewis so much as those characters who willfully reject the claims of osmosis. Among these truly damned are Ikey Sumpter in *The Cave* and Slim Sarrett in *At Heaven's Gate*, both of whom renounced the father, cut all their human ties, and vanished into the vicious and glittering isolation of New York City. Or sometimes the temptation is more subtle and human than that offered by New York, like the rich and powerful substitute fathers Bogan Murdock in *At Heaven's Gate* and Aaron Blaustein in *Wilderness*, glamorous figures who nearly seduce Jerry Calhoun and Adam Rosenzweig from the memory of their real fathers, the stooped and shabby ones. Or maybe the sin of rejection is committed in pride of modernity, as with the brash young fellow in "Ballad of a Sweet Dream of Peace" in *Promises*, who keeps calling his grandma "old fool" and "old bitch" until some supernatural hogs abruptly appear to chomp them both into the "oneness of Flesh" that is the book's mystical vision. And sometimes the osmosis is shunned not by reason of ignorance or a temptation towards wealth and glamour, but out of a fear of contamination. Thomas Jefferson's reluctance to shake Lilburn's hand with "the blood slick on it" is a case in point, and similar fear of contamination is delightfully portrayed in "Two Studies in Idealism," a poem in *You, Emperors, and Others* in which a Union soldier, a Harvard graduate of 1861, complains bitterly how a filthy old geezer fighting for the other side had the gall to forgive his death at the hands of the speaker:

> I tried to slay without rancor, and often succeeded.
> I tried to keep the heart pure, though the hand took stain.
> . . . .
> But they grinned in the dark—they grinned—and I yet see
> That last one. At woods-edge we held, and over the stubble
>   they came with bayonet.
>
> He uttered his yell, he was there!—teeth yellow, some missing.
> *Why, he's old as my father*, I thought, finger frozen on trigger.
> I saw the ambeer on his whiskers, heard the old breath hissing.
> The puncture came small on his chest. 'Twas nothing. The
>   stain then got bigger.
>
> And he said: "Why, son you done done it—I figgered I'd
>   skeered ye."
> Said: "Son, you look puke-pale. Buck up! If it hadn't been you,
> Some other young squirt would a-done it."

Like the serpent who "forgave all, and asked forgiveness, too" in *Brother to Dragons*, this rebel soldier offers a human communion transcending his loathsome appearance. To be sure, the Harvard graduate is too clothed in the Right of the Union Cause ("Touch pitch: be defiled" is his social creed) to accept the old geezer's dying gesture. But such acceptance of a human communion beyond right and wrong is what he needs to be saved, nonetheless, as opposed to his dependence on the "Treasury of Merit," which is Warren's term for the North's enduring sense of virtue in having fought for Right in the Civil War.

Warren's osmosis, then, postulates an ethic of community transcending self and family and tribe, and transcending too the separations worked by time or sin or ignorance. And in the end, the Warren protagonist must accept osmosis even as Jack Burden does, after the deep isolation of his Great Sleep and Great Twitch and Going West periods in *All the King's Men.* Having witnessed a procession of unsatisfactory father figures stream through his life—the Scholarly Attorney, the Tycoon, the Count, the Young Executive, the Judge—Jack Burden comes to accept the first (though not his biological) father in this Whitmanesque parenthesis: "So now I live in the house which my father left me. With me is my wife, Anne Stanton, and the old man who was once married to my mother. . . . (Does he think that I am his son? I cannot be sure. Nor can I feel that it matters, for each of us is the son of a million fathers.)"

The consummation of such osmosis of being on a social or family level is seen most strikingly in *Promises*, in a series of lyrics called "Ballad of a Sweet Dream of Peace." Here, in a macabre transition zone between the living and the dead, a brash young initiate is instructed in the mysteries of osmosis. In the following exchange between the initiate and his guide (whose role is much like Virgil's in Dante's *Inferno*), the initiate's speech is in italics, his guide's in regular print:

Out there in the dark, what's that horrible chomping?
Oh, nothing, just hogs that forage for mast,
And if you call, "Hoo-pig!" they'll squeal and come romping,
For they'll know from your voice you're the boy who slopped
    them in dear, dead days long past.
Any hogs that I slopped are long years dead,
And eaten by somebody and evacuated,
So it's simply absurd, what you said.
You fool, poor fool, all Time is a dream, and we're all one
    Flesh, at last,
And the hogs know that, and that's why they wait. . . .
                ("Go It Granny—Go It Hog!")

What the hogs wait for is to chomp one and all into the "one Flesh, at last" which their most fleshly of bodies symbolize. They begin, in the above poem, by devouring the initiate's grandma (the skeleton granny he had earlier called "old fool" and "old bitch"), and proceed thence—alarmingly—to the initiate himself, in a poem called "I Guess You Ought to Know Who You Are":

        . . . *But, look, in God's name, I am me!*
If you are, there's the letter a hog has in charge,
With a gold coronet, and your own name writ large,
And in French, most politely, "Répondez s'il vous plaît."

Our last view of the initiate shows him submitting at last to the doctrine of "one Flesh," as he meets the hour of his death in the traditional posture of humility—

Now don't be alarmed we are late.
What's time to a hog? We'll just let them wait.
But for when you are ready, our clients usually say
That to shut the eyes tight and get down on the knees is the
    quickest and easiest way.

Devouring their former devourers, these supernatural hogs provide in the otherworldly dark a universal eucharist, a compulsory last supper to which the guest comes to be eaten and absorbed into a collective final identity. This is real osmosis of being, then, its final object being a transubstantiation that merges (to return to Warren's *Sewanee Review* essay) "the ugly with the beautiful, the slayer with the slain," producing—in whoever can see this—"such a sublimation that the world which once provoked . . . fear and disgust may now be totally loved."

III

And so we come to the third major facet of Warren's osmosis: the metaphysical dimension, which is the most momentous in its price and rewards. The immediate price of osmosis is humility, which, seriously considered (as in Thomas Jefferson's case), is not easily come by; and the ultimate price is death: a permanent consignment of self to the oneness of Time and Flesh. This may well involve a final annihilation of the conscious ego, putting an end to that temporary and prideful separation from the larger collective being, but such a condition may prove desirable, and is in any case inevitable.

Part of Warren's concern with the father-son relationship bears upon this need to accept one's extinction, for in the natural world the father always comes bearing the gift of life in one hand and (this is the final meaning of the Billie Potts saga) a hatchet in the other: "What gift—oh, father, father—from that disservering hand?" "The father waits for the son," Warren says at the end of "The Ballad of Billie Potts," and so the son comes, at last, back to what looks like prenatal unconsciousness: "Back to the silence, back to the pool, back/ To the high pool, motionless, and the unmurmuring dream." And if he understands osmosis of being properly, he will come unwillingly, when he must, to bow his head to the hatchet-blow:

> And you, wanderer, back,
> . . . .
> To kneel
> Here in the evening empty of wind or bird,
> To kneel in the sacramental silence of evening
> At the feet of the old man
> Who is evil and ignorant and old. . . .

Similar illustrations of acceptance appear in Warren's fiction. In *The Cave*, Jack Harrick, stricken with cancer, at first resents his wife and son living on while he must die: "Old Jack Harrick wished she were dead, dead so he could love her, and not hate her as he did when he thought of her lying alone in her bed on a June night with moon coming in the window, and . . . her struggling against the need for a man-shape, simply a man-shape in the dark, not him, not Jack Harrick" and "I wanted my own son to die." But Jack comes to accept his extinction after he learns of his son's death in the cave. And in *Promises*, Warren's own parents, Ruth and Robert Warren, accept the price of osmosis, willing in their deaths that the generations supplant one another. "Child," the two skeletons tell their son in his vision at their gravesite, "We died only that every promise might be fulfilled." Later in *Promises* the skeleton granny who is devoured by hogs repeats this acceptance of sacrificial death: "I died for love."

Commitment to one Flesh is further enacted by a series of Christ figures in Warren's work, such as Jasper Harrick, the youth who dies in *The Cave* to "save" others (such as Ikey Sumpter: "*I'm saved*, he thought, and his heart overflowed with gratitude to Jasper Harrick who had saved him") and to bear guilt for their iniquity (Jasper is blamed for his younger brother's fornication). And Brother Potts in *Flood* makes the Christlike commitment, praying for a Negro convict who had spat on him without even wiping the spit away ("and it was running down some. It was a good gob, to run down. . . .") and spending his last days not in fear for the cancer that has already cost him an arm but preaching that "the life they had lived was blessed." Clearly, then, Warren's osmosis requires acceptance of one's annihilation: granny's whisper, "I died for love," means that she saw the self as a tool to be used and discarded to the advantage of a larger being that goes on and on.

But if the price of osmosis is high, meaning death for the conscious ego, the rewards are also high, meaning a kind of immortality through the ministrations of that shadow self so often shunned and loathed and locked out of the house of the psyche. For the shadow self, as made known in dream or animal intuition, is perfectly at ease in that infinitude of time and space which smites the conscious mind with anxiety that man and his Earth are a bubble in a cosmic ocean. The indestructibility of this deeper self was implied in its survival through *Eleven Poems*, despite the murder and burial in the cellar, and this immortality seems even clearer in *Brother to Dragons*, with particular reference to the serpent and catfish metaphors. In having "the face of the last torturer," the catfish is clearly associated with the "original sin" aspect of Warren's thought, but it also has redemptive possibilities not given to the conscious ego. (The ice in the following passage appears to divide the world of light and time and consciousness, above ice, from the timeless, totally dark world of unconsciousness—"unpulsing blackness"—under ice.)

> And the year drove on. Winter. And from the Dakotas
> The wind veers, gathers itself in ice-glitter
> And star-gleam of dark, and finds the long sweep of the valley.
> A thousand miles and the fabulous river is ice in the starlight.
> The ice is a foot thick, and beneath, the water slides black like
>   a dream,
> And in the interior of that unpulsing blackness and thrilled
>   zero
> The big channel-cat sleeps with eye lidless, and the brute face
> Is the face of the last torturer, and the white belly
> Brushes the delicious and icy blackness of mud.
> But there is no sensation. How can there be
> Sensation when there is perfect adjustment?

"Perfect adjustment" despite the awful cold and dark under ice is something the conscious self, in fear of naturalistic oblivion, might well envy. Warren becomes very Jungian indeed in what follows the above passages, for just as Jung saw the deeper self as both divine and demonic ("the unconscious [is] the only accessible source of religious experience," Jung says in *The Undiscovered Self*, even though it also embodies "the

general proclivity to evil . . . lodged in human nature itself"), Warren
sees this creature with the brute face of a torturer as being, in its total
osmosis with its environment, enviably "at one with God":

> . . . The blood
> Of the creature is but the temperature of the sustaining flow:
> The catfish is in the Mississippi and
> The Mississippi is in the catfish and
> Under the ice both are at one with God.
> Would that we were!

We are now clearly in the area of metaphysical speculation. In its
oneness with the total darkness under ice, the catfish need not fear, as the
conscious ego must, the awesome infinitude of time and cosmos above the
ice, where "the stars are arctic and/Their gleam comes earthward down
uncounted light-years of disdain." The catfish's brother image, the serpent, likewise evinces intimation of an immortality transcending the
naturalistic winter at the end of the book, where the snake, "looped and
snug," survives in "earth's dark inwardness" underneath the pitiful ruins
of the Lewis house, those "huddled stones of ruin" which "say the human
had been here and gone/And never would come back, though the bright
stars/Shall weary not in their appointed watch." Jasper Harrick gives
human embodiment to these metaphysical speculations when he describes
the cave as a place resembling the catfish's dark and timeless realm under
the ice: " 'It's a nice temperature down there,' he had said. 'It is not summer and it is not winter. There aren't any seasons to bother about down
there,' he had said, and laughed. . . . 'Blizzard or hot spell,' he had said,
'a lot of things don't matter down there.' " And Jasper goes on to state yet
another advantage of that dark underworld: it, and only it, can yield
forth the secret of final identity, the search for which has provided Warren's most recurrent theme over the decades: "He had said, 'Well, in the
ground at least a fellow has a chance of knowing who he is.' "

"Perfect adjustment," being "at one with God," and knowing at last
who you are—such are the final rewards of Warren's osmosis, though its
final price is the death of the conscious ego. "And the death of the self is
the beginning of selfhood," R.P.W. had said in *Brother to Dragons*, but
the new selfhood appears clearly superior to the old. Back in "The Ballad
of Billie Potts," Warren had indicated this supremacy of the unconscious
over the conscious self in a pair of memorable passages. The first lists
several modes of establishing a conscious identity as the world knows it:

> Though your luck held and the market was always satisfactory,
> Though the letter always came and your lovers were always true,
> Though you always received the respect due to your position,
> Though your hand never failed of its cunning, and your glands
>   always thoroughly knew their business,
> Though your conscience was easy and you were assured of your
>   innocence,

You became gradually aware that something was missing from
    the picture,
And upon closer inspection exclaimed, "Why, I'm not in it
    at all!"
Which was perfectly true.

But in contrast to the unease of the conscious self on finding "that
something was missing from the picture," the unconscious—as usual, embodied in a series of animal images—shapes the direction and meaning of
life through its secret, intuitive knowledge:

> (The bee knows, and the eel's cold ganglia burn,
> And the sad head lifting to the long return,
> Through brumal deeps, in the great unsolsticed coil,
> Carries its knowledge, navigator without star,
> And under the stars, pure in its clamorous toil,
> The goose hoots north where the starlit marshes are.
> The salmon heaves at the fall, and wanderer, you
> Heave at the great fall of Time. . . .)

Like these creatures, Billie crosses from the realm of conscious to unconscious direction in coming home to his father and thus to death and
eternity ("homeland of no-Time"): "You come, weary of greetings and the
new friend's smile,/. . . Weary of innocence and the husks of Time,/Pro-
digal, back to the homeland of no-Time."

Like "The Ballad of Billie Potts" and *Eleven Poems, You, Emperors,
and Others* (a book very ignorantly reviewed, for the most part) is very effective in setting off the conscious as against the unconscious identities, to
the great advantage of the latter. "Lullaby: Exercise in Human Charity
and Self-Knowledge," for example, is addressed to a sleeper who, being
unconscious, has lapsed out of the false identity provided in his conscious
life by name (Stanza 1), face (Stanza 2), and sex (Stanza 3), and who
therefore, in his unconsciousness, has access to an osmosis of being blend-
ing his identity with the whole universe: "And your sweet identity/Fills
like vapor, pale in moonlight, all the infinite night sky." Further emphasis
on the superiority of the unconscious to conscious reality appears in the
poet's advice in "A Real Question Calling for Solution," where conscious
life is so chaotic that "There is only one way, then, to make things hang
together,/Which is to accept the logic of dream" rather than such things
of consciousness as "Night air, politics, French sauces, autumn
weather,/And the thought that, on your awakening, identity may be
destroyed." Warren's headnotes sometimes prove relevant, too, as when
he refers to "a Roman citizen of no historical importance" and to Walter
Winchell's Mr. and Mrs. North and South America. According to
Warren's osmosis of being, all citizens are of historical importance—or
else none are—and even Mr. Winchell's phrase, as referring to a collective
self, might hold a meaning its originator never understood.

You, Emperors, and Others is especially concerned with imparting a

sense of power and vision through dream or animal intuition. "In the Tur-
pitude of Time" states overtly man's need for such animal intuition: "Can
we—oh could we only—believe/ What annelid and osprey know,/And the
stone, night-long, groans to divulge?" And "Prognosis" (the prognosis is
that you will die) tells quite plainly the advantage of knowing what annelid and osprey know. Here a woman doomed with cancer sleeps, after a
horrible day, and ". . . past despair,/Dreamed a field of white lilies
wind-shimmering, slow,/And wept, wept for joy. . . ." Fear of death,
moreover, is as irrelevant at this level of consciousness as it was to the catfish in his "unpulsing blackness" under ice; thus the woman says of her
impending death: "and I do not grieve to be lost in whatever awfulness of
dark. . . ." Intuition ventures past the awfulness of dark in some of the
"Nursery Rhymes" like "The Bramble Bush," where the speaker "now saw
past the fartherest stars" and "heard the joy/Of flesh singing on the
bone." The last word on osmosis of being is given by a grasshopper in the
final poem of *You, Emperors, and Others*. Unlike Ikey Sumpter or Slim
Sarrett, who cut all their ties and fled East (in *The Cave* and *At Heaven's
Gate*), the insect in "Grasshopper Tries to Break Solipsism" is trying to
establish connections: his grasshopper song is evidence of the humblest
creatures' need for each other. Solipsism, or the theory that the self is the
only existent thing, is the obvious enemy of osmosis, and as such, merits
the effort to "Break Solipsism" with which this book of poems closes.

IV

It is only just that we conclude this essay with a few lines from the
master of osmosis, Walt Whitman. In a conversation we once had, Mr.
Warren expressed misgivings about Whitman's work because of its undue
optimism—its lack of a sense of sin such as Hawthorne and Melville often
expressed. And certainly Warren's own continuing preoccupation with
delusion, betrayal, and depravity—or "original sin"—makes some of
Whitman's ringing affirmations seem innocent and sentimental by contrast. Warren distrusted Whitman, I think, because Whitman's osmosis
has no internal dimension, no psychological level of conflict and reconciliation within the self between conscious ego and humanity's black collective shadow. But on the other two levels, social and metaphysical, no
one has ever proclaimed the osmosis of being with the efficacy of Walt
Whitman. "And these tend inward to me, and I tend outward to them,"
Whitman says in *Song of Myself* after embracing all manner of folk in a
tremendous catalogue: "The pure contralto sings in the organ
loft . . . The deacons are ordain'd with cross'd hands at the altar . . .
The lunatic is carried at last to the asylum a confirm'd case,/(He will
never sleep any more as he did in his mother's bedroom) . . . The
malform'd limbs are tied to the surgeon's table/What is removed drops

horribly in a pail . . . The youth lies awake in the cedar-roof'd garret and harks to the musical rain . . . The old husband sleeps by his wife and the young husband sleeps by his wife . . . And of these one and all I weave the song of myself" (Stanza 15). Whitman's osmosis, like Warren's, embraces creatures long dead as well as those of the present: "In vain the mastodon retreats beneath its own powder'd bones." And most strikingly, Whitman's metaphysics are at one with Warren's in seeing one's cobweb connections to the entirety of past and future and in accepting the gift of death gracefully, as a welcome fulfillment or release into ultimate identity:

> Afar down I see the huge first Nothing, I know I was
> even there,
> . . . .
> Cycles ferried my cradle, rowing and rowing like
> cheerful boatmen,
> . . . .
> For it [my embryo] the nebula cohered to an orb,
> The long slow strata piled to rest it on,
> Vast vegetables gave it sustenance,
> Monstrous sauroids transported it in their mouths and
> deposited it with care.
> (*Song of Myself*, Stanza 44)

Like Warren's creatures under ice or his sleepers who do not fear "whatever awfulness of dark," Whitman is enabled by his osmosis to accept return to the oblivion that bred him:

> A few quadrillions of eras, a few octillions of cubic
> leagues . . .
> They are but parts, any thing is but a part.
>
> See ever so far, there is limitless space outside of that,
> Count ever so much, there is limitless time around that.
> (Stanza 45)
>
> And I say to any man or woman, Let your soul stand cool
> and composed before a million universes.
> . . . .
> (No array of terms can say how much I am at peace about
> God and about death.)
> (Stanza 48)

And as in Warren's metaphysics, this acceptance of death comes through the ministrations of an unconscious self, perceiving a pattern and meaning not available to the conscious ego:

> There is that in me—I do not know what it is—but I
> know it is in me.

Wrench'd and sweaty—calm and cool then my body
    becomes,
I sleep—I sleep long.

I do not know it—it is without name—it is a word unsaid,
It is not in any dictionary, utterance, symbol.
. . . .
It is not chaos or death—it is form, union, plan—it is eternal
    life. . . .

(Stanza 50)

Moved by these intuitions from the unconscious, Whitman can bend his
will, even as Warren's parents or old granny did in *Promises*, to commit
his identity to the osmosis of being: "I bequeath myself to the dirt to grow
from the grass I love,/If you want me again look for me under your boot-
soles." And as *Song of Myself* ends, even greater oneness is pending: "I
stop somewhere waiting for you."

Osmosis of being, in various manifestations, is not a new idea. It obviously motivated Emerson's conception of an Oversoul, for example, as
well as Wordsworth's pantheistic mysticism, his vision of "a spirit
that . . . rolls through all things" (*Tintern Abbey*). Ultimately, it dates
back to sacred writ; an idea of osmosis underlies both the Biblical ethic of
brotherhood, as preached by Isaiah and Jesus, and the Hindu metaphysics
of *Atman* (the soul), as seen in the *Bhagavad-Gita*: "I am the Atman that
dwells in the heart of every creature: I am the beginning, the life-span,
and the end of all . . . I am the divine seed of all lives . . . Know only
that I exist, and that one atom of myself sustains the universe" (Part
IX—"The Yoga of Mysticism"). With the declining influence of sacred
writ such as this in modern times, people look more than ever to the artist
for help in finding the meaning of their lives. One could do worse, I think,
than look to Warren's osmosis of being as a possible source of meaning.

"Toward an Analysis of the Prose Style of Robert Penn Warren"

Allen Shepherd*

The 'perfect' narrator-hero Tough Talker of our time is a man who can master both lowbrow and highbrow language, and he uses either to cast ironical doubt on the other. Naturally, his diction and rhetoric differ somewhat from the Hemingway Tough Talker, though they share many qualities of style. He can be a self-educated alumnus of the slums, like [Saul Bellow's] Augie [March]. Or he can be a formally educated or even aristocratic fellow who has repudiated his advantages to experience the hard knocks of the vulgar world. Such a one, possibly an important early example of the development I am describing, is Jack Burden, narrator of [Warren's] *All the King's Men* (1946).[1]

Certainly, Warren's imagery and command of texture, his concern with music and pattern, his sensitivity to language, all demand the freer form and tighter discipline of poetic form.[2]

Since *All the King's Men* is generally accounted Robert Penn Warren's best novel, it is probably natural that Walker Gibson in his study of modern American prose styles should focus his attention upon Jack Burden, Warren's premier Tough Talker, to the exclusion of the author's other protagonists. Burden is best[3] because he alone is an adequate spokesman-character, intellectually, morally and linguistically capable of articulating the issues at hand and of sustaining prolonged narrative focus. In *All the King's Men* the style is the man and vice versa.

The stylistic analysis undertaken here will appropriate and extend several of Gibson's insights and will survey eight of Warren's novels, from *Night Rider* (1939) to *Flood* (1964), with the aim both of describing and analyzing his prose style in these novels and of tracing, in so far as possible, its evolution over twenty-five years. As the most gifted of spokesman-characters, Burden is, by definition, unrepresentative of Warren's protagonists, but he does personify, in the style through which he is

*Reprinted with permission from *Studies in American Fiction*, 1 (1973), 188–202. Copyright © 1973 by Northeastern University.

made to address the reader, a problem endemic in Warren's fiction. Again, Gibson puts the matter succinctly.

> What are we to think of a graduate student in history and a sensitive soul who talks to us this way? What does the assumed author think of this manner of expression? . . . Is our quarrel with Jack Burden, a mixed-up young man, carefully contrived by his creator to display just these weaknesses? Is Jack ironically aware of his own tough-talking excesses? Or is our quarrel with the assumed author himself, who just possibly has not made up his mind who Jack is?[4]

While such questions may themselves intimate the sophistication, complexity, and ambiguity of this and other novels, it seems that the ironies in which Burden is swathed may in the course of a long novel lose much of their point. Burden is both character and chorus, embroiled in and yet detached from experience, participating in the event and then working up its meaning. Caught between the action and the meaning of that action, as he interprets it, he can look rather foolish, being solemn about the obvious or inconsequential or speciously knowledgeable about genuine mysteries.[5] In short, the "ironical doubt" to which Gibson refers in characterizing the Tough Talker's style seems to be shared by all hands, by protagonist, by author, and by reader.

Though one might order an examination of all of Warren's novels by application of the Tough, Sweet and Stuffy criteria of Gibson's study,[6] it seems preferable to consider as well other matters germane to stylistic analysis, to define the overall effect of Warren's prose by selecting and examining its most characteristic and important elements. Included among them are diction, sentence length and structure, syntactical relations, use of sentence rhythm, of imagery, of metaphor and simile, of multiple modifiers, and of sound devices. Amenable to less precise analysis but of at least equal importance is Warren's use of irony, rhetoric, the cliché, the cinematic technique, and the defining phrase.

One might begin with Warren's vocabulary, or better, vocabularies, readily identifiable as those of an educated and perceptive Southerner in the sense that the authorial narrative voice is punctuated by recurrent regionalisms and in that the voices of the characters accurately reflect their social and geographical origins. Whatever the reasons—"snobbish superiority or neurotic yearning"[7]—many readers have found the speech of Warren's backwoodsmen particularly attractive. Literal accuracy of recording is in fact of comparatively little importance for most readers, although one so inclined might easily do a bit of research in a linguistic atlas. Much of the effectiveness of the widely admired narratives of Willie Proudfit, Ashby Wyndham, and Munn Short,[8] all bravura performances, derives from the keenness of Warren's ear and the retentiveness of his memory. Wyndham's account is but one example of Warren's mastery of what might be called the fundamentalist Biblical idiom. Warren has stated on several occasions that he is a regular Bible reader, and has commended the Scriptures to aspiring writers. The extent of Biblical influence on his style is difficult to assess, but the not infrequent appearance of Biblical quotations, allusions, analogies, diction, and sentence rhythms would suggest that it has been considerable.

One notices that there are certain words, presumably favorites, which occur in all Warren's novels. While this is a decidedly minor matter, it is perhaps worthy of brief note. Some words, like "westering," as in "westering sun," have a vaguely poetic quality. One might call it a Faulkner word. Others, like "coiling," Warren finds equally apposite to physical description and to the suggestion of mental processes. Still others, like "enameled leaves," both represent an object and indicate obliquely the viewer's response. Warren also has his favorite names for characters: Sukie, Tolliver, Murdock, and Todd. "Sukie," for example, is Mr. Christian's name for his daughter Lucille in *Night Rider*, the apparently given name of Captain Marlowe's wife in *World Enough and Time*, the name of a slave woman in *Band of Angels* (1955), and the deputy warden's name for the electric chair in *Flood* (1964).

In the more common sense of the term, Warren makes frequent use of repetition, i.e., within a single paragraph. One thinks, perhaps, in this connection, of Jack Burden but Bradwell Tolliver, of *Flood*, is very similar, at least on this score. They are both great repeaters. When such repetition works, as it often does with Burden, the repeated words grow, expand, comprehend new levels of meaning, through the processes of accretion and evolution. Failure of the technique, manifest in narrative passages and Tolliver's monologues, shows in mechanical iteration, in lines which read like bad early Hemingway.

As an example of effective, almost incantatory repetition, there is the often quoted passage from *All the King's Men* on knowing, not knowing, and knowledge.

> The eye knows what's in the envelope, and it is watching you to see you when you open it and know, too. . . . It shivers cold inside you for it doesn't want to know what is in that envelope. It wants to lie in the dark and not know, and be warm in its not-knowing. The end of man is knowledge, but there is one thing he can't know. He can't know whether knowledge will save him or kill him. . . . There's the cold in your stomach, but you open the envelope, you have to open the envelope, for the end of man is to know.[9]

Though it has a number of other features to commend it, the passage nicely illustrates the glory and terror of knowing, that being the end toward which Burden takes his halting way throughout the novel.

From *Flood* comes the following Hemingway pastiche: "The hell it was. For there was the afternoon. He wondered what he, alone, would do in the afternoon. There would be the afternoon lengthening to shadow. There would be the night."[10] Well, yes, and after that the next morning, but this is poseur's prose, and conveys a shallow, tight-lipped and self-regarding intensity, which is perfectly appropriate to Tolliver, one might argue, but not readily distinguishable from much of the rest of the novel.

Although Warren demonstrates familiarity with the business and agricultural pursuits of Kentucky and Tennessee, the usual setting of his fiction, he does not in their description (as Hemingway, for example, often does) employ what could be called a technical vocabulary. One learns relatively little about the mechanics of finance in *At Heaven's Gate*, of movie-making in *Flood*, and not much more about tobacco farming in *Night Rider*. One does not doubt that Warren knows whereof he speaks, but he does not, contrarily, depend upon or display interest in that density of encyclopedic detail that distinguishes the fiction of his contemporary, James Gould Cozzens.

Warren's sentence structure is seldom particularly involved; if, for example, one has to re-read a sentence, it is usually because the narrator has undertaken a summary of events whose cumulative significance the reader is unprepared for. Occasionally sentences are rather long (150–200 words),[11] but the relation of dependent to independent clauses is clear, subjects and verbs are readily identifiable, and one sees nothing of Faulkner's raging confusion of pronouns. Warren sometimes employs a series of key sentences, or key first words in sentences, as a kind of defining sequence. Thus in the course of *Wilderness* there are nine sentences beginning with "If," each identifying a formative influence upon the hero, Adam Rosenzweig, together with his frustration at successive limitations on his will. In *All the King's Men* Warren secures a dramatic incremental effect by introducing a series of sharply etched descriptive passages with "Which was" (p. 216). Sentence rhythm is skilfully employed in narrative passages to suggest the state of mind of a character. Thus in the following sequence Adam Rosenzweig in a state of shock is wandering through New York in July, 1863, during the draft riots. He sees a Negro dangling from a lamp post.

> The blood had dried, dark blood on dark skin. Then he saw that one, last, slow, tumescent drop was falling from one foot. He looked at the foot. The toes had been cut off. His gaze wandered back up to the hands, tied primly before the body. He had thought—if he had thought anything—that the fingers were curled inward. Now he saw the truth. There were no fingers.[12]

The brief, blunt declarative sentences reflect Adam's dazed and horrified perception, his gradual and almost unwilling realization of the significance of what he sees hanging before him. The adjective series ("one, last, slow, tumescent drop") in slowing the movement of the sentence suggests both physical process, the drop forming, and his revolted fascination.

Some time later, having been rescued from the mob, he awakens in a bedroom in the house of Aaron Blaustein.

> His eyes opened to a high ceiling, light beige in color, the plaster worked in an intricate design of delicate craftsmanship. He felt the downy softness of the pillow under his head. He caught the starchy, clean, sun-bathed, herby smell of the sheet which lay across the jut of his chin. His eyes fell shut again, and in the hypnosis of that scent, he thought of lying on a high field, in late summer, smelling the gorse, watching the unmoving blueness of the sky (p. 37).

The sentences, with the exception of the second, have lengthened appreciably, and reflect Adam's leisurely and relieved perception of his new surroundings. Three of his senses—sight, smell and touch—are engaged, and both the detail of the first sentence, the color and design of the ceiling, and the adjective sequence of the third sentence intimate the lingering and perhaps self-defensive nature of his response, the idyll succeeding the horror, "the starchy, clean, sun-bathed, herby" sheet unsullied by that "last, slow, tumescent drop."

Sentence rhythm is used with comparable effect in *Band of Angels* (1955). Amantha Starr, in pride and fear of rejection, has just determined to leave her husband, to flee the past. The more she thinks of it, the more frightened she becomes at the prospect. "I would go to a strange place and I would walk down the street and be like everyone else, I would live in a cocoon of quietness, I would move in the sweetness of wanting nothing. . . ."[13] Each of the four preceding rather lengthy sentences had opened with "I would;" in this sentence, which seems spoken in one breath, and as if to convince herself, there is Manty's desperation in the rapid series of "I would's."

Perhaps because of his concern with the strange and almost infinitely ramifying relatedness of things, of cause and effect, beginning and end, Warren has frequent recourse to metaphor and simile. Although the following quotations are by no means exhaustive, they suggest, first, the range of his metaphoric manner. Often one encounters what might be termed a coordinate series of metaphors.

> And all the while that cold, unloving part of the mind—that maiden aunt, that washroom mirror the drunk stares into, that still, small voice, that maggot in the cheese of your self-esteem, that commentator on the ether nightmare, that death's-head of lipless rationality at your every feast . . . (*All the King's Men*, p. 280).

This six-member appositive series is unusually long, but is representative of one sort of metaphoric strategy. Each member seems coordinate, that is, as important as every other member, but the cumulative effect of the series is achieved by the increasing intensity of each successive metaphor. The danger of such a series, evident here, is that its latter members, e.g., "death's-head of lipless rationality at your every feast," will seem forced, shrill, exaggerated.

There are also instances, less frequent, of what might be termed the nearly-mixed metaphor. The speaker in the following passage is again Jack Burden, of *All the King's Men*, and he is recovering from the death of Judge Irwin, whom he has discovered to be his father.

> I felt that a story was over, that what had begun a long time back had been played out, that the lemon had been squeezed dry. But if anything is certain it is that no story is ever over, for the story which we think is over is only a chapter in a story which will not be over, and it isn't a game that is over, it is just an inning, and that game has a lot more than nine innings. When the game stops it will be called on account of darkness (p. 377).

Here, in three sentences, Burden's response is compared to a lemon, squeezed dry; a story, with untold chapters; something, played out; and a baseball game, with more than nine innings. The multiplicity and diversity of the metaphors create one problem, but the real difficulty arises in the second sentence, with the close proximity of the story and baseball. The relation established by any metaphor is not exact, but this association, of a story and a game with life, strikes one as foggy and forced, and as doing violence to both elements.

Here, as in a number of other places, one has to try to figure in the character's presumed state of mind. The Judge's suicide, along with preceding and succeeding events allied to it, Jack finds difficult to manage, at whatever chronological remove. Given the presumed cause, is Burden's speech appropriate? Or is the reader's quarrel, as Gibson asks, with the author? The latter seems the better answer, for the style of the passage cited, though not atypical of Burden, owes its infelicities to the author, not the character.

A third type of metaphor seems in its very brevity somewhat simpler, but is in fact in its allusiveness more complex. Thus the following passage: "But if Jeremiah Beaumont was a chip on the tide, he was a thinking and suffering chip" (*World Enough and Time*, p. 312). The allusion here, which is picked up some seventy-five pages later, seems to be to Pascal's formulation: "Man is but a reed, the most feeble thing in nature; but he is a thinking reed." The ultimate effectiveness of the metaphor, then, depends upon the reader's noting this allusion and reflecting upon the apparent opposition of the assumptions from which the statements, Warren's and Pascal's, derive. The passage also suggests the academic tone of Warren's later style, savoring of the commonplace book, most strikingly evident in *Flood*.

In addition to the usual brief garden-variety simile, Warren, particularly in his early novels, frequently employs similes in series, as in the following passage: "Then, looking down at him, as though he were some strange object washed ashore at her feet, some survivor from a distant storm whose most peripheral air had not even brushed her cheek, some kindly, awkward, humble monster which had wallowed up on the beach before her . . ." (*At Heaven's Gate*, p. 40). The possible result of such a practice is that the series ("object," "survivor," and "monster") will seem a substitute for but not an improvement on a single effective simile, or that there is no discernible development in the series.

The likely effect of a second kind of simile, of the elaborate and extended simile, is evident in the following.

> She [Lucy Stark] sat there, not eating much and keeping a sharp eye out for a vacant place on any plate and watching the jaws work, and as she sat there, her face seemed to smooth itself out and relax with an inner faith in happiness the way the face of the chief engineer does when he goes down to the engine room at night and the big wheel is blurred out with its speed and the pistons plunge and return and the big steel throws are leaping in their perfect orbits like a ballet, and the whole place, under the electric glare, hums and glitters and sings like the eternal insides of God's head, and the ship is knocking off twenty-two knots on a glassy, star-lit sea. (*All the King's Men*, p. 38).

This is a set piece, very well done, but the danger, perhaps potential rather than actual, is that the reader will become so involved in the extended figure of speech that he loses track of the referent, that the point of association of Lucy Stark and the chief engineer will be forgotten.

Viewed in a slightly different perspective, however, the similitude may be seen as one of an extensive and complex series of mechanical images which permeates the novel and which serves to define Jack Burden's concept of a mechanistic universe, this opposed to and succeeded by Cass Mastern's spider web theory of mutual complicity and responsibility, articulated in the novel's central image. Though Warren does make expert and extensive use of such patterns of imagery throughout his fiction, it is still the case that an image or figure of speech must work, must speak to the reader, in its immediate context before it can function effectively as an element in a larger structure.

In several of the passages quoted above, there have been instances of rather lengthy adjective series, of a sort commonly encountered in Warren's work. Usually the adjectives are simply strung out before the noun: "the sober, metallic, pure, late-light, unriffled glint of the water" (*All the*

King's Men, p. 82), or "the hammer-headed, antediluvian, saurian, earth-colored, as out of earth, crusted heads of the mules" (*At Heaven's Gate*, p. 276), but occasionally the effect of the series is periodic, that is, the last adjective reforms the meaning of those preceding it. Thus: "the *Advocate* was logical, insistent, fearless, violent, eloquent, and scurrilous" (*World Enough and Time*, p. 91). Or there may inhere in an adjective series a cumulative irony: "each set between two, small, conical, bright-green, non-indigenous and non-thriving conifers" (*Flood*, p. 5).

Warren's penchant for hyphenated adjectives is marked and not always felicitous in its issue. "It was as though all those hairy, flea-bit, underfed, iron-rumped and narrow-ass-ted, whooping and caterwauling, doom-bit bastards, on hammer-headed nags" . . . (*Flood*, p. 258). This is badly overwritten, but does not approach the following, which records one of the many carnal reveries of Bradwell Tolliver, one of the twin heroes of *Flood*: ". . . set off by chalk-whiteness around, and seeing the discreet gleam of the orchidaceously blossoming brown-petaled, self-offering, immolation-inviting, crimson-winking, crimson-hearted slash" (p. 420). Walker Gibson's question, a little out of context, comes to mind again: "Or is our quarrel with the assumed author himself?" To which the answer is probably yes, although, unhappily, the style is perfectly appropriate to the character.

As in his poetry, Warren often in his fiction employs onomatopoetic alliteration, the continuing effectiveness of which he sometimes tends to overestimate. Thus the following, which could be duplicated on any of four successive pages: "The earth was so sodden that firm turf quaked underfoot and squelched, and if you stood still you could hear the faint susurrus and hiss of water shifting in its place in the spongy earth or being squeezed from the surface by your own motionless weight" (*World Enough and Time*, p. 109). Or, for a more restrained sample, this from Warren's first novel: "There would be the slow, somnolent, saddening sound of water" (*Night Rider*, p. 161). It puts one in mind of John Crowe Ransom's "murdering of innumerable beeves."

The term which seems most frequently to be applied to Warren's style is "rhetorical." Although it is sometimes difficult to determine what is meant by the term, to tell whether the style is thought "poetic" and full-bodied or simply "Southern," full of sound and fury, "rhetorical" is often employed in the common pejorative sense of a use of language in which manner and sound are more important than matter and sense. The distinction between "good" and "bad" rhetoric is of course highly subjective, but it seems demonstrable that Warren in recent years has come to depend upon or to permit himself a kind of rhetoric which may be regarded as non-functional or inorganic, that is, rhetoric which might easily and profitably be excised.

To define with any precision the nature or the time of the change in Warren's style, from "non-rhetorical" to "rhetorical," is difficult but not profitless. One might begin by comparing his first and eighth novels, *Night Rider* and *Flood*. The prime difference between them is clearly evident: *Night Rider* is a modest and plainly told narrative, while *Flood* is a rather diffuse opus. One is impressed in the first novel by Warren's spareness and economy of language, if not of incident. The protagonist, Percy Munn, is an introspective man, but Warren maintains a detachment which inhibits both the strained intensity of lyrical flights and the swollen splendor of extended tragic soliloquies. In *Flood*, however, Warren often allows his characters free rein, and since most of them are almost hysterically compulsive talkers, they are hard to stop. Much that they do or think or see is mountainously over-described and over-elaborated, so much so that Warren's aim seems total inclusiveness and the characters' malady logomania.

When between 1939 and 1964 did the change in style occur? Clearly, this is not an answerable question. Moving backward from *Flood*, one comes to *Wilderness* (1961), which is in its length, at least, rather deceptive. In the interests of a direct, allegorical approach to meaning, Warren has stripped from the tale much of the vividly realized detail and circumstantiality which usually distinguish both his fiction and his poetry. The result, however, is often either another character's lecturing Adam Rosenzweig or the stationing of Adam on center stage, rapt in soliloquy, and in the closing pages of the novel, italics, which in Warren's fiction identify the thoughts, often significant, of the protagonist, begin to come thick and fast. Although one sees in *The Cave* (1959), as in *Wilderness* and *Flood*, that the final pages of Warren's novels are the most vulnerable, that is, the most rhetoric-prone, the prose of *The Cave*, earthy and dynamic, is some of the best Warren has written. Thus the impossibility of any rigid or straight-line formulation of the development of Warren's prose style.

Band of Angels (1955) is unsatisfying largely because of its narrator, Amantha Starr, whose self-consciously literary reflections are fairly represented in the following passage.

> But no, that darkness of the past into which Rau-Ru had walked was not, I suddenly knew, the darkness of the thing fulfilled. No, it was, rather, a teeming darkness, straining soundlessly with forms struggling for recognition, for release from that dark realm of undifferentiated possibility (p. 262).

Amantha is for a number of reasons a rather unattractive character, her voice pseudo-female at best, the style of her speech highly wrought and improbable. Writing of the book and the author's presumed intentions, Leslie Fiedler says, "Since reading *Band of Angels*, I have become aware that what he [Warren] has been approaching for so long is something not very different from nineteenth-century Italian opera: a genre full of conventional absurdities, lapses of good taste, strained and hectic plots—all aimed at becoming myth and melody."[14] The aim, perhaps, is not subject to dispute, but the result is certainly open to criticism.

World Enough and Time (1950) may well seem a special case, and strangely enough it was only the British reviewers[15] who commented favorably upon Warren's expert creation of a Byronic idiom for his pro-tagonist, Jeremiah Beaumont. In this novel, full-blooded romantic rhetoric is functional, in so far as it defines Beaumont and his world, although it can make for decidedly heavy going for the reader. The novel also contains several instances of Warren's habit of inserting a Dos Passos-like survey in the middle of dialect passages or period descriptions. Thus as Beaumont is riding along toward Frankfort, where he will murder Col-onel Fort, his benefactor, the passage reads: "Now the highways, 31 W and 31 E, glittering with concrete or asphalt, slash north across the Knobs, and in no time you can make it to Louisville (The Fall City), Bardstown ('My Old Kentucky Home'), Frankfort (Historic Frankfort), or Lexington (The Dimple of the Bluegrass)" (p. 244). The contrast, pointed up by the archivist-historian who has assumed overall narrative respon-sibility, is functional, relating as it does past and present, but the jux-taposition is jarring nonetheless.

In *All the King's Men* (1946) there is fully established a narrative style, that of Jack Burden, the Tough Talker, which had been haltingly developed in *At Heaven's Gate* (1943) and which was later revitalized in *The Cave*. It seems overall a breezy, cynical style, occasionally jour-nalistic, but is essentially an amalgam of a number of styles, most of them complementary. There is, for example, a style resembling that of Mickey Spillane: "And all of this [Anne Stanton] done up in a swatch of gray flan-nel which pretended to a severe mannish cut but actually did nothing but scream for attention to some very un-mannish arrangements within" (p. 255). There is an unusually violent naturalistic rendering of the pro-cess of cigarette lighting, emblematic in so much slick fiction of "reality." "She [Sadie Burke] fished a cigarette out of the desk and lighted it. The flare of the match jerked the face out of shadow. She whipped the match flame out with a snapping motion of her arm, then spewed the first gulp of smoke out" (p. 394). Or there is the elaborated, semi-lyrical style, undercut at the end of the sentence.

> The season was like the fine big-breasted daughter of some poor spavined share-cropper, a girl popping her calico but still having a waist, with pink cheeks and bright eyes and just a little perspiration at the edge of her tow hair (which would be platinum blond in some circles), but you see her and know that before long she will be a bag of bone and gristle with a hag face like a rusted brush hook (p. 281).

Or there is the high poignancy-of-sweet-recollection style. "She [Anne Stanton] had seemed to be again the little girl who had, on the day of the picnic, floated on the waters of the bay, with her eyes closed under the stormy and grape-purple sky and the single white gull passing over, very high" (pp. 328–29).

To many modern ears the term "rhetorical," despite its long and honorable history, suggests oratorical emptiness, and "rhetoric," as Isocrates once noted, "the art of making great matters small, and small things great." One sense in which "rhetorical" may be applied to *All the King's Men* refers to Willie Stark and his remarkable powers as a public speaker. Warren is fully master of a style appropriate to the mature Stark, confident of his powers, at one with his audience, contemptuous of his enemies, but Warren also conveys nicely Stark the amateur, suffering through his first campaign, wooden, uninspiring, ignorant of what issues will move his audience, fully prepared with reams of statistics. So carefully attuned is Warren's ear that T. Harry Williams, in *Huey Long*, suggests that one academic estimate of Long's early forensic ineptitude, "sharply at variance with the recollections of others and with contemporary accounts, . . . is suspiciously similar to Warren's description of Willie Stark in his first campaign."[16]

If only by a process of elimination, it has now become evident that the rhetorical element is first plainly discernible in Warren's style in *At Heaven's Gate*, which is to say, very early. The reasons for the change in style, when compared with that of *Night Rider*, one can only speculate about. There are, however, two surmises. Warren in his first novel preserved an unbroken detachment from Percy Munn and his concerns; this detachment seems to have exercised a restraining influence upon the overt representation of Munn's most deeply felt fears and desires. In *At Heaven's Gate*, Warren maintains less distance between himself and his characters, some of whom are given to dark reflections and highly emotional outbursts. Whatever the depth of their introspection and the violence of their speech, however, the principal characters in the novel are not equal to, have not the capacity for, the adequate expression of Warren's philosophical themes. Thus it is that he was led to depend upon "bad" rhetoric, sound and manner, for the expression of these themes.

One might also gather from *At Heaven's Gate*, as from other novels, that Warren has little fear of the verbal cliché. Such fearlessness, in fact, has remained a constant element in his style. To note but one example: "She thought of Jerry Calhoun, somewhere in a plane, high up in that clear sky to the north, and was struck by a stab of envy, a sense of being trapped and earthbound and betrayed" (*At Heaven's Gate*, p. 5). Certainly neither the "stab of envy" nor the "sense of being . . . betrayed" is overly original. One could cite a number of other comparably stale locutions, but that would be to miss an important point. More often than not, when Warren closes with a verbal or intellectual cliché, the effect is not carelessly or lazily to hand it on to the reader, but rather to examine it critically and either to extract from it a kernel of revivified truth or to explode the hollow shell.

The stylistic technique which Warren perfected in *At Heaven's Gate*, and which he has regularly employed ever since, is a kind of modified cinematic technique, the sort which would readily appeal to a movie audience. The action is highly dramatic, or melodramatic, is related exclusively in the third person, that is, from the outside, and is developed through a predictable series of highly conventionalized sounds, appeals, gestures and responses as is the case in the following scene. Three people are in the room, Dorothy Murdock, her husband, Bogan, and Private Porsum, a long-time business and political associate of Mr. Murdock. Mrs. Murdock has just told her husband, untruthfully as it turns out, that she and Porsum have recently had an affair. Mrs. Murdock, who is among other things an alcoholic, had appeared in "a pale blue negligee and her bare feet were in mules, her face was fixed in a distant, unapproachable, abstract, pale, saintly smile. . . ." She speaks falteringly, and then laughs, with a "brittle, glassy intonation." The negligee opens, exposing her bosom; she pays it no mind. Bogan Murdock speaks, "spacing the words out precisely, half in question, half in echo." He picks up a convenient pistol, Porsum denies the charge, Mrs. Murdock urges her husband on. "He is lying, Bogan." Then the pistol "sank a fraction of an inch." Mrs. Murdock taunts her husband: "You're afraid, Bogan." Bogan tells Porsum to leave: "Get out!" Mrs. Murdock seconds her husband's command: "Get out!" Then "his [Porsum's] steps retreated across the hall, and the hall door was shut with its solid, dull, authoritative sound. Then, an instant later, there was the sound of a motor starting" (pp. 344–47).

Such a scene, which might be duplicated in a number of the author's other novels, is perfectly conventional in structure, content, and style. Warren is taking chances with the crisis of the Murdocks and Porsum: that it is written according to formula, that they are not quite real. But it might well be observed that the patterned exchange itself dramatizes one of Warren's central contentions about the Murdocks: that they aren't quite real, that they are self-created abstractions. They speak and behave as they are.

Though court room scenes are often encountered in Warren's fiction, he has fully developed in his eighth novel, *Flood*, a stylistic technique which he will probably continue to find useful. This is the inclusion in the narrative of brief, sometimes fragmented, character sketches and of trial transcripts. The sketches, which include scraps of dialogue, serve both to introduce certain characters who will later appear in person, at length, and to give the reader a kind of sociological cross-section of the community. The transcripts, recorded in question and answer form, are employed not only to suggest the character and motives of the participants but also to inject a bit of court-room drama. Whatever else may be said of such techniques, they do illustrate something of what is meant when Warren is termed a "popular" novelist.

Warren has a positive gift for what might be called the defining phrase, the sort of phrase which a reviewer or quarterly essayist in search of a guiding generalization inevitably fastens upon. There is, for example,

Amantha Starr's first utterance: "Oh, who am I?" (*Band of Angels*, p. 3). Here, in brief, the problem of identity. Or there is, for topical relevance, the narrator's description of the fanatic Percival Skrogg, in *World Enough and Time*: "his race has multiplied and become the glory and the horror of our time" (p. 86). Or there is Jack Burden's final reflection, which no critic has missed, that Adam Stanton and Willie Stark represent "the terrible division of their age" (*All the King's Men*, p. 462).

The defining phrase is not simply a "quotable quote" or a tip to the slow reader. It is a commonplace and perfectly legitimate practice, offering valuable insight and capable of considerable refinement. There is, however, a difference to be noted among the three quoted passages. The first, Amantha Starr's loaded question, strikes the reader full force on the first page of her narrative, and in its heavyhandedness is not unrepresentative of the author's practice throughout. The second, the archivist's aside, is markedly, perhaps excessively topical, perhaps gratuitous. Burden's closing observation, on the other hand, issues from and is validated by the whole of his recorded experience.

It is surely appropriate to conclude a consideration of Warren's prose style by returning to Jack Burden, aristocrat, Tough Talker, master of both highbrow and lowbrow language. He is alive to the concrete, the immediate, the sensuous, yet displays a ready grasp of the conceptual, the abstract. Burden also registers and illustrates his creator's pleasure in and sure control of folk speech, dialect, and speech mannerisms. Though there are many important points of difference, C. Hugh Holman put the case well when he says, speaking of Thomas Wolfe, "the particular linguistic combination that Wolfe used—the combination of concrete detail, accurate speech and incantatory rhetorical extravagance is also present to a marked degree in the works of Faulkner, particularly since 1932, and in the novels of Robert Penn Warren."[17]

Admirers of Warren's style are prone to speak of his "gusto," his "prodigality," his "masculine force"; those less impressed are inclined to remark upon his "gothicism," his "derivative intellectualism," his "regionalism." Yet what one sees on almost every page of Warren's novels belies the easy tag. Perhaps that is why there have been so few extended studies of his prose style. Faulkner and Hemingway appear to be the fathers of the style, which is, in its purified form, a special heightened language about midway between verse and mannered prose. Though one could well expatiate on the triumphs of this style, most notably in *All the King's Men* and *The Cave*, it seems also appropriate to note that the style is strong enough to sustain the reader's interest in several novels whose philosophic drive is limited, as is true of *World Enough and Time*. Though his style is his own, Warren has not been an innovative stylist. Thus his management of point of view, or his treatment of stream of consciousness: always clear, always conventional. Both of these elements of style contrast markedly with Faulkner's common practice.

In the eight novels whose style has been examined, finally, there are, in creative tension, the Southerner's sensuous apprehension of the word and the professor and critic's detachment and ease with abstraction. There are the exact, almost doting observation of the physical world and the sensitive exploration of the shadowy, ambiguous inner darkness. And there are the anguished voices of characters mired in closed systems and the beauties of the occasional nature lyric. Or, again, the bookish metaphor and the exuberant simile. Overall, a style that is flexible, rich, dynamic, comprehensive.

Notes

1. Walker Gibson, *Tough, Sweet* and *Stuffy: An Essay on Modern American Prose Styles* (Bloomington: Indiana Univ. Press, 1966), p. 64.

2. Leslie Fiedler, *No! in Thunder: Essays on Myth and Literature* (London: Eyre and Spottiswoode, 1963), p. 126.

3. I have also made this point in "Percy's *The Moviegoer* and Warren's *All the King's Men*," *Notes on Mississippi Writers*, 4, No. 1 (1971), 2–14.

4. Gibson, p. 66.

5. For further observation on the point, see the present writer's "Robert Penn Warren as a Philosophical Novelist," *Western Humanities Review*, 24 (1971), 157–68.

6. For illustration of Gibson's linguistic techniques, see his "Appendix A: Style and Statistics," pp. 113–40.

7. Robert Penn Warren, *Brother to Dragons: A Tale in Verse and Voices* (New York: Random House, 1953), p. 43.

8. Characters in, respectively, *Night Rider* (Boston: Houghton Mifflin, 1939), *At Heaven's Gate* (New York: Harcourt, Brace and Co., 1943), and *World Enough and Time* (New York: Random House, 1950). All subsequent quotations will be identified in the text.

9. Robert Penn Warren, *All the King's Men* (New York: Modern Library, 1953), pp. 11–12. Subsequent quotations will be identified in the text.

10. Robert Penn Warren, *Flood* (New York: Random House, 1964), p. 30. Subsequent quotations will be identified in the text.

11. The best and most frequently cited example of such a sentence is that which opens *All the King's Men*.

12. Robert Penn Warren, *Wilderness: A Tale of the Civil War* (New York: Random House, 1961), p. 31. Subsequent quotations will be identified in the text.

13. Robert Penn Warren, *Band of Angels* (New York: Random House, 1955), pp. 334–35. Subsequent quotations will be identified in the text.

14. *No! in Thunder*, p. 133.

15. See, for example, "Fables for Our Times," *Times Literary Supplement*, 27 Nov. 1959, p. 692.

16. T. Harry Williams, *Huey Long* (New York: Alfred A. Knopf, 1969), p. 203.

17. " 'The Dark Ruined Helen of His Blood': Thomas Wolfe and the South," in *South: Modern Southern Literature in Its Cultural Setting*, ed. Louis D. Rubin, Jr. and Robert D. Jacobs (Garden City, N.Y.: Dolphin Books, 1961), p. 189.

"A Meditation on Folk-History: The Dramatic Structure of Robert Penn Warren's *The Ballad of Billie Potts*"

William Bedford Clark*

In his intriguing "reconsideration" of Coleridge's *Ancient Mariner*, Robert Penn Warren notes that the "fable" of Coleridge's poem is centered around the problem of "crime and punishment and repentance and reconciliation."[1] Significantly, the same elements play a vital role in much of Warren's own poetry and fiction; and, while Warren's vision of the human condition within historical process is not "orthodox" in the strictest of terms, it clearly involves a reworking of certain concepts basic to western religious *mythos*. For Warren man exists in a fallen state in which evil is an inescapable fact; he is not simply the innocent pawn of cosmic forces but a more-or-less responsible agent who desperately needs to come to terms with himself in order to be reconciled with that larger reality of which he is a part. In focusing his attention upon man and the circumstances of human experience, Warren begins with the most basic and self-evident of premises. "A man ain't nuthin but a man," he writes by way of prefacing *Incarnations*, echoing the words of the American folk-hero John Henry; and in poem after poem, speaking as a man to men (to use Wordsworth's phrase in a special sense), Warren addresses himself to an all-embracing "you"—the dual-functional ambiguity of that pronoun enabling him to direct his statements simultaneously toward the individual reader and toward humanity at large, identifying as it were the collective human lot with one man's individuated experience. In this connection, the poem "Clearly About You" yields a convenient synopsis of both the focus and function of much of Warren's poetry:

> Whoever you are, this poem is clearly about you,
> For there's nothing else in the world it could be about.
> Whatever it says, this poem is clearly true,
> For truth is all we are born to, and the truth's out.[2]

* Reprinted with permission from *American Literature*, 49 (1978), 635–45. Copyright © 1978, Duke University Press.

Such poetry, confronting us with unavoidable truths about ourselves and our condition, is as insistent as man's fate itself. There is no satisfactory way out. We must come to terms with the truth and with ourselves.

These initial observations provide a useful point of departure for a reevaluation of one of Warren's most interesting and significant poems, *The Ballad of Billie Potts*. From a thematic standpoint, it is an especially rich and elaborate presentation of the poet's characteristic view of man as engaged in a symbolic progression from sin to ultimate reconciliation. Yet, while most students of Warren's writing acknowledge the importance of *Billie Potts* in relation to the poet's canon as a whole, few have failed to express reservations about its structure.[3] The fact that the poem alternates between two levels of language, reflecting radically different levels of awareness, does seem at first to raise some serious questions as to its final unity; and for this reason it is best to begin with a consideration of the work's formal peculiarities before moving on to an explication of its thesis, although here, as elsewhere in Warren, theme and form are in the end inextricably related.

Formally *The Ballad of Billie Potts* is conveniently divisible into two distinct elements. The first is narrative in nature, and the second might be termed reflective. The narrative element consists of the "ballad" itself, a Kentucky folktale the poet tells us he first heard from an elderly female relative. While not metrically a ballad, the narrative contains unmistakably balladlike qualities. It tells a violent tale with tragic implications. Like innumerable traditional ballads, it becomes dramatic through the introduction of frequent dialogue. Finally, it utilizes a "refrain" that grows increasingly suggestive as the tale unfolds: "the land between the rivers." The language is vernacular, specifically the speech of rural Kentucky characterized by provincialisms and vivid, "folksy" figures. At the outset, the narrator likens the elder Potts's "gut" to a "croker of nubbins" (3,4); at the end of the narrative, the reader last sees Potts bending over the body of the son he has unwittingly murdered, his mouth gasping "like a fish for air" (16, 21).[4] Understatement, a sardonic staple of Anglo-Saxon wit, is also much in evidence. The narrator tells how the younger Potts spends ten years in exile without once writing home, declaring that "Little Billie never was much of a hand with a pen-staff" (9, 12). In keeping with the rustic decorum of the narrative, the narrator's vocabulary is singularly free of euphemisms. He does not shy from the use of such genteel unmentionables as "snot" and "piss."

The overall effect of these "folk" characteristics—when coupled with the twisted meter of the narrative's versification—is one of wry and uninhibited humor, as in the passage relating the events immediately following Little Billie's abortive effort at assassination:

> Oh, Billie didn't tarry and Billie didn't linger,
> For Billie didn't trust the stranger's finger
> And didn't admire the stranger's face

And didn't like the climate of the place,
So he turned and high-tailed up the trace,
With blood on his shirt and snot in his nose
And pee in his pants for he'd wet his clothes,
And the stranger just sits and admires how he goes,
And says, "Why that boy would do right well back on
    the Bardstown track!"

(8, 13–21)

The humor of these lines is the more remarkable in that they treat the aftermath of an attempt at cold-blooded murder. Yet the humor remains pervasive and infectious throughout the narrative segments of the poem, although the tale's climax, taken out of context, seems to be the stuff of tragedy. It recounts with relentless irony the unnatural murder of a man by his parents and their subsequent realization of what they have done. Such an archetypal situation, rich with mythic overtones, might well have provided the foundation for a tragic drama along Sophoclean lines. But the voice of the folk narrator undercuts the tragic potential until the ironies strike the reader as grimly funny rather than tragically profound.

While the narrative sections of *The Ballad of Billie Potts* have obvious roots in the tradition of native American humor, notably that of the Old Southwestern school, and recall the worlds of Davy Crockett and Sut Lovingood in which violence and death are often rendered laughable, the lyrical and introspective sections belong quite properly to a self-consciously "literary" tradition and reflect a sensitive, cultivated consciousness at work. In contrast to the Anglo-Saxon diction of the "ballad," the diction of the "literary" passages if often latinate. The first three adjectives in the narrative, "big," "stout," and "wide," typify its concrete unpretentiousness. The verbal character of the more introspective and speculative passages proclaims itself in three representative adjectives from the first verse paragraph in parentheses: "fetid," "astute," "magnificent." In contrast to the homely similes used to describe characters in the narrative sections, the speaker in the parenthetical passages relies upon figures of speech conventionally "poetic" and sometimes abstract. To his intricate and imaginative perception, the face of an aged hill man is "seamed and gutted like the hill,/Slow under time, and with the innocent savagery/Of Time . . ." (4, 16–18). While the vocabulary of the narrative sections is peculiar to a given time and place, that of the sophisticated sections is highly diversified in origin. Science, religion, metaphysics, and everyday experience alike contribute images and phrases to their poetic texture. Both the language of the "literary" intrusions and the cerebral level of experience it expresses resemble other poetry written by Warren in the same period—roughly the early 1940's. The prevailing tone and tenor of poems like "Terror," "Pursuit," and "Question and Answer" illustrate the likeness. It is a carefully contrived, most complex poetry, a poetry that synthesizes serious philosophical speculation with bristling paradoxical wit: it is a far cry from the seemingly naive artlessness of the folktale element in *Billie Potts*.

Initially the perplexed reader is prone to wonder why Warren was not content to present his "ballad" in isolation. It is a skillful, charming achievement at the folk level of expression, convincingly demonstrating the poet's ability to exploit his regional acquaintance with an oral tradition. A brief passage from Warren's *Brother to Dragons* sheds considerable light on this problem. There the poet, R.P.W., tells Thomas Jefferson that once he contemplated writing a ballad about the violent deeds of the former president's nephews, the Lewises, who murdered a slave boy out of what appears to be innate perversity. R.P.W. goes on to recite an excerpt from that aborted work, verses which bear remarkable stylistic resemblances to the narrative sections of *The Ballad of Billie Potts*. "But," R.P.W. continues,

> the form
> Was not adequate: the facile imitation
> Of a folk simplicity would never serve,
> For the beauty of that simplicity is only
> That the action is always and perfectly self-contained,
> And is an image that comes as its own perfect explanation
> In shock or sweetness to the innocent heart.

The form is inadequate because

> our hearts are scarcely innocent,
> And any pleasure we take in the folk simplicity
> Is a pleasure of snobbish superiority or neurotic yearning.[5]

Further, the ballad form alone proved inadequate to contain the full implications of the Lewis case. The significance of that tragedy is not "self-contained" in the events. It could only be realized from the vantage point of that "any time" and "no place" which dominates *Brother to Dragons*. Nor could Warren, a contemporary poet whose heart is no longer innocent, have been content to recount the earlier Billie Potts story in simple terms. To remain true to the intricacies of his vision, he was compelled to push beyond the boundaries of folktale. The parenthetical, meditative passages serve to elevate the Potts legend to that level of myth at which particularized events take on universal significance. Taken this way, folktale provides the impetus for philosophy.[6]

Thus it may be said that *The Ballad of Billie Potts* presents a highly sensitive consciousness coming to terms with the raw materials of the past as they are embodied in a local legend reputedly based upon fact. Recognition of the poem's final unity depends upon a realization of the extent to which its form is essentially *dramatic*. *The Ballad of Billie Potts*, like *Brother to Dragons*, attempts to penetrate beyond the bare facts of a human event in order to grasp at general "truths." The image of Amantha

Starr, the heroine of Warren's *Band of Angels*, poring over the chaotic pages of a congressional report on the New Orleans riots in an effort to understand her own place in history can serve to represent what is being dramatized in *Billie Potts*. While Warren's poem is not, strictly speaking, a "meditation on history"—to use William Styron's admirable description of his *The Confessions of Nat Turner*—it does recreate a meditation on folk-history, a kind of history that already points toward myth. The meditative sections which interrupt the progress of the narrative represent the efforts of a philosophizing speaker, like the R.P.W. of *Brother to Dragons*, to raise image to symbol, to render a set of specifics universal. The poem not only makes a far-reaching statement about the nature of man and his experience; it dramatizes the way in which a contemporary consciousness formulates such a statement out of the raw stuff of life.[7]

The first three verse paragraphs of the poem form part of the narrative proper and introduce the principal *dramatis personae*: Potts senior, his wife, and Little Billie. They also locate the action of the narrative in a specific place, "the land between the rivers," that portion of Kentucky which lies between the Cumberland and the Tennessee. Seemingly struck by the emphasis placed upon the narrative's setting in these introductory lines, the meditative voice intrudes to survey that locale from the vantage point of time present. The "land between the rivers" is still there in a physical sense, and the observer is able to describe it with vivid certainty. However, this first of his intrusions ends upon a note of uncertainty. The reader is presented with a snatch of conversation between the speaker and an unnamed hill man. The speaker asks the old man if he is on the right road to Paducah, and the man answers, "They names hit so, but I ain't bin" (4, 19). The old man's response points out a distinction between personal experience and second-hand information, and the epistemological implications of that distinction bear upon the observer's situation as he looks back at the Billie Potts story. Though the setting of the story exists relatively unchanged, its actual substance remains hearsay from a lost time. The observer is denied historical certitude.

That the observer understands this limitation on his perspective appears in the second parenthetical passage. After a brief return to the narrative during which the reader learns that the elder Potts established an inn, the observer launches into a second revery. In his mind's eye, he visualizes Potts and one of his guests as they walk toward an arbor. This imaginary glimpse, however, is as close as he can come to recreating the past. Though the figures' lips move, the observer cannot hear their words, nor the snap of a "trodden twig" nor the singing of nearby birds (4, 32). The past exists but is never quite reclaimable. The speaker wistfully realizes that the names of myriad other such early settlers "are like the leaves, but are forgot" (5, I). On this elegiac note, the vision fades out almost cinematically as the two figures from the past enter the arbor.

The narrative resumes at this point, and the reader learns that the source of the elder Potts's prosperity lies in the fact that he is inclined to arrange the robbery and murder of prosperous-looking guests. And now the narrative is interrupted with an explicit confession of the observer's inability to recapture the past as it was. Though history has its beginning and end, contemporary man, locked within his experiential present, cannot comprehend them. The figures from the past, themselves confined within their segment of time, "pace a logic merciless as light" (5, 27) and cannot convey the actualities of their world to a man who contemplates them in the present. The latter must rely upon an agonizing "speculation" that "rasps its idiot nails/Across the dry slate" of attempted understanding (5, 32–33): "The answer is in the back of the book but the page is gone" (5, 34). Even though the past continues to live in the memories of certain old people "who bear/History like bound faggots, with stiff knees" (6, 4–5), the old ones, like dumb beasts of burden, cannot sufficiently communicate "the infatuate weight of their wisdom" verbally (6, 2). They too inhabit a world aloof, which suggests the static serenity of "fresco, vase, or frieze" (6, 8).

As the narrative resumes, the reader learns that Little Billie, in an effort to please his loving parents, sets out to plunder a guest on his own. "He always was a good boy to his darling Mammy," the rustic narrator concludes (6, 36). From the viewpoint of the philosophical observer, however, Little Billie's initiative is not funny. Now the speaker's focus on events shifts from his concern with epistemology to an attempt to read the ballad's significance as metaphor. He becomes less concerned with Little Billie and the stranger in themselves than with an effort to see their encounter as an archetypal confrontation between would-be murderer and intended victim. Raising the question of identity that is to play a vital role in the rest of the poem, the speaker asks the reader, "Which are you?" Then, implying the problem of the nature of man, the work's final concern, he extends the range of his query: "What [are you]?" (7, 17; brackets mine).

Following this shift of the observer's perspective, the narrative returns to the younger Potts's ludicrously unsuccessful debut as a criminal, the episode earlier quoted from at length. The upshot of the affair is that Little Billie is banished from the "land between the rivers." Victor Strandberg has noted a parallel here between *The Ballad of Billie Potts* and the Biblical account of Adam and Eve.[8] Translated literally, Mesopotamia, the traditional locus of the Garden of Eden, means "the land between the rivers." It is possible, then, to regard the banishment of Little Billie, like the expulsion of Adam and Eve from the Garden, as punishment for original sin; but the reader should guard against carrying this analogy too far. The setting of Warren's work is no Edenic realm of innocence. Little Billie's attempted crime does not bring evil into the world; it initiates him into that world where evil is already an established fact.

It is significant that Little Billie, like many of his counterparts in Warren's fiction, seeks escape in the West.[9] In certain respects the West in Warren's writing is associated with the world of experience in which man is compelled to act and interact with other men. Little Billie's trip west symbolically reflects his lapse from a state of relative personal innocence into full participation in the human condition. However, in keeping with traditional attitudes toward the West as a land of perpetual promise and renewal, Billie naively looks upon his western flight as a satisfactory escape from the consequences of his guilt. The West seems to offer the fugitive an endless series of new beginnings and fresh identities, but the observer, in his meditation on the narrative, is not deceived. He realizes that the new identity Billie seeks to assume is nothing more than a reflection on the surface of water. From this point forward in the poem, water imagery begins to play an increasingly suggestive role. Beneath the superficial image of self on the surface, "the water coils and goes/And its own beginning and its end only the water knows" (9, 23–24). Though there are many rivers, they all contain the same element—water. The observer evokes a metaphorical vision which suggests at once the Heraclitian river of ceaseless change and the archetypal Sea of Being, that ultimate level of existence which both transcends and permeates earthly reality. A resulting tension between two levels of being, one eternal and unified and the other transient and diversified, is implied to form a basis for the set of ambiguities which begin to surround the concepts of time and identity in the speaker's musings:

> Time is only and always beginnings
> And is the redemption of our crime,
> And is our Saviour's priceless blood.
>
> For Time is always the new place,
> And no-place.
> For Time is always the new name and the new face,
> And no-name and no-face.
>
> (10, 10–16)

Time on the one hand, is the world of the West, a world of individuated experience. On the other hand, time is also the mystical unity of being into which all distinctions are absorbed. This ontological duality provides the foundation upon which the observer's ultimate assessment of human destiny will be based.

Finding no abiding peace in the West in spite of his worldly success there, Billie Potts returns home to find himself; and the narrative concludes around this motif of return.[10] The observer sees the events of the legend as symbolic of man's need to return to a lost state of innocence. It is hardly possible to regain such innocence in this world, however; it may be regained only by exchanging the individuated self for nonself, by being washed in the redemptive waters of Time. Plunged again into the Sea of Being, man is at last reconciled and at peace. Death, significantly brought about by one's parents, who, ironically, are responsible for one's earthly existence in the first place, serves as the final act of atonement. It makes possible reunification with the source and ground of all existence, or, in religious terms, with the divine.

This, then, is the truth about what it means to be human as the observer in the poem begins to understand "truth." It is interesting to note how strongly his view resembles that of the old man at the end of *All the King's Men*, who writes that "separateness is identity and the only way for God to create, truly create, man was to make him separate from God himself, and to be separate from God is to be sinful."[11] While the tone and language of this statement, taken out of context, may suggest a kind of Manichaean otherworldliness, it would be a serious error to accuse Warren of devaluing life. Man, in Warren's scheme of things, lives out his life in a world where evil is a constant factor, but, through self-awareness and an acceptance of personal responsibility, he is nevertheless capable of rising above his fate at times. It is this that lends a "glory and power" to his fallen state.[12]

Thus, for all its structural peculiarities, *The Ballad of Billie Potts* is the kind of poem the reader might logically expect its author to write. Not only is its thematic thrust typical of some of Warren's best-known work, its structure, viewed in dramatic terms, may be seen to be an obvious outgrowth of one of his most characteristic preoccupations as a writer— an overwhelming need to come to terms with the significance of the past, whether it comes to us from the printed page, or, as in *The Ballad of Billie Potts*, through the oral history of the folk.

Notes

1. "A Poem of Pure Imagination," *Kenyon Review*, 8 (1946), 391–427.

2. *You, Emperors, and Others: Poems 1957–1960* (New York: Random House, 1960), p. 3.

3. The attitude of Leonard Casper, who finds the poem mannered and lacking in unity, is a typical one. See *Robert Penn Warren: The Dark and Bloody Ground* (Seattle: Univ. of Washington Press, 1960), pp. 72–75. Charles H. Bohner likewise views the poem as flawed. See *Robert Penn Warren* (New York: Twayne, 1964), p. 57.

4. Parenthetical entries denote page and line numbers in the text of *The Ballad of Billie Potts* as it appears in Warren's *Selected Poems: 1923–1943* (New York: Harcourt, Brace and Co., 1944). Although Warren revised the poem for *Selected Poems: Old and New* (New York: Random House, 1966), I prefer to base my essay on the earlier version because in it the contrasts between vernacular and "literary" elements are more fully apparent.

5. *Brother to Dragons* (New York: Random House, 1953), p. 43. Floyd C. Watkins was, so far as I know, the first critic to note the relevance of this passage to *The Ballad of Billie Potts*. See his discussion of the poem in "Billie Potts at the Fall of Time," *Mississippi Quarterly*, 11 (1958), 19–28.

6. The creative act as "a process of discovery and exploration" on Warren's part is treated intelligently by Curtis Whittington, Jr., in his essay, "The Earned Vision: Robert Penn Warren's *The Ballad of Billie Potts* and Albert Camus' *Le Malentendu,*" *Four Quarters*, 21, No. 4 (1972), 79–90.

7. Warren's concern with grasping the human significance of past events, whether real or fictitious, is a manifestation of the contemporary writer's desire to extract sense from the whole sweep of man's seemingly inchoate experience. He writes that the "philosophical" writer is one "for whom the documentation of the world is constantly striving to rise to the level of generalization about values." For such a writer, "image becomes symbol," and "The urgency of experience, no matter how vividly and strongly experience may enchant, is the urgency to know the meaning of experience." See Warren's preface to Conrad's *Nostromo* (New York: Modern Library, 1951), p. xxxviii.

8. *A Colder Fire: The Poetry of Robert Penn Warren* (Lexington: Univ. of Kentucky Press, 1965), p. 115.

9. See Joe Davis's article "Robert Penn Warren and the Journey West," *Modern Fiction Studies:* Special Robert Penn Warren Number, 6 (1960), 73–82.

10. See Sam Hynes's handling of this theme in "Robert Penn Warren: The Symbolic Journey," *University of Kansas City Review*, 17 (1951), 279–85.

11. *All the King's Men* (New York: Modern Library, 1953), p. 462.

12. *All the King's Men*, p. 463.

"All the King's Men and the Shadow of William James"

Cushing Strout*

Robert Penn Warren has told us that reading William James was part of the matrix of *All the King's Men*.[1] The "scholarly and benign figure" of the philosopher cast his shadow on the creation of the novel's Southern demagogue, Willie Stark.[2] This genesis would seem to fit with the fact that Warren's group of poet-critics, often called the Southern Agrarians, has been identified with a traditionalist criticism of "the dislocation of modern sensibility," a plight supposedly produced by the "modern intellectual movement variously known as positivism, pragmatism, instrumentalism."[3] In support of this explanation one might make the point that the novel is a study of the divided character of the dictator and even more of the narrator's struggle for personal integration. Furthermore, Warren invokes through the "historical" inset-story of Cass Mastern a Christian consciousness that knows "the world is all of one piece," a lesson that the history student Jack Burden comes to learn for himself in the modern world. Yet, in spite of all this, a close reading of both the novel and the philosophy of pragmatism, looking at each alternately over the shoulder of the other, discovers a quite different connection—a remarkably close convergence of the two points of view. Whether or not Warren himself would consider his novel to stand in such a close relation to the philosopher, the juxtaposition of them clarifies a story that has provoked a variety of interpretations. Moreover, it subverts the historical myth, fostered by some apologists for the Southern Agrarians, of an untragic, pragmatic Northern mind posed in contrast to a tragic, passionate Southern mind, informed by classical humanism and Christian faith.[4] Warren himself undermines this facile polarity not only by his own rejection of moral absolutism, but also by his projection of an aspect of pragmatism into his creation of an archetypal Southern demagogue.

On historical grounds it is not surprising that James should have come to Warren's mind when he began the verse drama that ultimately led to *All the King's Men* in Mussolini's Italy of 1938. When Warren left Louisiana State University, where he had taught in the days of Huey

*Reprinted with permission from *The Southern Review*, NS6 (1970), 920–34. Copyright © 1970 by Cushing Strout.

Long's regime, he took "the myth of 'Huey' " with him to Perugia. Long's dictatorship has sometimes loosely been called fascist, and Mussolini himself said in 1926: "James taught me that an action should be judged rather by its results than by its doctrinary basis. I learnt of James that faith in action, that ardent will to live and fight, to which Fascism owes a great part of its success."[5] Some self-styled "experimentalist" progressives, notably the journalist Lincoln Steffens, did defend Mussolini on the historicist ground that "the wave of the future" could not be ridden by men hobbled by liberal moral and political principles, and a few pragmatic liberals were briefly attracted to Mussolini's "corporatism." But Warren himself must also have known that some conservatives in sympathy with the Agrarians, notably the editor of the *American Review* to which they frequently contributed, incongruously identified a romantic reactionary monarchism with both Mussolini and Huey Long.[6] Many Italian pragmatists, however, were anti-fascists; James was an anti-imperialist and anti-militarist, a defender of Dreyfus; and Warren supported the New Deal.[7] These facts are consistent with Warren's own qualifying reference to "the scholarly and benign figure" of James.

What the novel finds in Willie Stark's political "realism" is a populistic version of James's skepticism about the finality of any particular social balance of conflicting ideals. Justifying his scorn for his Attorney General who has resigned for moral and legal reasons, Willie Stark argues that you have to make the Good up as you go along out of whatever you need to do business:

> I'm not denying there's got to be a notion of right to get business done, but by God any particular notion at any particular time will sooner or later get to be just like a stopper put tight in a bottle of water and thrown in a hot stove the way we kids used to do at school to hear the bang. The steam that blows the bottle and scares the teacher to wet her drawers is just the human business that is going to get done, and it will blow anything you put it in if you seal it tight, but you put it in the right place and let it get out in a certain way and it will run a freight engine.[8]

Willie's persuasiveness borrows from the "anti-formalist" spirit of American social thought in the early twentieth century, although he has extended this pervasive mood to a rationalization of the Machiavellian tactics of fear, favor, force, and fraud. What wins our limited sympathy for him is his populist feeling for the social welfare of the hill folk of his state, too long neglected by the inertia and the class bias of the ruling gentry from the Delta. A new social balance does need to be struck, and his awareness of the need dignifies his demagoguery. Willie's rationale is a vulgar echo of James's own analysis of the relativity of law and custom:

> There is nothing final in any actually given equilibrium of

human ideals, but that, as our present laws and customs have fought and conquered the other past ones, so they will in their turn be overthrown by any newly discovered order which will hush up the complaints that they still give rise to, without producing others louder still. . . . These experiments are to be judged, not a priori, but by actual finding, after the fact of their making, how much more outcry or how much appeasement comes about. Every now and then . . . some one is born with the right to be original, and his revolutionary thought or action may bear prosperous fruit. . . . He may, by breaking old moral rules in a certain place, bring in a total condition of things more ideal than would have followed had the rules been kept.[9]

Just as Willie's apologia is qualified by the story, showing how in fact he has become corrupted by an inordinate egotism, a vindictive passion for revenge, and a relentless drive for power over others, so also is James's analysis critically qualified by his own moral sensibility, tuned to a sense of justice that found "hideous" any bargain by which millions might be "kept permanently happy on the one simple condition that a certain lost soul on the far-off edge of things should lead a life of lonely torture."[10] And he concluded with characteristic tolerance that the moral victory philosophically to be prayed for was that of the side "which even in the hour of triumph will to some degree do justice to the ideals in which the vanquished party's interests lay."[11] But when philosophers must speak out in the press of events about a particular course of action, they can only fall back, James believed, on "the dumb willingnesses and unwillingnesses of their interior characters, and nowhere else," for then what is on trial is their "personal aptitude or incapacity for moral life."[12] Similarly, Warren's novel moves away from generalized defense of, or attack on, Willie's regime in order to look in this Jamesian fashion into the "interior characters" of both Willie and Jack Burden, probing their aptitude or incapacity for moral life. Even in history, both Warren and James would agree, character counts.

The closest the novel comes to a justification of the Boss is in Jack Burden's speculation that the "theory of historical costs" would entail the idea that "maybe a man has to sell his soul to get the power to do good." But Burden describes this theory as "a high historical view from a chilly pinnacle" that perhaps only "a hero" could act on (p. 418). Later he does come to believe in Willie's greatness, whatever had happened to pollute it, but this belief does not prove that Jack has accepted the "theory of historical costs." On the contrary, he plans to go into politics with Hugh Miller, who resigned on principle as Attorney General because the Boss would not give comfort to his enemies by firing a corrupt state auditor. Miller tells Jack: "History is blind, but a man is not" (p. 462). Men living in the midst of things cannot abstract from their situation by rising to some "chilly pinnacle" but must use whatever insight and conscience they have in the world. The novel does not rely on historicism as Willie does—and as "wave of the future" apologists did in the 1930s—but instead shows its formerly cynical narrator forming the intention in his very last line to go out "into the awful responsibility of Time."

All the King's Men is a philosophical novel in Warren's definition of the term: "The philosophical novelist, or poet, is one for whom the documentation of the world is constantly striving to rise to the level of generalization about values, for whom the image strives to rise to symbol, for whom images always fall into a dialectical configuration, for whom the urgency of experience, no matter how strongly experience may enchant, is the urgency to know the meaning of experience."[13] James's major themes of the place of the hero in history; of free will versus determinism; of the mediating role of truth in relation to past and present experience; and of "the twice-born sick soul" of the converted and unified self, are remarkably close to the novel's main drama of Jack Burden's reflective and emotional transformation into a responsible agent in a moral and historical world.

James dealt with one of the major concerns of *All the King's Men* in his reflections on the causal role of the great man in history. He affirmed that "the causes that make communities change from generation to generation" are "the accumulated influences of individuals, of their examples, their initiatives, and their decisions." He acknowledged that the environment could adopt or reject, preserve or destroy, the great man for "a given genius may come either too early or too late." But he protested against the fatalistic vagueness of Herbert Spencer's theory that "a real explanation" of the changes brought about by individual leaders "must be sought in that aggregate of conditions out of which both he and they have arisen." Such a fatalistic position is no different, James pointed out, from "the Oriental method of replying to whatever question arises by the unimpeachable truism, 'God is great.' "[14] In *All the King's Men*, Jack Burden, in mid-career, speculates on historical causation as if he were "God brooding on History":

> You could look at the crowd out there and hear that undertone in its cry, hoarse like surf, and think that the crowd there could cause the event. But no, in turn it could be replied that Willie Stark merely gave the Legislature the opportunity to behave in the way appropriate to its nature and that MacMurfee, who sponsored the election of those men, thinking to use their fear and greed for his own ends, was truly responsible. But no, to that it could be replied that the responsibility belonged, after all, to that crowd of people, indirectly in so far as it had allowed MacMurfee to elect such men, and directly in so far as it had, despite MacMurfee, elected Willie Stark. But why had they elected Willie Stark? Because of a complex of forces which

had made them what they were, or because Willie Stark could lean toward them with bulging eyes and right arm raised to Heaven? (pp. 161–62)

Burden does not resolve this problem until he has come out from under the spell of his vision of the naturalistic determinism of "The Great Twitch." When he learns that his own research into the past has tarnished his girl friend's image of her father and led her in disenchantment to become Willie Stark's mistress, Jack flees West. He escapes from his own culpability by a philosophy of mechanical determinism, symbolized by Dr. Adam Stanton's transformation of a personality by a brain operation on a catatonic schizophrenic. Only when he has come to believe in the personal reality of his mother's love for Judge Irwin, of the Judge's honor, despite his flaws, and of Willie's resurgent idealism, displayed in his project for a public hospital and in his return to his wife, does Jack take personal responsibility for what has happened because of his own blackmailing research for the Boss. At the same time he comes to believe that Lucy Stark was right in thinking that Willie was a great man: "And believing that Willie Stark was a great man, I could think better of all other people, and of myself. At the same time that I could more surely condemn myself" (p. 452).

Willie's greatness had its environmental occasion in the inertia and class bias of the earlier conservative administrations of the state. Burden finally sees, however, that Willie's own eloquence and energy, his corrupted idealism, has played a significant role. The old image of Willie as "Cousin Willie from the country, the boy with a Christmas tie," a deluded and gulled hick, begins to fade in Jack's mind and is replaced by a less patronizing one. When Anne is attracted to the Boss as a man, Jack sees the orator's virile face, as if for the first time: "Funny, I had never seen it before" (p. 346). Willie himself believes "it might have all been different" (p. 425). This theme of indeterminism may seem to be countered in the novel, however, by Jack's conclusion that Adam and Willie were "doomed" to destroy each other because each was "incomplete with the terrible division of their age." But this doom "had nothing to do with any doom under the godhead of the Great Twitch." If they were doomed, they lived "in the agony of will" (p. 462). The necessity in their conflict is not causal.

Their relationship in the novel is dialectical, linked by their opposing tendencies, their mutual distance from the norm of integrated reason and will, thought and action, morality and politics; and their incompleteness is politically expressed in the gap between the Delta aristocrats and the poor hill folk. In the novel's climax of action they briefly exchange roles, Willie idealistically dedicated to building a public hospital, Adam seeking revenge with a gun. If this dialectical confrontation and implied synthesis suggest Hegel rather than James, it is partly because we have forgotten

James's own view of the mediating function of pragmatism. Its strongest appeal, he felt, lay in its role as "a mediator of tender-mindedness and tough-mindedness," of "going by principles" and "going by facts."[15] In this perspective the novel contrasts Adam's rationalistic "tender-mindedness" with Willie's empirical "tough-mindedness" in the characteristic division of their age. In the end the Boss's divided nature, his failure of integration, leads to his downfall because his henchmen, who resent his idealism, and Adam Stanton, who resents his affair with Anne, conspire together to kill him.

James's conception of truth was also mediatorial: "new truths thus are resultants of new experiences and of old truths combined and mutually modifying one another."[16] Pragmatism emphasizes the "leading" function of true ideas, their pointing towards "consistency, stability and flowing human intercourse." And the success of mediation is to be measured subjectively by the individual's appreciation.[17] Jack Burden has trouble with his historical thesis because he cannot appreciate the meaning of Cass Mastern's story until he also has some sense of the direction of his own life. Speaking about the day of the assassination, Jack says that its meaning came to him only afterwards, for "reality is not a function of the event as event, but of the relationship of that event to past, and future, events." It is a pointing process that matters; "direction is all" because "our own identity is dependent upon this principle" (p. 407). Jack's own identity depends upon his ability finally to accept his past, and thereby to have a future. His mother's cry of love for Judge Irwin, the Judge's refusal to defend himself by pleading his paternal relation to Jack, and Willie's own chastened response to his son's death are crucial experiences that give Jack the respect needed to accept his past by forming new truths. He now knows that truth-finding is not mere reporting, and he can grasp his own connections with the tragic bit of past history that his ancestor, Cass Mastern, had lived. Like him, Jack has been part of a process of events that has led to the suicide of another man. And just as Cass could not bear the eyes of his slaves upon him, so Jack cannot bear the winking eye of Tiny Duffy upon himself, implying that they are bound together in a "monstrous conspiracy." Only the acceptance of his own guilt, and his deliberate refusal to compound it further, enables Jack to escape what James called "the block universe" of mechanism in which all are bound together, as Jack ironically puts it, "by the Holy Grace of the Great Twitch whom we must all adore" (p. 442).

In his *The Legacy of the Civil War* Warren points out that the Civil War was a clash between two absolutistic ways of thinking, "the higher law" of the Abolitionists and the "legalism" of the defenders of slavery and states rights, and this conflict paved the way, he suggests, for the development of pragmatism.[18] Men who act pragmatically know that their conduct cannot simply be controlled either by absolute legality or absolute morality, since neither stance takes account of the qualifying particularity of a specific historical situation. In the novel two characters, Cass Mastern of the 1850s, the ancestral subject of Jack's graduate thesis, and Ellis Burden, Jack's legal father, represent an absolutistic religious sense of morality that unfits them both for living in the world. Cass, agonized by his own sins and the crime of slavery, concludes: "Perhaps only a man like my brother Gilbert can in the midst of evil retain enough of innocence and strength . . . to do a little justice in the terms of the great injustice" (pp. 195–96). And Jack Burden at the end of novel suggests that Gilbert is rather like Judge Irwin, Jack's real father, a man whose sins had not prevented him nevertheless from being a good judge, a person whom Jack cannot condemn too harshly for "a man's virtue may be but the defect of his desire, as his crime may be but a function of his virtue" (p. 463). Jack's legal father, a pious recluse who had "walked away" from his past, was charitable: "But his goodness had told me nothing except that I could not live by it" (p. 375). Though eventually Jack charitably takes the senile old man into his home, left him by Judge Irwin, it is his flawed natural father whom he respects and loves. Gilbert Mastern and Judge Irwin, neither complacent nor agonized, have reacted to their loss of innocence without the obsessive guilt of Cass, the cynical self-mistrustful "moral neutrality" of Jack, the pathetic withdrawal of his legal father, or the resentful ruthlessness of Willie Stark, embittered by his knowledge that he has been gulled by other politicians. How they react to their fall from innocence—suggested by the title itself—is an index of their capacity or incapacity for moral life in the world.

The end of innocence is a theme easily related to Biblical theology, but in the modern American postwar world the theme was widely developed in secular terms, a reflection of the end of continental security, of laissez-faire capitalism, and of the myth of irreversible progress. This is not to say that Warren does not make effective *dramatic* use of Protestant themes and rhetoric, but if the novel's references to traditional Christian ideas are taken seriously on philosophical rather than on moral grounds, they tend to confuse the story's intention. This difficulty parallels some of James's own philosophical problems in using religious ideas.

The relevance of Warren's novel goes beyond politics because of our modern interest in the theme of personal identity. Jack's transformation at the end of the story is a kind of moral second birth in contrast to Adam Stanton's surgical transformation of the schizophrenic's personality. How a self becomes a new self is really the burden of Burden's story, the major chord of the novel, including Willie's search for identity within it. The "twice-born sick soul" is also the basic category in James's analysis of the psychology of conversion in *The Varieties of Religious Experience*. For him it need not necessarily be Christian or even moral:

> The new birth may be away from religion into incredulity; or
> it may be from moral scrupulosity into freedom and license;
> or it may be produced by the eruption into the individual's life

of some new stimulus or passion, such as love, ambition, cupidity, revenge, or patriotic devotion. In all these instances we have precisely the same psychological form of event,—a firmness, stability, and equilibrium succeeding a period of storm and stress and inconsistency. In these non-religious cases the new man may also be born either gradually or suddenly.[19]

James's conception of conversion in religious cases, however, emphasized the precedent sense of sin, sorrow, and despair. Even more striking is the analogous fact that for James himself mechanistic determinism had been a part of his own identity crisis in his early manhood, just as it was for Burden during the worst period of his despairing reaction to the loss of his girl to Willie. In the French philosopher Renouvier's idea of free will James found the intellectual support for refusing "to blink the evil out of sight" and for taking the moral posture of an active will, determined to resist evil, which was "as real as the good."[20]

If both Burden and James come out of a despairing belief in mechanism to accept free moral action, there is a difference. Burden finds salvation in accepting his own *guilt*, understanding the wink which Duffy gives him as a fellow conspirator; James found his salvation in a sense of his own *worth*, previously inhibited by his father's scorn for human "merit." It says much about the cultural distance of Warren's outlook from that of the late nineteenth century, still in James's case close to the felt power of the Calvinist tradition of original sin, that the more modern writer should turn to guilt in order to restore a moral universe. But there is a strong analogy in the fact that James's father preached original sin in his own theologically heretical way, just as Jack Burden's legal father did, convinced that God had to create evil as an index of his glory and power so that "the creation of good might be the index of man's glory and power. But by God's help." He maintains that man's separateness is his identity; and to be created is to be separated from God and therefore sinful. James's father would have agreed—selfhood *is* sin. At the end of the novel Jack is able to say about his legal father's theology: "I was not certain but that in my own way I did believe what he had said" (pp. 462–63). Similarly, James wrote *The Varieties of Religious Experience* to testify to his own respect for "Father's cry that religion is real," and he too accepted some of his father's theological concerns in his own more agnostic and empirical way. The twice-born "sick soul," he believed, has essential insights into reality, lacking in the optimistic gospel of the once-born "healthy-minded" soul because "the evil facts which it refuses positively to account for are a genuine portion of reality; and they may after all be the best key to life's significance, and possibly the only openers of our eyes to the deepest levels of truth."[21] The reader of *All the King's Men* is entitled to expect that when Jack Burden finishes his thesis on the guilt-haunted "sick soul" of Cass Mastern he too will have understood the insights of his ancestor in more secular terms. While Cass believed that theologically it was a "human defect" for him to believe that he could know now himself by knowing another, instead of seeing himself in God's eye, Jack's "new picture of the world" was, in fact, given to him by his appreciation of the reality of other persons. (pp. 184, 458).

Warren's novel comes to a sharp divergence from James's position in its use of the metaphor of a seamless world. Cass had believed that "the vibration set up in the whole fabric of the world" by his act "had spread infinitely and with ever increasing power and no man could know the end" (p. 189). Jack himself comes to believe "that the world is all of one piece," an enormous spider web which if touched at any point causes the spider to "inject the black, numbing poison under your hide" (p. 200). In giving Willie's murderer the name of Adam, Warren implies the primer's saying, "In Adam's Fall We Sinned All." By these allusions he transforms the mechanistic universe of the Great Twitch into a moral universe, but by his evocation of Original Sin he may appear to substitute a spiritual mechanism for the old one, leaving it still, in James's terms, "a block universe," seen from the point of view of omniscience. Monism, James often pointed out, is more appropriate to justifying our stake in having "a moral holiday" than in taking responsibility. Burden believes that by not sleeping with Anne years ago, because of his need to protect his innocent image of her and his own mistrust of the future, he has led her "by an obscure and necessary logic" (p. 329) to become the mistress of Willie. But Willie comes to believe that "it might all have been different," a conclusion that Jack also accepts. And Jack acts on his own only when he breaks a chain of events by refusing to tell the "trigger-happy" Sugar Boy that Tiny Duffy has plotted against the Boss. The resolution of these seeming inconsistencies lies in seeing that the logic of intelligibility that makes sense out of history is not the logic of mechanical sequence.

In *The Legacy of the Civil War* Warren speaks of the need to try to determine the limits of responsibility in experience, and he opposes any historicism that would make the North "merely the bright surgical instrument in the hand of God, or History."[22] James would have agreed. Metaphysical indeterminism, he pointed out, with its commitment to the "ambiguity of future volitions," is entirely compatible with the *psychological* fact that decisions, by granting consent to one possibility and withholding it from another in a "self-luminous and self-justifying" way, can "transform an equivocal and double future into an inalterable and simple past."[23] Looking backwards, the historian (like Jack Burden) tries to make the past intelligible, but this intelligibility, like the self-luminous quality of decisions, does not make the future determined. Similarly, James's pluralism is not incompatible with Warren's demonstration that Jack's and Willie's fictional histories are, "in one sense, one story" (p. 168). While actual histories "interlace and interfere at points," James pointed out, "we cannot unify them completely in our minds." Thus "the world appears as something more epic than dramatic."[24] Jack's and

Willie's stories are partially unified because both characters are in need of integrating their own natures and experiences. Only then can their worlds metaphorically appear to be "all of one piece."

James was willing to concede that the idea of free will could be made compatible with the idea of Providence, "provided you do not restrict the Providence to fulminating nothing but *fatal* decrees." Providence itself would then carry out its own thinking in the category of possibilities as well as actualities. This compromise, he noted, would not stand if God were considered to be a timeless mind. But he believed that the timeless mind was "a gratuitous fiction," only another way of "whacking upon us the block-universe, and of denying that possibilities exist—just the point to be proved."[25] His own matured personal predilection was against any notion of a world "already saved *in toto* anyhow," but on his own grounds he had to conclude that "in the end it is our faith and not our logic that decides such questions."[26] Burden's resolution of his problems is made in the same way. He no longer believes in "the Great Twitch" because he has "seen too many people live and die" (p. 461). If he and Anne, leaving Burden's Landing at the end of the novel, are "going out of history into history and the awful responsibility of Time," Warren's use of the capital letter even points towards James's own theory of a Providence that is subject to temporality (p. 464).

Warren's novel, far from being a protest against pragmatism, as exemplified in Willie Stark's demagoguery, is instead a dramatic exploration of the major themes of James's philosophy. If as a social reformer the Boss illustrates James's point about the way in which a new and needed social balance is struck, as a dictator he also exemplifies the danger of a pragmatic ethic abstracted from the moral sense and metaphysics that James notably had, though too many of his critics seldom give him credit for articulating them, as if he had not coined the memorable phrase about "the bitch-goddess—SUCCESS."

The skeptical reader may feel inclined to protest at this point that at least Warren's own aesthetic view of the novel as a form places him outside pragmatism. A novel, he says, is knowledge *by* and *of* form, and that includes, "most emphatically, those elements drawn from the actual world and charged with all the urgencies of actuality," but transmuted into a vision of experience that yields an image of man himself, "a paradigm of his inner life." Warren adds that the gift of art does not merely feed "the life of contemplation, for the soul does not sit in self-regarding trance, like Rachel before a mirror all the day, in Dante's *Purgatorio*. No, that gazing prepares for the moment of action, of creation, in our world of contingency."[27] Probably because of the fact that his brother was a novelist with a taste for aesthetic theory, William James unfortunately never did relate pragmatic theory to aesthetics, a conspicuous mark of the incompleteness that he lamented in his philosophy. But he had first studied drawing and painting, and he wrote his brother: "Away from art, as we live, we sink into a flatter, blanker kind of consciousness and indulge in an ostrich-like forgetfulness of all our richest potentialities . . ."[28] In seeing the novel as a paradigm of the inner life that prepares us for action in a contingent world, Warren has proposed an aesthetic that James might have found highly congenial.

If Warren consciously drew on James only for an element of Willie Stark's "toughmindedness," he loosely exploited pragmatism with a poet's privilege of distortion. Certainly the philosopher himself would have seen much of pragmatism in Jack Burden's transformation into a moral agent. Because James's philosophy was "too much like an arch built only on one side," it was his fate to be superseded by the more systematic Dewey.[29] In that development, pragmatism lost much of the inwardness, moral drama, and metaphysical speculation that serve the novelist's imagination. If *All the King's Men* has become a modern classic, it is testimony not only to its remarkable energy and poetry of language but to the persisting vitality of those intellectual issues that it shares with the "benign figure" of William James.

Notes

1. "Louisiana Politics and *All the King's Men:* The Matrix of Experience," *Yale Review*, 53 (1963), 166.

2. Introduction to *All the King's Men* (New York: Modern Library, 1953), p. vii.

3. Robert Wooster Stallman, "The New Criticism and the Southern Critics," in *A Southern Vanguard*, ed. Allen Tate (New York: Prentice-Hall, 1947), p. 37.

4. Herbert Marshall McLuhan, "The Southern Quality," in *A Southern Vanguard*, p. 116.

5. Ralph Barton Perry, *The Thought and Character of William James* (Boston: Little, Brown and Co., 1936), II, 575.

6. See Alfred E. Stone, Jr., "Seward Collins and the *American Review:* Experiment in Pro-Fascism, 1933–37," *American Quarterly*, 12 (1960), 3–19; John Diggins, "Flirtation with Fascism: American Pragmatic Liberals and Mussolini's Italy," *American Historical Review*, 71 (1966), 487–506.

7. Robert Penn Warren, "Knowledge and the Image of Man," *Sewanee Review*, 63 (1955), 183.

8. *All the King's Men* (New York: Harcourt, Brace and Co., 1946), pp. 273–74. All quotations are from this edition.

9. "The Moral Philosopher and the Moral Life," in William James, *Essays on Faith and Morals*, ed. Ralph Barton Perry (New York: Longmans, Green and Co., 1947), pp. 206, 207, 208.

10. "The Moral Philosopher and the Moral Life," p. 188.

11. "The Moral Philosopher and the Moral Life," p. 205.

12. "The Moral Philosopher and the Moral Life," p. 215.

13. Introduction to Joseph Conrad's *Nostromo* (New York: Modern Library, 1951), p. xxxviii.

14. "Great Men and Their Environment," in *Selected Papers on Philosophy* (London: Everyman's, 1947), pp. 166, 176, 179, 180.

15. *Pragmatism: A New Way for Some Old Ways of Thinking* (New York: Longmans, Green and Co., 1919), p. 269.

16. *Pragmatism*, p. 169.

17. *Pragmatism*, pp. 6, 215.

18. *The Legacy of the Civil War* (New York: Random House, 1961), pp. 19–20.

19. *The Varieties of Religious Experience: A Study in Human Nature* (New York: Longmans, Green and Co., 1928), p. 176.

20. For a psycho-historical analysis of James's identity crisis see Cushing Strout, "William James and the Twice-Born Sick Soul," *Daedalus*, 97 (1968), 1062–82.

21. *The Varieties of Religious Experience*, p. 163.

22. *The Legacy of the Civil War*, pp. 99–100.

23. "The Dilemma of Determinism," *Essays on Faith and Morals*, p. 158.

24. *Pragmatism*, pp. 143–44.

25. "The Dilemma of Determinism," pp. 180–81.

26. *Pragmatism*, pp. 295–96.

27. "Knowledge and the Image of Man," pp. 191–92.

28. *The Thought and Character of William James*, I, 327.

29. William James, *Some Problems in Philosophy* (New York: Longmans, Green and Co., 1911), p. viii.

"The Case of the Vanishing Narratee: An Inquiry into *All the King's Men*"

Simone Vauthier[*]

While the narrator in *All the King's Men* has received much critical attention, his partner in the act of communication has been rather neglected. Yet not only are the two images of narrator and narratee[1] always dependent on each other but in Robert Penn Warren's novel the polarity is all the more marked because, contrary to common usage, the addressee is first to appear on the scene:

> To get there you follow Highway 58, going northeast out of the city, and it is a good highway and new. Or was that day we went up it. You look up the highway and it is straight for miles coming at you, black and slick and tarry-shining against the white of the slab . . . and if you don't quit staring at that line and don't take a few deep breaths and slap yourself hard on the back of the neck you'll hypnotize yourself and you'll come to just at the moment when the right front wheel hooks over into the black dirt shoulder off the slab, and you'll try to jerk her back on but you can't because the slab is high like a curb, . . . But you won't make it, course. . . . Then a few days later the boys from the Highway Department will mark the spot with a little metal square painted white and on it in black a skull and crossbones. . . .
>
> But if you wake up in time and don't hook your wheel off the slab, you'll go whipping on into the dazzle . . . Way off ahead of you, at the horizon where the cottonfields are blurred into the light, the slab will glitter and gleam like water, as though the road were flooded. You'll go whipping toward it, but it will always be ahead of you, that bright, flooded place, like a mirage.[2]

And on for two pages before the narrator-agent makes his appearance. Thus it is the narratee who is first made to take the trip to Mason City, to

[*]Reprinted with permission from the *Southern Literary Journal*, 6, No. 2 (1974), 42–69. Copyright © 1974 by the Department of English, University of North Carolina at Chapel Hill.

see the hypnotic road and the changing countryside, to face destruction or regeneration through baptismal waters that may be only part of a mirage. The narratee is shocked into awareness of a dangerous future in the extradiegetic world. But unwittingly he has been embarked on the perilous journey of the narration. And the man for whom God's mercy is implored at the end of the second paragraph, ("God have mercy on the mariner"), is not simply the man in the car, in "this age of the internal combustion engine," but the man on the road of the narration, the wedding guest suddenly turned mariner, whose precarious voyage through the text this paper proposes to retrace.

The trail of the narratee is not always easy to follow. In the first place the tracks which he leaves in the text are now very broad, now rather faint. Certainly, for long stretches, pronouns may clearly reveal his presence, either the recurrent "you" that proclaims the allocutor, as in the example just quoted, or the occasional "we" that includes the narrator and the receiver as in "we can be quite sure that Hubert had not named the behind guy . . ." (p. 320) or that embraces the interlocutors and the generality of men:

> We get very few of the true images in our heads of the kind I am talking about, the kind which become more and more vivid for us as if the passage of the years did not obscure their reality . . . (p. 118).

Sometimes a change in tenses signals that the orientation of the utterance has changed and become more narrowly focused on the addressee:

> It *was* just the shade of question, of puzzlement.
> But that *is* something. Not much, but something. It is not the left to the jaw and it does not rock them on their heels . . . Nothing lethal, just a moment's pause. But it *is* an advantage. *Push* it (p. 237, italics added).

The passage from narrative to commentary marks the rise of the narratee who is confided in, enlightened, advised, and finally urged to act, with an imperative that introduces him directly in the text. Less obvious still is the network of rhetorical questions that riddles the narration. Sometimes they may be questions which the narrator asks of himself but which might also come from some interlocutor, like the following:

> Judge Irwin had killed Mortimer L. Littlepaugh. But Mortimer had killed Judge Irwin in the end. Or had it been Mortimer? Perhaps I had done it (p. 353).

The narrator may also be challenging his audience: "A clam has to live, hasn't it?" (p. 265) or taunting his self-pitying narratee: "You bloody fool, do you think you want to milk a cow?" (p. 76). Occasionally, however, the narratee puts his oar in:

[Jack Burden] might come out and take a drink or take a hand of cards or do any of the other things they did, but what was real was back in that bedroom on the pine table.

What was back in the bedroom on the pine table?

A large packet of letters, eight tattered black-bound account books tied together with faded red tape, a photograph . . . (p. 160).

Needless to say, the narrator knows what is on the table; only a narratee impatient to be told can ask the question from the narrator, who simply relays it. This device is used repeatedly, often as a transition: *What had I read? I had read this*. . . . Some of the narratee's interrogations are not formulated but are revealed by a reiteration of some words or phrases: "Then all at once something happened, and the yellow taste was in the back of my mouth. This happened" (p. 417). Indeed repetitions—a mannerism of the narrator's style—often convey that an impression has to be made on an addressee:

People still came here for picnics. Well, I had come here for picnics, too. I knew what picnics were like.

I knew what a picnic was, all right (p. 116).

Explanations also imply an allocutor who must be informed as accurately as possible about what is going on in the diegesis[3] (e.g. "the papers—the administration papers, that is") or in the narration ("I am merely pointing that . . ."). Negations that are in fact assertions suggest that he has to be set right, or reassured: "The fabricator had, on this item, allowed himself the luxury of a little extra material. Not too much. But enough" (p. 104). Many sentences begin with an assertive "no," or "yes," or "oh," and numerous phrases—all right, no doubt, as I say, true, well—answer an implicit remark, objection or question of the addressee. In short, clues to the narratee's presence are abundantly scattered throughout the novel.

Yet, pervasive as it is, this presence remains elusive and after a first reading, one has only a blurred image of the narratee, who, on further investigation, turns out to be a many-sided character. For the sake of brevity, only aspects of the narratee as "you" will be examined here, although other elements of the narration—the questions and pseudo-questions, the intimations and assertions, and the many analogies and comparisons that convey something of the allocutor's habits, attitudes and knowledgeability would also yield precious information. Obviously the addressee of the cited speeches (especially that of Willie's incantatory political speeches) would deserve examination; such a study might throw light on the receiver of the narration but cannot be undertaken here.

The identities of the "you" are so many that some attempt at classification must be made. If we consider the relation of the "you" to the diegesis, we have, at one end of the spectrum, a narratee that is extradiegetic. Such is the case of the "you" that brings the addressee close to the reader. For instance after the narration has depicted at some length Sugar Boy driving the Governor's Cadillac, the narrator speculates upon the narratee's reaction: "No doubt, you thought Sugar Boy was a Negro. But he wasn't. He was Irish." Clearly, to entertain such a thought the person addressed must not have been given a sight of Sugar Boy; he is drawing an incorrect conclusion from his name and therefore he must stand in the position which the reader occupies. More obviously still, the person who is concerned by the remark, "Any act of pure perception is a feat, and if you don't believe it, try it sometime" (p. 35), is challenged to accomplish an action in the extradiegetic world, and may be identified provisionally with the (mock) reader, as is the "you" earnestly advised to "burn his home movies" (p. 272). At the other end of the spectrum, the "you" represents diegetic characters. Theodore and Adam are briefly addressed; Lois is saluted: "Goodbye, Lois, and I forgive you for everything I did to you" (p. 308). A longer passage of the narration is donated to Lucy:

> Yes, Lucy, you have to believe that. You have to believe that to live. I know that you must believe that. And I would not have you believe otherwise. It must be that way, and I understand the fact. For you see, Lucy, I must believe that, too (p. 427).

Sometimes the "you" refers to Willie Stark:

> One time I had wondered why the boss never had the house painted after he got his front feet in the trough and a dollar wasn't the reason you got up in the morning any more (p. 22).

Sometimes the "you" is a collective group of anonymous people, like those who send telegrams of condolence to the governor: "You couldn't tell that praying [i.e., getting off the telegram] would do any good, but it certainly never did anybody any harm" (p. 384). A third position of the narratee as regards the diegesis must be briefly mentioned; in Chapter Four, Cass Mastern, being a metadiegetic narrator, can only have metadiegetic narratees.[4] These include an explicit "you," Gilbert, to whom Cass's letters are addressed, and implied narratees, inasmuch as Cass's diary is oriented towards himself ("I write this down" that "if ever pride is in me, of flesh or spirit, I can peruse these pages and know with shame what evil has been in me," [p. 161]) and also towards God, in the light of whom the young man tries to judge his life, and who is once directly addressed, "O God and my Redeemer!" (p. 166).

The appearances of the purely diegetic and extradiegetic narratees are few and far between in comparison with those of yet another category to be studied next. But with the exception of the metadiegetic narratee, restricted to the confines of Chapter Four, they are distributed fairly regularly throughout the novel. And significantly the appeal to a diegetic "you" that is at once most developed in terms of the utterance and most significant in terms of the theme, namely that to Lucy, is placed towards the end. Worthy of notice, too, a "you" is made to represent Willie only in the chapters describing his early career. Although *comparatively* little represented, these categories are important insofar as they project a full range of positions and by setting up a number of secondary narratees, to whom the narration is only addressed occasionally, increase the complexity of the "implied dialogue" which, as Wayne Booth has observed, goes on among author, narrator, the other characters, the reader, and it must be added, the narratees.[5]

Furthermore, since, as narrator-participant the "I" has a dual nature, so has the narratee; the duality is evidenced in the report of Willie's rhetorical power over listening crowds: "I would wait for the roar. You *can't help it*. I knew it would come, but I would wait for it" (p. 146, italics added). In this case the "you" includes both a diegetic character—the experiencing self—and an extradiegetic person—the narrating self[6] distancing himself from Jack Burden the participant—plus an undetermined someone, also extradiegetic—any man in the same kind of situation. Or take the passage, too long to be quoted here, when Jack muses on "the Friend of Your Youth [who] is the only friend you will ever have, for he does not see you" (p. 234). The "you" designates again an undetermined man, who can bear any name, "Spike, Bud, Snip, Red, Rusty, Jack, Dave,"[7] exemplifying a common human experience. But the "you" addressed at the end of the meditation is so close to the experiencing self that he is then called Jack: The Friend of Your Youth "speaks your name . . . saying, 'Well, Jack, damned glad you came, come on in, boy!' " (p. 235). The time flow of the narrative was interrupted, as Adam Stanton came to the door to greet Jack, for a disquisition on "The Friend of Your Youth"; we then are smoothly let back into the narrative by the reduction of the "you" to one of its components, the narrator, who now hears the words his friend has been speaking. Moreover many occurrences of the second-person belong to the level of the enunciation rather than to that of the diegesis, introduced as they are in the images brought up by the locutor (e.g., "[I could] let all the pictures of things a man might want run through my head . . . and let them all slide off, like a deck of cards slewing slowly off your hand. Maybe the things you want are like cards" (p. 99).

Confronted therefore with a multiplicity of "you's" the reader finds himself trying to assess the referential extension of specific instances, wondering how big or limited is such and such a "you." In some cases, the second-person is, so to say, all-inclusive:

> After a great blow, or crisis, after the first shock and then after
> the nerves have stopped screaming and twitching, you settle
> down to the new condition of things . . . (p. 355).

This we may call, in parody of Jack Burden, The Aphoristic You. (Of course, the Aphoristic You can only embody the wisdom of mankind as filtered through the unconscious assumptions of the narrator.) A more limited but still fairly extensive "you" is the Mythical American:

> For that is where you come, after you have crossed oceans and eaten stale biscuits while prisoned forty days and nights in a stormy-tossed rat-trap, after you have sweated in the greenery and heard the savage whoop, after you have built cabins and cities and bridged rivers, after you have lain with women and scattered children like millet seed in a high wind, after you have composed resonant documents, made noble speeches, and bathed your arms in blood to the elbows, after you have shaken with malaria in the marshes and in the icy wind across the high plains. This is where you come to lie alone in a bed in a hotel room in Long Beach, California. Where I lay . . . (p. 309).

We have here the Archetypical American Hero, already described though less ambiguously, by Tocqueville,[8] and epitomizing American history. In another version, the historical archetype is resolved into distinct roles—murderer, gold-rusher, Greeley's young man, etc.—which reveal more clearly the American nightmare along with the American dream.

> For West is where we all plan to go some day. It is where you go when the land gives out and the oldfield pines encroach. It is where you go when you get the letter saying: *Flee, all is discovered*. It is where you go when you look down at the blade in your hand and see the blood on it. It is where you go when you are told that you are a bubble on the tide of empire. It is where you go when you hear that there's gold in them-thar hills. It is where you go to grow up with the country. It is where you go to spend your old age. Or it is just where you go (p. 270).

The Mythical American is easily reduced into the Average American: "When you don't like it where you are, you always go west" (p. 309). Indeed the Average American and his experiences are often invoked. On occasion he is even provided with a family:

> It was like a showing of a family movie, the kind the advertisements tell you to keep so you will have a record of the day Susie took her first little toddle and the day Johnny went off to kindergarten and the day you went up Pike's Peak and the day of the picnic on the old home farm and the day you were made chief sales manager and bought your first Buick (p. 272).

Little Susie reappears at least twice as the average child of the Average American, *you*. Occasionally, the Average American turns Southerner: "You don't get rich being an Attorney General in a Southern State" (p. 219). Clearly determined by the narrative situation is the case of the Attentive Observer, who has the opportunity to watch the characters in action, although sometimes the observer is only the Virtual Observer: "the atmosphere would have reminded you of a morgue" (p. 367). Determined and yet indefinite is the Equivocal Participant, the "you" that "represents" both a diegetic character and an allocutor *persona*, singular or plural:

> The gentlemen from the city persuaded Willie that he was the savior of the state. I suppose that Willie had his natural quota of ordinary suspicion and cageyness, but those things tend to evaporate when what people tell you is what you want to hear (p. 66).

A particular variety of the Equivocal Participant, the Disguised Narrator, is a recurrent figure: the above-mentioned passage on the Friend of Your Youth furnishes a typical example. Hesitation as to the identity of the Disguised Narrator is possible because somehow our expectancy is not answered. For instance we naturally expect the "you" in the following sentence to encompass the allocutor:

> For after the dream there is no reason why you should not go back and face the fact which you have fled from (even if the fact seems to be that you have, by digging up the truth about the past, handed over Anne Stanton to Willie Stark), for any place to which you may flee will not be like the place from which you have fled, and you might as well go back, after all, to the place where you belong, for nothing was your fault or anybody's fault, for things are always as they are (p. 311).

But although in the main sentence the second-person generalizes and covers a multitude of experiences, on which the immediate context and the many allusions to the myth of the West throw light, we realize with something of a jolt that the "you" in the parenthesis can only refer to Jack Burden, since he alone can have done the particular action mentioned. Then the other "you's" of the passage are felt as representing the narrator.

But such examples also provide us with a clue to the functioning of the second-person. Often it is made to stand for the first-person in a figure that can be called *speaker/addressee (destinateur/destinataire) commutation.*[9] In *All the King's Men* commutation of the interlocutors is a systematic device which deserves closer scrutiny.

Destinateur/destinataire commutation is by far the most frequent. Avowedly the story of Willie's rise from "Cousin Willie" to Governor Stark, the narration is therefore apparently oriented towards outsiders who have some knowledge of the Boss's career, without being in possession of all the facts and, above all, of the meaning of them. But even before the narrator discloses personal information about himself, long before he owns that this "is [his] story, too," Jack Burden betrays the autobiographic nature of his narrative when he makes the "you" a reflection of his self, and the outside allocutor an inner auditor. (Amusingly enough, this is symbolized in one minor detail: when Willie exerts his oratorical spell on the Mason City crowd, "you could hear one insane and irrelevant July fly sawing away up in one of the catalpa trees . . ." (p. 9). If here the "you" can represent the anonymous listeners, in the following repetition of the notation, the "you" can no longer do so and the present tense underlines that the sensation is one of the narrator's: "there was only the sound of the July flies, which *seems* to be inside your head as though it were the grind and whir of the springs and cogs which are you . . ." (p. 11).

But when the narrator declares "I have a story. It is the story of a man who lived in the world and the world looked one way for a long time . . ." and then goes on to summarize his evolution in third-person terms for three paragraphs (pp. 435–36), he uses a *terminal/non-terminal commutation* to put some distance between his past self and the regenerated self, which, however, is grammatically and dramatically reborn at the end of the last paragraph: "It looks as though Hugh will get back into politics and when he does I'll be along to hold his coat." And reborn, too, complete with a past still active in the present as indicated by the tense: "*I've had* some valuable experience in that line" (p. 436, italics added). Seeing Willie for the first time, Jack Burden is, unknowingly, meeting fate, so this is how the narrator reports the occasion:

> Metaphysically it was the Boss, but how was I to know? Fate comes walking through the door and it is five feet eleven inches tall and heavyish in the chest and shortish in the leg and is wearing a seven-fifty seersucker suit . . . and a stiff high collar like a Sunday-school superintendent and a blue-striped tie which you know his wife gave him last Christmas and which he has kept in tissue paper with the holly card ("Merry Christmas to my Darling Willie from your Loving Wife") until he got ready to go to the city, and a gray felt hat with the sweat stains showing through the band. It comes in just like that and how are you to know? It comes in, trailing behind Alex Michel (p. 14).

In the whole paragraph, Willie is referred to by an a-personal pronoun, except in the relative clause which deals with his personal life, symbolized by the Christmas *tie* and represented by a new correlation *my-your*, where, incidentally, one expects *his*. However, when after the introduction of Willie as husband the narration returns to Willie as the embodiment of Fate, not only is the a-personal "it" resumed, for an effect which is now more marked than in the first occurence from being pointedly repeated; but with the repetition of the transformed question and the use of "you," (how are you to know?), both narrator and narratee are made responsible for the *person/non-person commutation*, which betrays their common unawareness of Willie's potentialities and of the mysterious ways of fate. *Definite/indefinite commutations* are also to be found (e.g. "*They* called that Idealism in *my* book I had when I was in college" p. 30, italics added). But since such turns are common enough in everyday speech they need not be emphasized. An arresting sentence may be mentioned here:

> In a hanging you do not change a man's personality. You just change the length of his neck and give him a quizzical expression, and in an electrocution you just cook some bouncing meat in a wholesale lot (p. 317).

One would rather expect something like: a man's personality is not changed, and only the length of his neck is changed, clauses that would leave the responsibility for these drastic measures unassigned, whereas the "you" involves the allocutor in the executioner's role or in society's meting out of punishment.

Apart from commutations—the substitution of one person (or non-person) for another on the paradigmatic axis of the narration—permutations—a substitution on the syntagmatic axis—also play a prominent part in *All the King's Men*. In Chapter Four, the narrating self assumes toward a period of his own life, with a measure of self-parody, the detached stance which the acting self took as history graduate toward Cass Mastern, the object of his research.[10] The first-person narrator then turns into a third-person character, "Jack Burden" and "he," while Cass, a third-person in the diegetic narration, now becomes a speaking "I," whose letters and journal are abundantly cited. As a consequence of this permutation, the "you" of the overall narrative situation can become a "we."

> [The journal] did not report what book it was that Gilbert's riding crop tapped. It is not important what book it was. Or perhaps it is important, for something in *our* mind, in *our* imagination wants to know that fact. *We see* the red, square, strong hand ("my brother is strong-made and florid") protruding from the white cuff, grasping the crop which in that grasp looks fragile like a twig. *We see* the flick of the little leather loop on the page, a flick brisk, not quite contemptuous, but *we cannot* make out the page (p. 164, italics added).

Here the first-person plural, while it excludes the first person singular subject of the embedded utterance, includes four kinds of participants in the act of communication—the implied author whose fairly discrete presence in the sequence is here made manifest, "Jack Burden," the narratee(s), and the reader; all four stand on almost equal footing in respect to the fact under scrutiny since to all of them (or us) it is something out of the past, fictive or real, which has to be deciphered. Obviously the "I" of the diegetic story can never say "we," meaning himself and his narratee and/or reader, when he tells or ponders about acts of his own life, but only when he speculates or moralizes on the human condition. (And as a matter of fact there are a few such cases of a universal "we.") He could, of course, write: "We wonder what books Cousin Willie read in the lonely, cold upstairs room." But this would shape a different relation between narrator and narratee from that which is firmly established from the opening sentence of the novel and the narrator never uses the first-person plural to puzzle out the enigma that is Willie Stark.

Commutations and permutations, as might be expected, often interact, creating complex moves across the narrational chessboard.

> (1) At night you pass through a little town where you once lived, and you expect to see yourself wearing knee pants, standing all alone on the street corner under the hanging bulbs. . . . (2) You expect to see that boy standing there under the street lamp, out too late, and you feel like telling him to go to bed or there will be hell to pay. (3) But maybe you are at home in bed and sound asleep and not dreaming and nothing has ever happened that seems to have happened. (4) But, then, who the hell is this in the back seat of the big black Cadillac that comes ghosting through the town? (5) Why, this is Jack Burden. Don't you remember little Jack Burden? He used to go out in his boat in the afternoon on the bay to fish, and come home and eat his supper and kiss his beautiful mother good-night and say his prayers and go to bed at nine-thirty. (6) Oh, you mean old Ellis Burden's boy? (7) Yeah, and that woman he married out of Texas—or was it Arkansas?—that big-eyed, thin-faced woman who lives up there in that old Burden place now with that man she got herself. Whatever happened to Ellis Burden? Hell, I don't know, nobody around here had any word going on years. He was a queer 'un. Damn if he wasn't queer, going off and leaving a real looker like that woman out of Arkansas. Maybe he couldn't give her what she craved. Well, he gave her that boy, that Jack Burden. Yeah.
>
> You come into town at night and there are the voices (pp. 40–1).

In the first sentence, we may take the "you" to be the narratee (n) and a projection of the narrator (N) who has just been telling about such a ride to Burden's Landing; "yourself wearing knee pants" is a reduction in time of N + n, a past self of both narrator and narratee. But this past self takes on an independent life and becomes a third person, *that boy, he*, in sentence (2). The "you" of sentence (3) seems to be N + n again, with the difference, however, that n seems to have dwindled in size: the first narratee could be almost any reader of the male sex with a smalltown background; whereas now the possibility that the narratee could also be the reader is more radically excluded since n is perhaps asleep—which the reader of *All the King's Men* cannot be, of course. With the question of sentence (4) a *voice* is heard, which, as the answer makes clear, implies a speaking "I." However, this "I" cannot be the first-person narrator since *he* is now ensconced in the text as the referent of the query, the man in the back seat of the Cadillac. The voice can only be the voice of n. Nor is the transformation of N + n complete inasmuch as n further splits into two dialoguing characters, one who recognizes "little Jack Burden" (n_1) and one (n_2) who has to be reminded of the identity (through blood kin, a misleading index) of Jack Burden. By now neither can be considered indefinite, extradiegetic addressees. Absorbed into the story, they also become active participants in the narration as they take over the narrating role, providing the reader with new information on Jack Burden's background. The permutation is complete when the knowledgeable n_1 uses the first person "Hell, *I* don't know." Yet this is an empty "I," whose outlines will never be filled and whose sole function is to displace the narrating self, who could have given us this kind of information, and thus modify the addressee, an effect which is enhanced by the fact that the typography—the absence of commas, the juxtaposition of question and answer—makes it impossible at the end of the dialogue to discriminate with certainty between the two interlocutors.

Another interesting transformation of the "you" can be observed in the following passage.

> (1) Which is nonsense, for whatever you live is Life. (2) That is something to remember when you meet the old classmate who says, "Well, now, on our last expedition up the Congo—" or the one who says, "Gee, I got the sweetest little wife and three of the swellest kids ever—" (3) You must remember it when you sit in hotel lobbies, or lean over bars to talk to the bartender, or stand in a dark street at night, in early March, and stare into a lighted window. (4) And remember little Susie in there has adenoids and the bread is probably burned, and turn up the street, for the time has come to hand me down that walking cane, for I got to catch that midnight train, for all my sin is taken away. For whatever you live is Life (pp. 239–40).

After comprehending N + n + n + n . . . in sentence (1), the extension of "you" progressively diminishes until in the last part of sentence (3) it coincides with N, the narrator who happened to be staring into a lighted window on an early March night when he went into this philosophical mood. Yet with sentence (4) and the imperative *remember*, which modulates the earlier *it is something to remember*, followed by *you must remember*, the "you" designates a definite singular n; only, in this case, the narratee is revealed as an alter ego of the narrator, who then reappears as "me" and then "I." But, although defined through grammatical marks and through the situation (Jack Burden in on his way to catch the night train to Memphis and to uncover Judge Irwin's guilty secret), the "I" is in fact more—therefore less—than Jack Burden's self: it is the indefinite "I" of the popular song, the blues and the spiritual, as phrasing and rhythm connote, so that it can easily become again the generalizing, aphoristic "you" at the end of the paragraph: Whatever you/one/man live[s] is Life. In short, the narratee is a Protean figure who alternately dilates and contracts and keeps changing positions in the narration, with the result that the distance separating it from the other figures increases or decreases accordingly, and the pattern of relationships between them shifts like a kaleidoscope.

Throughout all this, the characteristic feature of the narratee is his dependence on the narrator. Even at the farthest distance—as fictive reader—the "you" is dependent for his very existence on the "I" that projects him as an image of the Other. And this Other, notwithstanding his more checquered career (as outlaw or family man, for instance) is not very different from the experiencing self. The composite narratee has participated in some of Jack's experiences, been subjected to the fascination of Willie, seen Anne Stanton as a young girl, taken the meaningful trip to the West, and has had, in a word, an American education. Although he may be unaware of certain aspects of the South, since things have to be described to him, he is still very familiar with Southern life as many analogies show, and he knows for example what it feels like to have "a sizable chunk of dry cornpone stuck in [his] throat." A man of culture, he can pick up allusions to Prometheus (p. 394) or echoes of Poe in the wind that "didn't chill us or kill us in the kingdom by the sea" (p. 103). More significantly, the narratee has Jack Burden's inquisitive mind—witness all the passages developed through questions—and he shares in his basic assumptions on life as evinced in the many generalizations. Thus he reveals Jack's need to extract private meaning out of public events and to socialize personal meaning in a dialectic process. (To this extent, the frequent use and the nature of the adjunctive "you"[11] partly reflects and shapes Jack's attempts to "re-establish his values within a different social framework" from that of Burden's Landing.[12]) Even in his talents as a quick-change artist, the addressee mirrors the narrator, a self-confessed *Svengali*. Thus in his choice of narratees, Jack Burden betrays both his anxiety at being limited, defined, limited *because* defined, and his desire for self-definition.

For to turn to the Other is to meet the Self, but to face the Self is to encounter the Other. *Je est un autre*. And in *All the King's Men*, the "you" is an *alter* ego—not a past vanished self, however, to whom the narrator would talk across the gap of years, in the typical autobiographical stance. (Needless to say there is such a distance in time and identity between the narrating and the acting selves, but it is marked through a number of elements, temporal adverbs, tenses, whole comments [*that was what I thought I had learned*] and an episodic use of the third-person, etc.—which cannot be studied here.) On the contrary, the "you" would seem to speak for a "not-dead" self since he relives in an intemporal, almost dream-like present some of the experiences of Jack.

> But as the train pulls away, a woman comes to the back door of one of the houses—just the figure of a woman for you cannot

make out the face . . . She goes back into the house. To what is in the house . . . but you cannot see through the walls to the secret to which the woman has gone in.

The train pulls away, faster now and the woman is back in the house where she is going to stay. She'll stay there. And all at once, you think you are the one who is running away and who had better run fast to wherever you are going for it will be dark soon. . . .

But nothing happens, and you remember that the woman had not even looked up at the train. You forget her, and the train goes fast, and is going fast when it crosses a little trestle . . . [You] see the cow standing in the water upstream near the single leaning willow. And all at once you feel like crying. But the train is going fast, and almost whatever you feel is taken away from you, too.

You bloody fool, do you think that you want to milk a cow?

You do not want to milk a cow.

Then you are at Upton (p. 76).

Against the increasing speed of the train, (although it moves through "cloying," "syrup"-like air), is balanced the stagnancy of the "you," the self becalmed in the treacly waters of an eternal present, unable to detach himself from the images and feelings which Jack believes have been taken away from him but which "stay there" forever.[13] And surely, the woman appearing only to disappear, going back to her secret behind the walls, and even the cow with her milk now forever unavailable remain there in the narrator's *speech* because their verbal evocation reanimates older images, older feelings—the longing for a mother's love, the desire to know the secret behind the parents' door. (This is, however, a privileged example, insofar as the metonymical chain of desire is short and the repressed material can be perceived through the actual iamges.) But it would be absurd to say that the disjunctive "you" is Jack Burden's unconscious self. Rather when he addresses this "you," the narrator projects a split state of consciousness. Nor can this "you" be called Jack's "bad" self, for he is as guilty as but no guiltier than the "I." In fact, he is a *double* whose *raison d'être* seems to be his non-subjectivity. Jack Burden suffers from a sense of unreality which makes him see others as unreal too: "Oh, they are real, all right, and it may be the reason they don't seem real to you is that you aren't very real yourself" (p. 58). Unable to see himself clearly, he posits in the disjunctive "you" the double that embodies him, that makes *him* visible because *he* can address it. *Percipi est esse*, and to speak is to make oneself perceived.

Therefore, if the polarity of "you" and "I" points to the disassociation of Jack Burden's personality, what can hold Jack-as-Humpty-Dumpty together is precisely the hyphen of the interlocutory act. Furthermore the disjunctive "you" performs its part in the act so satisfactorily that it is

truly a "didactic you." By in fact telling parts of his story—the trip to
Mason City, the trip to Burden's Landing, the trip to Upton, in particular—through a second-person, the first-person narrator shows that he
is not yet fully aware of all the aspects of his own life or is at any rate
reluctant to face them. The "you" which conveniently separates and
distances experience also clarifies it, and assumes the function which
Michel Butor assigns to the second-person, making "a progress in self-
consciousness, the very birth of language, or of *a* language."[14] Indirect
confirmation can be found in the Cass Mastern episode. Cass, who is convinced of his personal guilt and can explain his sinfulness in theological
terms, simply records his testimony through a straight-forward first-
person narration, although he is aware that his present "I" is different
from his past "I." So "you" is a form of address which, with but one exception (p. 175), he reserves for a "real" allocutor and whenever he wants
to generalize he uses a-personal forms (such as *it is dishonorable to spy
upon another*) or the indefinite *man* (*Man is never safe*) and "one" (*One
can only know oneself in God*, p. 173). Direct confirmation is brought by
the gradual disappearance of the disjunctive "you" in Jack Burden's
speech. Already the last chapter contains noticeably fewer occurrences
and there are none after the visit to Lucy, which marks a high point in
Jack's acceptance of Willie Stark and of himself.

From the beginning, in any case, balancing the egocentrism and
disintegration of a self refracted in a multiplicity of "you's" there is the
structure that both shapes and expresses the relation of Jack to the world.
Despite all temptations to disengage himself, to retreat to the solitude of
the anonymous room in Long Beach or, more drastically, into the Great
Sleep, Jack also needs to establish relationships with an other. Thus, in his
relation, discourse, "a statement presupposing a locutor and an auditor,
and in the first named an intention of influencing the second in some
way" predominates over a "récit," a "narrative of past events."[15]
Although passages from the former type of utterance to the latter and
back are frequent, *All the King's Men* is overwhelmingly a discourse.
Consequently, it is difficult to agree entirely with Franz Stanzel's statement that

> the first-person narrator's eccentric position is the reason why
> long stretches of the novel contain no real first-person
> references. . . . From a given page of such a section it is often
> impossible to decide whether the work is a first-person novel or
> a third-person novel.[16]

Although the narrator may not be present, he is represented in the text
often through his faithful companion, the narratee. See, for instance, the
many signs of the latter in the description of Willie's early career, which
the narrator reconstructs. The permanence of the addressee, whether the
disjunctive "you," the adjunctive "you," or the truly non-subjective per-

son, testifies to the protagonist's deep need for relatedness. Besides, the narratee does not usually condescend to his allocutor, although he may be something of an authoritarian, enjoining behavior (*you ride*) or ideas (*you think*). On occasion too he may give him a piece of advice: "If you ask something quick and sharp out of a clear sky you may get an answer you never would get otherwise" (p. 207). But insofar as the narratee is often made, through comments and analogies, to carry part of the ideological burden of the novel, his experience is necessarily considered to be as valid as that of the narrator.

This points to another of the many functions of the narratee. He does not simply contribute to the characterization of the narrator but plays a part in the elaboration of the ideas and themes of the novel. In the generalizations and similes, the adjunctive "you" provides the clarifying parallel and guarantees the general application of whatever Jack may feel or think. Making the story more natural, the narratee also makes its ideological message more acceptable, because apparently accepted within the textual dialogue. To him, indeed, is delegated one of the functions which Robert Penn Warren assigned to his narrator, that of chorus,[17] for which it is better suited than Jack Burden, being collective, anonymous, and already aware of the public aspects of the drama whose hidden patterns Burden is seeking to trace out. Because it is changeable and unobtrusive, this chorus does not harden temporary half-truths into eternal verities, thus preserving the dialectic complexity of the novel. Because it is undefined, it can enhance both the American dimension of the action and the "tragedy of incomplete personalities"—which, beyond the Southern or American affabulation, is the real theme of the work.[18]

The relation of narratee and theme is even more interesting. For one thing, if in *All the King's Men*, "a plurality of heroes is one symbol of a riven world,"[19] so is a multiplicity of narratees a further symbol of a riven self in a riven world, as the contrast between Jack Burden's narration and Cass Mastern's emphasizes. Yet regeneration, rebirth, in other words a newer integration, remains possible, partly because through language can be discovered anew the "complicity of relatedness." Moreover, although identity, contrary to what some of the characters may believe, is not fixed and unchanging, man is nonetheless responsible for his actions—a lesson for which Jack pays with "blood." While the Protean "you" becomes the mask of an uncertain, shifting self, the pronominal permanence of the "I"—despite a few eclipses—asserts the continuity of moral responsibility, notwithstanding. Conversely the persistence of the "you's" in the part of the narration concerned with the *discovery* of meaning affirms again that self-realization depends on the realization of the Other. Thus the autobiographical narration can be both the recognition and the acting-out of man's accountability.

If we go into the functioning of the text, the complex moves of the interlocutors, the permutations and commutations mirror the central metaphor of the novel, the image of the web. Just as "the world is all of one piece," so is speech: if you touch the "web of things" and the web of words—"however lightly, at any point," "the vibrations ripple to the remotest perimeter" (p. 188). With every change of addressee, the narrator sends ripples that modify not only the arrangement of the verbal parts of his utterance but his relations to the allocutor, to the message and hence to the world. These substitutions also undercut the antimony of the "I" and the "you," the ego and the non-ego, the self and the world, which are then seen to be dialectically generating one another. "Direction is all."

In addition, the chess-like moves of the interlocutory figures may also serve to modalize the narrator's conscious attitudes. Alone in his car, Jack finds comfort in a sense of depersonalization:

> They say you are not you, except in terms of relation to other people. If there weren't any other people there wouldn't be any you because what you do, which is what you are, only has meaning in relation to other people. That is a very comforting thought when you are in the car in the rain at night alone, for then you aren't you, and not being you or anything, you can really lie back and get some rest. It is a vacation from being you . . . (p. 128).

By the use of the introductory "*they say*," and of the conditional tense, as well as by the flippancy of his tone in the rest of the passage, Burden seems to discount the theory even as he expounds it—a characteristic stance of Jack, who likes to have his cake and eat it. But the text yet hints at a different story. The "I" installs an insistent "you" in place of itself, thus suggesting inter-subjectivity and the inversibility of "I" and "you." This seemingly bears out the idea that you are not you except in the presence of people. At the same time, it suggests that the idea is acceptable only at a certain level. Even in solitude the "I" can posit a "you" to relate to, in the socialized structure of language. Jack Burden, indeed, manipulates language so resourcefully that he convinces us that man, the speaking animal, can never be really alone: language provides him with a built-in allocutor.

No wonder then that the relationship of narrator and narratee shapes the process of self-knowledge which is the protagonist's central experience. At the beginning of his narration which not only tells about but mirrors his quest, Jack Burden who has little sense of identity, confronts himself with a series of narratees, who, whether imaginary or "real," represent faces of the self he is looking for. He commits what Cass Mastern, who lived in a world where men were more complete, less scattered and could relate more easily to a transcendence, considers a human error, the error of trying "to know oneself by the self of another" instead of in "God's eye" (p. 173). In "the age of the internal combustion engine," however, it would seem to be a less a defect than a normal pattern of behavior. And the protagonist achieves maturity through what Robert Penn Warren calls elsewhere an "osmosis of being which in the end does not deny, but affirms his identity."[20] With its use of narratees, its permutations and commutations, its disjunctive and adjunctive "you's" that overlap and may fade out into one another, the narration embodies the process of interpenetration[21] and of readjustment of perspectives. Through the shifting patterns of relations, "new perspectives" and "new values" are being created and Jack comes to discover his kinship with other men, i.e. his participation in human guilt at the same time as he realizes his unavoidable isolation. Hence, as has been pointed out, the need for the disjunctive "you" reflecting the split self and for the adjunctive "you" mirroring the defining Other diminishes.

As Jack's quest for identity passes through tentative and incomplete identifications with father figures that he in a sense kills, for "the truth always kills the father," so does his struggle for integration pass through incomplete cleavage of the self, for "separateness is identity." And he can get rid of the obsessive inner narratee when, having been reborn, he is at last able to tell his version of the "family romance" to Anne Stanton: "I had to tell it to somebody," he says to Anne, "I had to say it out loud—to be sure it's true [that he is changed]. But it is true. . . . It's my mother, you know" (p. 435). Jack can now tell the significant encounter with his mother and the return to Anne without any mediation. Similarly, the next-to-last generalization of the novel is one that stresses no longer the interrelatedness of the subjective to the non-subjective but the relation between the one and the many, the individual and mankind. "For *each of us* is the son of a million fathers." No doubt as he goes out into "the convulsion of the world," Jack Burden will be involved in new patterns of relationships. No doubt the self-knowledge he has acquired is incomplete but he has achieved an awareness that enables him to stand alone and yet say "we," whether the "we" includes only his wife, or all of us, the children of a million fathers. Having told his story the narrator can make a *new* beginning and, turning historian, write the formerly abandoned life of Cass Mastern whom he "now may come to understand." And in the Life, *récit* ought to prevail over discourse, narrative over narration, in conformity with a scholarly code that Burden can now accept because he has found his true language.

In short, the narratee has become expendable. And his fate also concerns the reader. True, reader and narratee are not to be confused. But by the same polarity that creates the dependence of the narrative "you" and the narrative "I," the reversibility of "you" and "I" works not only within the story-telling situation but, to some degree, within the reading situation. I, the reader, cannot help feeling somehow implied in the "you" that is being addressed so insistently, even as I realize that this is a doubly fictive you with a fictive experience which may be quite remote from mine.

The brilliant introduction that whizzes the narratee over the road to Mason City and the "great mirage" of the meaning of the novel may help set up the reader's partial identification with the narratee before he has had the opportunity to begin establishing the more usual identification with the protagonist and perhaps it brings him thus closer to the authorial *persona*. In any case, the reader is perforce implicated in the experience of the narratee, if only to the extent that he has to strip off his masks, and keep track of who and where he is. Thus the transformations of the narratee upset the reader's facile certainties and engage him in a quest of his own which parallels that of the narrator. Should he refuse to identify provisionally with the protagonist and to share in his burden of human guilt, he is jolted into awareness of his guilt as virtual narratee, whether the latter is cast in the role of conventional brigand or less conventional executioner. *L'hypocrite lecteur, mon semblable, mon frère* must acknowledge himself an accomplice of either the acting self, or the narrator, or the narratee—if not of all three of them. But he is thereby offered the chance—together with the advice—to "be baptized to be born again," too. Redemption is available to every reader willing to change, to "burn his home movies," to accept his commitment as reader and play the metonymic and metaphoric game of the novel.

Yet woe to the unwary reader who has accepted in good faith the role of next-of-kin to the narratee. When the regenerated "I" throws overboard the now useless "you," he may feel like a castaway, may at least experience a sense of depletion.[22] Having been allowed the freedom of many squares across the board, he now discovers that his moves are severely restricted, and few positions open to him from which to view the narrator's "picture of the world." But he had had his warning in the introduction with its recurrent images of car-wrecks and the perils of water. So he too is, in a sense, back at the beginning, as Jack Burden is back at his dissertation grappling with the task of understanding Cass Mastern and relating his story. The task for the reader is to start assessing anew the characters' half-truths (Cass Mastern's and Willie Stark's and Jack Burden's) in the light of the whole truth. But the whole truth, of course, can, in this case, only be that embodied in the novel, a "myth" of "human nature's trying to fulfill itself,"[23] Humpty-Dumpty poised back on his wall by the grace of *All the King's Men*. To that extent too, it is a form in which the reader collaborates in the dialectical process of reading, and for which he must therefore assume some responsibility. God have mercy on all reading mariners.

Notes

1. I am indebted for this term to Gerald Prince whose two seminal articles ("Notes Towards a Categorization of Fictional 'Narratees,' " *Genre*, 4 [1971], 100–05, and "Introduction à l'étude du narrataire," *Poétique*, 14 [1973], 178–96) greatly helped me to categorize and define my interpretation of the allocutor in *All the King's Men*.

2. Robert Penn Warren, *All the King's Men* (New York: Bantam Books, 1955), p. 1. Page references are to this edition.

3. These are in a somewhat simplified version the concepts established by Gérard Genette in *Figures II* (Paris, 1972), p. 202, and *Figures III* (Paris: Editions du Seuil, 1972), pp. 72, 238, 241 *et passim*. Diegetic is what belongs or refers to the time-space of a story within a story (the metadiegesis). Let us add that, for simplification's sake, we have said that the "I" *refers* to or *represents* Jack Burden, while the "I" can refer only to the individual speech act in which it is uttered, designating the locutor—as "you" only designates the allocutor.

4. Gérard Genette, one of the first critics to have paid any attention to the narratee, writes: "Comme le narrateur, le narrataire est un des éléments de la situation narrative et il se place nécessairement an même niveau diégétique" (*Figures III*, p. 265).

5. Wayne C. Booth, *The Rhetoric of Fiction* (Chicago: Univ. of Chicago Press, 1961), p. 155. Not only breadth but depth of communication is thus achieved, as a simple example will illustrate:

> It was, in a sense, proper that Cass Mastern—in the gray jacket, sweat-stiffened and prickly like a hair shirt, which it was for him at the same time that it was the insignia of a bedgrudged glory—should have gone back to Georgia to rot slowly to death. For he had been born in Georgia, he and Gilbert Mastern and Lavinia Mastern, in the red hills up toward Tennessee. "I was born," the first page of the first volume of the journal said, "in a log cabin in north Georgia, in circumstances of poverty . . ." (p. 161).

Here the implied narrator, who is a *persona* of the extradiegetic narrator, the "I," who has been telling the story so far, comments on the destiny of Cass (it was *proper*) for the benefit of a narratee. What with the anaphoric "he," the string of names, the redundancy of the Mastern surname, the phrasing (in *the* red hills *up toward* Tennessee) and the rhythm of the explanation, the illusion of a voice is created, thus emphasizing the encounter between locutor and allocutor. But when the narrator quotes Cass's journal, he does not simply substantiate his own statement. In the quotation, not only is a different locutor speaking but a different allocutor is addressed. So, redundant as the information on Cass's birthplace really is, it is not received at the same level and the reader, who is in a sense the ultimate addressee, must himself assume different roles at different levels and shift positions.

6. Franz Stanzel has made use of these two concepts in his analysis of *All the King's Men*. *Narrative Situations in the Novel: Tom Jones, Moby-Dick, The Ambassadors, Ulysses* (Bloomington: Indiana Univ. Press, 1971), pp. 63–64.

7. Since Robert Penn Warren is known to his friends as "Red," one may wonder if this is not a secret signature, a tiny image of the author hiding in the crowded canvas of the novel, like a medieval painter's self-portrait. More, it might suggest that one of Jack's names is RPW; but on the testimony of this same passage the RPW *persona* is to be sought behind the masks of the narratees as well as behind that of the narrator.

8. "Le peuple américain se voit marcher lui-même à travers ces déserts, desséchant les marais, redressant les fleuves, peuplant la solitude et domptant la nature. Cette image magnifique d'eux-mêmes ne s'offre pas seulement de loin en loin à l'imagination des Américains, etc." ("Sources de poésie," *De la démocratie en Amérique* [Paris: Gallimard, 1961], I, 79).

9. The following categorization of commutations is that of J. Dubois *et al.* in *Rhétorique Générale* (Paris: Larousse, 1970), pp. 159–70.

10. The reasons for the change of reference may be more complex than suggested above. But Franz Stanzel's explanation seems, in any case, inadequate: "the author was evidently faced with the problem of avoiding any confusion which might arise between the two first-person narrators while at the same time preserving the sense of immediacy in the content of the journal. His solution was to transform the original 'I' of the main narrator into an objectified third-person novel figure and retain the first-person narrative situation of the journal"

(p. 63). The interpretation disregards in particular the resort by the first-person to a terminal/non-terminal, subjective/non-subjective commutation in scattered parts of the novel. See pp. 40, 103, 309, 311, 323, for instance.

11. We shall call disjunctive the "you" that represents a fragment of the self and adjunctive the "you" that subsumes a plural experience, in which the "I" can be included.

12. Louis D. Rubin, Jr., *The Faraway Country: Writers of the Modern South* (Seattle: Univ. of Washington Press, 1970), p. 125.

13. Although time seems to freeze, this is not "a moment of frozen action," such as Robert Penn Warren observed in Faulkner's fiction ("The Art of Fiction XVIII: Robert Penn Warren," *The Paris Review*, reprinted in John L. Longley, Jr., ed., *Robert Penn Warren: A Collection of Critical Essays* [New York: New York Univ. Press, 1965], p. 33). There is, in fact, continuous movement in the diegesis. And if the distance between narrative time and fictional time seems to decrease, it is not because, as happens in the last section of the novel, they have come to coincide. Narrating time dominates narrated temporality and almost conjures it away. Nor is the moment a suspended *memory of the narrator*, insofar as the experience is ascribed to a "you" which only exists in the present utterance of the "I." The "I" does not describe a recollection, he names—i.e. creates—the experience for the "you" as he goes on speaking: "you cannot make out," "you cannot see," "you think," "you remember," "you forget." Far from constituting a moment of frozen time, the passage exemplifies a "continuous creation."

14. "Si le personnage connaissait entièrement sa propre histoire, s'il n'avait pas d'objection à la raconter ou à se la raconter, la premiére personne s'imposerait . . . Ainsi, chaque fois que l'on voudra décrire un véritable progrès de la conscience, la naissance même du langage ou d' un langage, c'est la seconde personne qui sera la plus efficace." Michel Butor, "L'usage des pronoms personnels dans le roman," in *Essais sur le roman* (Paris: Gallimard, 1969), p. 81. Symbolical of this growth in self-awareness is the high recurrence of the "you" in the travel sequences which function as metaphors for Jack's Pilgrim's Progress.

15. "Il faut entendre par discours dans sa plus large extension: toute énonciation supposant un locuteur et un auditeur, et chez le premier l'intention d'influencer l'autre en quelque matière," Emile Benveniste, *Problèmes de Linguistique Générale* (Paris: Gallimard, 1966), pp. 241–42.

16. Stanzel, p. 63.

17. See Warren's introduction to the Random House edition of *All the King's Men* where he tells of his need for "a character to serve as a kind of commentator and *raisonneur* and chorus" (p. iv).

18. Robert Heilman, "Melpomene as Wallflower; or, the Reading of Tragedy," reprinted in Longley, p. 83.

19. Heilman, p. 81.

20. Robert Penn Warren, "Knowledge and the Image of Man," reprinted in Longley, p. 241.

21. Interpenetration in *All the King's Men* does not concern only the animate world. Norton R. Girault has pointed out Jack's attempts to lose himself in nature ("The Narrator's Mind as Symbol: An Analysis of *All the King's Men*," *Accent*, 7 [1947], 220–34). One amusing example, not mentioned by Girault and more directly related to our approach, is the passage where Jack sees himself from the point of view of a cow and then sees himself transformed into a cow: "The cow would stand there knee-deep in the mist and look at the black blur and the blaze and then, not turning its head, at the place where the black blur and blaze had been with the remote, massive unvindictive indifference of God-All-Mighty or Fate or *me*, if I were standing knee-deep in the mist and the blur and the blaze whizzed past and withered on off between the fields and the patches of woods. But I wasn't standing there in the field in the dark, with the mist turning slow around *my* knees and the ticking no-noise of the night inside *my* head" (p. 36, italics added).

22. Might not this account for the reaction of the critics who find the ending weak?

Leonard Casper, for instance, has perceived something like "sheer fatigue or the weakness of insufficient resolution" in the conclusion. "It requires a faith equal to Jack's in Willie to believe that this is only the last effect of the purge that must precede the great appetite," Leonard Casper, *Robert Penn Warren: The Dark and Bloody Ground* (Seattle: Univ. of Washington Press, 1960), p. 132. But the kind of self-knowledge which Jack achieves can only bring about a chastened, not an exultant mood. After all, in the words of *Brother to Dragons*: "The dream of the future is not/Better than the fact of the past, no matter how terrible./For without the fact of the past we cannot dream the future" (New York: Random House, 1953), p. 193. What faith the book requires is not to be applied to Jack's capacity for renewed life but to our readiness to integrate Jack's experience and language—and our capacity to keep that "speck of green" on our hope that, according to the epigraph, promises us redemption.

23. This definition of "good fiction" is to be found in the essay on Ernest Hemingway in Robert Penn Warren, *Selected Essays* (New York: Random House, 1958), p. 116.

"Brother to Dragons: The Fact of Violence vs. the Possibility of Love"

> "We are but shadows—we are not endowed with real life, and all that seems most real about us is but the thinnest substance of a dream—till the heart be touched. That touch creates us—then we begin to be—thereby we are beings of reality, and inheritors of eternity."— Letter of Nathaniel Hawthorne to Sophia Peabody

Now that we have in Warren's *Selected Poems, 1923–1975* the artist's own sense of the shape of his career as a poet, the importance of *Brother to Dragons* as a turning point in his development emerges in sharp perspective. The publication in 1953 of Warren's *Tale in Verse and Voices* marked his rediscovery of the possibilities of the poem, a form which he had abandoned for nearly a decade, while it introduced the new and more personal voice which the artist was to exploit successfully from *Promises* to the present. The transitional nature of *Brother to Dragons* has been suggested over the years by the writer's several brief accounts of the genesis of the work, of his struggle to find the appropriate form for his material.[1] The early Warren is best remembered for his prose, especially *All the King's Men*, for which he received the Pulitzer Prize in 1946, a handful of short stories collected and republished in 1948, and three or four critical essays, the best of which appeared before 1951. In his later career, although his historical and journalistic essays are widely respected, Warren's laurels have come chiefly through his poetry. *Promises*, the most personal and affirmative of his later works, won the Pulitzer Prize for poetry in 1957. Following and confirming this pattern, *Brother of Dragons* began in the late forties as a novel and was transformed in the process of composition into a "dialogue in verse." Warren considered and abandoned fictional and dramatic and ballad forms (all of which he had used previously) before he created this new "hybrid genre,"[2] a free-flowing dialogue which combines the qualities of both prose and verse,

*Reprinted with permission from *American Literature*, 49 (1978), 560–79. Copyright © 1978, Duke University Press.

lyric and drama. *Brother to Dragons* was no casual experiment, however, but the result of a prolonged reassessment on Warren's part of the relation of his art to his own life.[3]

Brother to Dragons is, critics agree, an act of moral accounting, an attempt to balance the books on two hundred years of American experience since the Declaration. In it Warren examines a crime committed by the nephew of Thomas Jefferson as an image of the tragic core of American history, thus renewing the large, uncomfortable questions which arose in all his more youthful work. In fact, Warren's exploration of this nightmare of the American past treats of so many themes from his early development that the extent to which it also breaks with that previous work has seldom been recognized and never fully explored.[4] Though the newness is partly elusive, it may be sensed immediately in the lifting, at the end of the poem, of the gloom pervasive in his earlier work. The stoical acceptance of *At Heaven's Gate* and *All the King's Men* now gives way to joyous affirmation; even the darkness of *Night Rider* and *World Enough and Time* appears to be dispelled. Far more significant, however, is the writer's invitation to read this work autobiographically. The artist, identified simply as "R.P.W.: the writer of this poem,"[5] has become a character in the work; and what the action finally dramatizes is a profound change in him—the change, one assumes, which led to the work itself. As his first self-portrait, the character "R.P.W." represents more than a culmination of the gradual movement away from T. S. Eliot's conception of the artist as an impersonal, invisible "catalyst" and Warren's arrival at an open, confessional stance from which the writer speaks undisguisedly in his own voice. It represents a wholly new dimension in Warren's work, a new willingness to take the direct risks of self-involvement in the issues he raises. It announces that events in the author's own life—specifically, his discovery in a new relationship of the nature of love—have become, in a sense, the source and the subject of the poem.[6]

I

Seen in the context of this change in the writer, it seems appropriate that *Brother to Dragons* be as much an inquiry into the nature of love as a reconstruction of an ax murder. In spite of its nearly overwhelming impact, the slaying serves not as the center of the action but as an occasion for a wide-ranging dialogue between the protagonists, R.P.W. and Thomas Jefferson. Lilburn Lewis's crime functions largely to image one of the "constants" of human experience; it stands for the ineradicable worst at which the two men must look. The act of violence is balanced throughout the action, however, by a consideration of what love is or what it might be. In Warren's depiction of the slaying, love is the murderer's dominant motive; love, or the need for love, pervades every recess of the dark interior world which Lilburn inhabits. Whatever understanding of the nature of love is to be possible in the drama, it must, consequently, accommodate and subsume the form it takes in him; it must "tally" with the fact of murder.

The meaning of this violent fact, however (and the facts, as always in Warren, appear to bear a number of constructions), becomes the issue between Jefferson and R.P.W. Though Jefferson and R.P.W. represent antithetical character types with opposing points of view, stubbornly adhered to, the points of view of neither character remain static; both change as they move toward a common ground of understanding.[7] Initially, Jefferson appears in the throes of a profound "moral shock . . . caused by the discovery of what his own blood was capable of . . ." (p. xi). Knowledge of his nephew's brutality has turned his optimism at the human prospect to gall and driven him into a sour misanthropy. Jefferson represents one of the familiar "idealist" figures in Warren's work who are wedded to some abstract conception which proves eventually destructive to themselves and others.[8] In this case Jefferson's belief in human perfectibility is also one of the most cherished and, according to Warren, dangerous and superficial of our national myths. Jefferson's moral revulsion at his nephew's crime is presented as the other face of his Enlightenment optimism, and both are projections of his self-pride.

Warren's characterization of himself is subtler and more interesting. He portrays himself as a combined historian and detective, visiting the site, sifting through the old court records, and pondering the motives which led to the slaying. While Jefferson is presented as a disillusioned idealist, R.P.W. appears as a cynical realist, devoid of optimistic illusions. Lacking both Jefferson's intellectual and emotional range, he is neither taken in nor even attracted by utopian visions. He has instead a dogged, nagging determination to test every conclusion, to measure every generalization of Jefferson's against all the facts at his disposal. But his worrying of every question from all possible sides seems to reflect a deep strain of anxiety as well as skepticism. If R.P.W. is "afflicted with logic" as with a disease, it is perhaps because his compulsion to analyze indicates a tacit, not wholly conscious acceptance of "naturalism," a view of the world as meaningless mechanism. How far his preoccupation with causation brings him toward this form of nihilism is not clear. His assertion at one point in the dialogue, however, that power, "power empty and abstract," is ". . . still, in the last analysis, the only/Thing worth the struggle" (p. 92), is certainly symptomatic of that typically modern malaise. On another level R.P.W.'s interest in the sordid seems almost a parody of the preoccupations of some self-styled literary "naturalists," who shared R.P.W.'s conclusion (or his fear) that the "facts" were necessarily ugly.

In any event, Warren's characterization of himself seems hardly intended as a model of sanity or all-encompassing wisdom.[9] On the contrary, that laconic, fact-ridden, alternately shrill and mundane voice belongs to a man who stands as much in need of "redemption" as Jefferson. In the two of them, in fact, Warren has personified the two chief heresies of modernism: a too facile optimism about progress and human perfectibility; the nihilism which comes from staring too long into the abyss. The excesses of R.P.W.'s rhetoric—a "Seneca in the meat-house," according to Leslie Fielder[10]—resemble, particularly in the early speeches, the excesses of Jack Burden in *All the King's Men*. The rhetorical styles of both serve a similar function: to indicate stress and their half-successful, half-foolish attempts to control it. The R.P.W. who first visits the site of the murder, for instance, moves through a landscape alive with terrifying visceral and sexual images. Both the landscape and his encounter with the blacksnake in the ruins of the old Lewis mansion provide perfect correlatives for his state of mind. The irrational terror which the snake evokes is fear of himself, of his own as well as the world's "intolerable inwardness":

> . . . In some black aperture among the stones
> I saw the eyes, their glitter in that dark,
> And suddenly the head thrust forth, and the fat, black
> Body molten flowed, as though those stones
> Bled forth earth's inner darkness to the day,
> As though the bung had broke on that intolerable inwardness,
> And now divulged, thus focused and compacted,
> What haunts beneath earth's primal, soldered sill,
> And in its slow and merciless ease, sleepless, lolls
> Below that threshold where the prime waters sleep.
> Thus it flowed forth, and the scaled belly of abomination
> Rustled on stone, rose, rose up
> And reared in regal indolence and swag.
> I saw it rise, saw the soiled white of the belly bulge,
> And in that muscular distension I saw the black side scales
> Show their faint flange and tracery of white.
> And so it rose and climbed the paralyzed light.
> On those heaped stones it was taller than I, taller
> Than any man. . . . (p. 33)

The imagery of the scene associates the snake with primal evil and that "darker self" which manifested itself in Lilburn in the meat-house but is also present in every man, in R.P.W. himself. Here that specter of the writer's own potential is manifest in a terrifying, almost supernatural dimension: ". . . it was taller than I, taller/Than any man." To regain his composure the writer has to name over to himself, as if reciting a charm, the familiar and scientific names which designate this apparition as mere snake, as *Elaphe obsoleta obsoleta*. In thus attempting to exorcise the symbolic dimensions of the encounter, he substitutes a naturalistic view for the metaphysical one which terrifies him. The scene thus raises one of the main issues in the work: whether evil is a reality or (the pun is perfect) an "obsolete" conception. At the same time the scene reveals a split in the psyche of the character: the rough, garrulous exterior of a man who believes in nothing and is surprised at nothing barely conceals a deep-seated, almost hysterical revulsion at what he suspects to be his true nature.

There must consequently be a double movement towards a redemptive vision of life in *Brother to Dragons*. Jefferson and R.P.W., originally the poles of a dialectic dramatic structure, end in reconciliation and affirmation. The ax murder by the nephew of Thomas Jefferson which is the subject of their dialogue is, paradoxically, both the means by which reconciliation comes about and the thing to which they must be reconciled. To confront the horror is to dispel it, and in this sense, as Victor Strandberg has pointed out, the action has strong Jungian parallels.[11] The language of their debate frequently evokes the image of a "labyrinthian" descent into the unconscious self, though the purpose of that descent is not to slay the Minotaur, but to drag the monster to light. This confrontation involves the discovery by both Jefferson and R.P.W. of themselves in Lilburn; each eventually acknowledges Lilburn's act as a fulfillment of qualities latent in himself. Once he accepts responsibility for the disillusionment and suicide of his own "near son," Meriwether Lewis, Jefferson can see Lilburn's self-justification as an extension of his own.[12] Similarly, R.P.W. comes to recognize as his own the murderer's compulsion to strike at any cost through the fog of uncertainty to "Truth" and the peace of some single definition.

Initially the "facts" of the reconstructed slaying seem to bear out Jefferson's contention that a perverse moral duplicity pervades all. All acts, he believes, stem (like Lilburn's crime) from a blind, devouring egotism where murderer and victim alike conspire together to satisfy their deepest needs, where even George, who returns to "wreak his merciless frailty on Lilburn" (p. 139), may be a party to the crime. In Jefferson's disillusioned view, human nature is worse than bestial; it is monstrous. It is ruled by a disguised and acknowledged Minotaur that lurks somewhere in the Labyrinth of self:

> . . . and in that dark no thread,
> Airy as breath by Ariadne's fingers forged.
> No thread, and beyond some groped-at corner, hulked
> In the blind dark, hock-deep in ordure, its beard
> And shag foul-scabbed, and when the hoof heaves—
> Listen!—the foulness sucks like mire.
>
> The beast waits. He is the infamy of Crete.
> He is the midnight's enormity. He is
> Our brother, our darling brother. (p. 7)

Or, more precisely, he is Jefferson's nephew. Jefferson sees Lilburn as an embodiment of that monster, a waking, daylight manifestation of the nightmare lurking in every self. And in that composite image Jefferson discerns (so he thinks) the underlying truth, the real nature of things. Thus, to Jefferson, as to Faulkner's Addie Bundren, words are a disguise, a mask of rationalization. The actuality, the "doing," is the brutal service of the beast's needs. Lilburn's fatal ax had been lifted in vindication of his "love"—actually an unacknowledged incestuous yearning for his mother. "Love," then, is the most insidious form of self-deception in a world in which everything is a charade, everything is flatteringly disguised as its moral opposite. In Jefferson's horrified definition,

> . . . all love, all kinds, descriptions, and shapes,
> Is but a mask to hide the brute face of fact,
> And that fact is the immitigable ferocity of self,
> And once you find it in your blood, and find even
> That the face of love beneath your face at the first
> Budding of the definitive delight—
> That every face, even that one, is but a mirror
> For your own ferocity, a mirror blurred
> And breathed upon and slicked and slimed with love,
> And through the interstices and gouts of that
> Hypocritical moisture, the cold eyes spy out
> From the mirror's cold heart, and thus self spies on self
> In that unsummerable arctic of the human alienation.
> (p. 47)

Love is a weapon, meekness is betrayal, forgiveness is "desire/Gone craven with placation, / . . . the self's final ferocity/Whetted in sweetness as a blade in oil" (p. 49). Tirelessly through this charade, the conscious self plays out its self-deceptive, self-vindicating roles as it serves the monster-self within. Ultimately, Jefferson concludes, only the pain is real:

> . . . So let us name the truth, like men.
> We are born to joy that joy may become pain.
> We are born to hope that hope may become pain.
> We are born to love that love may become pain.
> We are born to pain that pain may become more
> Pain, and from that inexhaustible superflux
> We may give others pain as our prime definition. . . .
> (pp. 131–32)

The pain which Lilburn inflicts on George is therefore the absolute authentication of his own existence at the same time it is (to Jefferson) the concrete image and indictment of *all* existence.

II

However dark Jefferson's view of experience, it is clear that he speaks from a point of view which is moral, even though inverted. In the cruel charade he describes, evil masquerades as good. R.P.W.'s pessimism is subtler. His analysis of the possible sources of the slaying in the psychology of the participants tends, in its cumulative effect, to reduce the significance of Lilburn's act to zero, to another datum in an infinite series of pathetic, meaningless human acts. And just as Lilburn's story seems initially to confirm Jefferson's disillusionment but eventually transcends his views of it, the story also *appears* initially to confirm R.P.W.'s nihilism, his view of man as helpless automaton. R.P.W. discovers (or invents) in the background of the slaying all the elements of a psychological case study: an unhappy, loveless marriage in which the mother seeks companionship in her son, the Oedipal rivalry in her two sons, the nursemaid who competes with the mother for the son's love, and the son's wife who is unwittingly a surrogate for his mother. In addition, Lilburn's path is strewn with all the tragic mischances and coincidences necessary to disaster. Insofar as this chain of cause and effect appears adequate to explain the tragedy, it must follow that Lilburn "had" to do what he did. And having had no choice in the matter, he (and, ultimately, mankind in general) must be absolved from guilt. The same logic, however, "absolves" his action, or any action, from significance. This has been Warren's underlying objection to naturalism throughout his career and the reason for his stubborn defense of "contingency" as opposed to determinism. The attraction of naturalism, he acknowledges, lies not only in the "absolution" it confers but in the convenient distance which it puts between us and our actions:

We feel that the force now driving Lilburn on
Is but part of the unleashed and unhoused force of Nature,
Mindless, irreconcilable, absolute:
The swing of the year, the thrust of Time, the wind.
But we also feel a need to leave that house
On the dark headland, and lift up our eyes
To whatever liberating perspective,
Icy and pure, the wild heart may command,
To escape the house, escape the tightening coil
And mathematical constriction: and so the glimmering
                                   night scene and storm under
The incalculable and distant disdain of starlight, serve,
                                              therefore,
As an image of lethal purity, the incessant
And whirling dream of desperate innocence,
The infatuate glitter of the land of Platonic ice.

> It is an image to free us from the human trauma,
> And the wind drives unremitting, and the oak will bend. (pp. 95–96)

As the action makes clear, however, there is no escape from the "human trauma," no sufficiently "liberating perspective." Here and in the lines just preceding the quotation, Warren images the seeming helplessness of Lilburn in the oak bending before the pressure of the "wind," one of his favorite metaphors for the blind forces of nature:

> The powerful boughs that crook and lift are iron, and lifeless.
> The oak's comment is anguish, but the oak stands.
> The oak is Jacob, and all night in anguish wrestles the
> > incessant
> And pitiless angel of air. The stars are arctic and
> Their gleam comes earthward down uncounted light-years
> > of disdain,
> And on the exposed headland the oak heaves,
> And in radius of more than a thousand miles the continent
> Glitters whitely in starlight like a great dead eye of ice.
> The wind is unceasing, and the stars likewise. (p. 95)

These images of immense cold and infinite space evoke a powerful sense of the bleakness of the nonhuman universe, devoid of both sentience and value.[13] Only the intrusion by the poet of what is ostentatiously a "pathetic fallacy," an allusion to Jacob's anguish and an *illusion*, purposely not sustained, of sentient, purposeful behavior on the part of the elements (the "pitiless angel of air"), reminds us of the human perspective, which is practically synonymous here with the capacity for anguish. The passage delineates sharply the boundary between the human and the "natural," implying at the same time that to dissolve Lilburn wholly into the natural (as a deterministic view would do), to merge him wholly with the image of the unconscious and "lifeless" oak acted upon by the "wind," would be a falsification, an error as obvious as the attribution of pitilessness to the wind or disdain to the stars.

The fact of consciousness itself, that capacity for anguish and self-delusion, remains to be accounted for, both in the passage and in the events leading up to the murder. To be aware of the mechanisms of nature without being free of them appears to be the anomalous human burden. Because of it, there can be no "perfect adjustment" of conscious mind with unconscious nature; the gulf between them, Warren implies, is absolute. In one of the most quoted passages in the book, the artist imagines an existence in the flow of time in which being and sustaining environment *are* in perfect harmony:

> A thousand miles and the fabulous river is ice in the starlight.
> The ice is a foot thick, and beneath, the water slides black
> > like a dream,

And in the interior of that unpulsing blackness and
thrilled zero
The big channel-cat sleeps with eye lidless, and the brute face
Is the face of the last torturer, and the white belly
Brushes the delicious and icy blackness of mud.
But there is no sensation. How can there be
Sensation when there is perfect adjustment? The blood
Of the creature is but the temperature of the sustaining flow:
The catfish is in the Mississippi and
The Mississippi is in the catfish and
Under the ice both are at one with God.
Would that we were! (p. 94)

This image of *un*conscious being is the antithesis of human existence, the essence of which is not "perfect adjustment" but "sensation"—or, as Jefferson insists, pain.

From this inexplicable but stubborn fact of consciousness comes, Warren has always maintained, the human need to wrest significance out of pain, to find sanctions, to bestow value on the "unpulsing blackness" which encompasses man.[14] In addition to the endurance of pain, then, the essence of consciousness involves the perception of—or rather the creation of—values, the making of a context for "virtue." That is to say, man necessarily creates a frame of reference in which his actions may acquire meaning. To be conscious is to live by discriminations, to judge, and to require therefore a definition of "good" as well as of "self." Hence, the paradox (which R.P.W. affirms) of value existing within a naturalistic world: ". . . despite all naturalistic considerations,/Or in the end because of naturalistic considerations,/We must believe in virtue" (p. 29). Elsewhere, Warren has explained more fully the nature of these "values." "Against all reason," he has argued, "man insists . . . on creating and trying to live by certain values. These values are . . . 'illusions,' but the last wisdom is for man to realize that though his values are illusions, the illusion is necessary, is infinitely precious, and is . . . his only truth."[15] The fragility of such values is self-evident: self and self-concept, the world and one's vision of it, can never perfectly coincide. But yet, in some manner, "all life lifts and longs toward its own name,/And toward fulfillment in the singleness of definition" (p. 121).

Ultimately Lilburn's story confirms that yearning. Longing for some transcendent moment of what Warren calls "glory," a moment of intensity great enough to stand for meaning and force all the objects of his interior world to coalesce into meaning, Lilburn—in part, and in some sense of the word—*chooses* the moment in the meat-house. The seductive promise of a single, defining act to redeem him from the "anguish of complication" is the real motive for his crime: ". . . any act,/Any act at all, the bad, the good, affords,/Or seems to afford, the dear redemption of simplicity:/The dear redemption in the mere fact of achieved definition,/Be what that may" (p. 56).[16]

The universality of this struggle to wrest coherence out of chaos is suggested throughout the work in many ways. Charles Lewis, the father of the murderer and in some ways the source of the family problems, describes his own actions in similar terms:

> I built the house, left Albermarle and ease,
> Took wife and sons, slaves, chattels, beasts, and goods,
> Potions and pills, picked-lint, and scalpel, all
> My marks of rank and occupation, all
> *Those things, intangible and tangible, that men*
> *Clutch round them like a cloak against the time*
> *The wind will shift,* and sit sudden in the dire
> Airt, and the cold creep.
> *I took those things, for they are like*
> *The shell the shellfish spins from the slick slime*
> *And deliquescence of itself to fend*
> *That self, and its poor palpitation, boxed in dark.*
>   (pp. 12–13, italics mine)

Similarly, the deep need of all the characters to be purified and freed by projecting their guilt elsewhere (as in the ancient Hebrew ritual of the scapegoat) illustrates, however pitifully, the necessity of constructing a "moral universe" around oneself. It is as if all the main characters unconsciously assume the existence of a retributive moral order to which they are personally accountable and a savage god which they must propitiate. The god, of course, is within, and perhaps but another version of the blind beast of egotism. The charade which Jefferson describes appears to be performed for its benefit; all of experience is bent to accommodate it:

>   . . . yes, every one,
> The saints and angels, too, who tread, yes, every
> And single one, but plays the sad child's play
> And old charade where man puts down the bad and then
>   feels good.
> It is the sadistic farce by which the world is cleansed.
> And is not cleansed, for in the deep
> Hovel of the heart that Thing lies
> That will never unkennel himself to the contemptible steel,
> Nor needs to venture forth ever, for all sustenance
> Comes in to him, the world comes in, and is his. (p. 42)

While Lilburn may realize at some level that *he* is the betrayer, he suppresses that knowledge and invents the treacherous and conspiratorial servants who try to obliterate his mother. Jefferson's revulsion at Lilburn is a similar evasion by projection, a way of denying the existence of the same potential in himself. This convenient externalization of evil and the pro-

jection of it onto others takes myriad forms; it may, as in the case of
R.P.W., emerge as an image of a monster-self which is really *other*-than-
the-self, a demon alien for whom one is not really responsible.

This false exorcising of one's own evil seems a kind of mental game, a
set of moral gymnastics universally indulged in. If it were the whole story,
Jefferson's darkest utterance about man's nature would be understatement. But the very fact of this charade, the universal necessity to ra-
tionalize sadism and lust into virtues, implies that lust and sadism are not
all: ". . . Lilburn's heart-deep need/To name his evil good is the final
evidence/For the existence of good" (p. 144). Lilburn's sordid act, then,
cannot stand as a definitive image of human nature; it must stand instead
as a tragic possibility, ever present, of the perversion of good.

Lucy Lewis, the mother of the killer and a kind of catalyst in the process of R.P.W. and Jefferson's enlightenment, becomes the means through
which this idea is explored. Of all the characters in the drama who struggle toward some self-vindicating definition of good, she is the only one
who does not blind herself through some secret (and unreal) dream of self,
or turn experience into alibi. "The human curse," she discovers, "is simply
to love and sometimes to love well,/But never well enough" (p. 123), and
she resists, successfully, the temptation to deny the evil consequences of
her love for her son. "I accept," she says:

> . . . the responsibility of my love,
> And know, somehow, that my love was infected with failure.
> No, I must maintain that my love in some part,
> Some part at least, was love. Else how had I lived?
> But even my love had infected my son's heart. (pp. 187–88)

That one's best gifts may kill or corrupt is a bitter but crucial recognition
which frees her from the self-deceptions that limit the understandings of
the others. It is Lucy (the bearer of light) who loves unstintingly and sees,
therefore, what Jefferson cannot, that in Lilburn's brutal act were mingled his best as well as his worst qualities: "He saw poor George as but his
darkest self/And all the possibility of the dark that he feared,/And so he
struck, and struck down that darkest self . . ." (p. 189). Even in his moment of sadistic self-gratification, then, Lilburn affirms in some twisted
way that he is more than brute. He kills for the highest value he is capable
of recognizing, performs his evil deed in the name of good. If he thus par-
ticipates in the charade which Jefferson described, so do they all. To reject Lilburn as a monster, then, is to compound his crime and to repeat it
in its essence.

III

The universality of the need to wrest meaning out of experience is
suggested in yet one other way, in an analogy implicit between the pro-

cess of individual self-definition and an artist's act of creation. The individual's creation of a moral universe in which to act and the artist's shaping of his materials into form manifest the same deep, imaginative process. Out of both come the fragile human artifacts: order, meaning, and value. In Warren's characterization of himself in *Brother to Dragons* we observe that *process* as well as its results. We see the artist assembling the sources and records of his story, pondering the motives of the participants, groping for a *form* adequate to its complexity, and inventing at one point where the records are silent the necessary and ironical engine of Lilburn's destruction, the faithful hound who betrays him. And if we miss the import of that spectacle there remains the conversation in which R.P.W. broaches the subject of artistic form to his own creation, Jefferson. To the artist's comments on the inadequacy of certain genres, Jefferson replies:

> . . . There is no form to hold
> Reality and its insufferable intransigence.
> I know. I know, for I once tried to contrive
> A form I thought fit to hold the purity of man's hope.
> But I did not understand the nature of things. (p. 44)

Form in art and the "myth" which one makes of experience are thus nearly interchangeable terms; both impose meaning and pattern on essentially inert materials. They are equally attempts to make comprehensible an intractable "universe" of experience. As Warren remarks in the introduction to the book, ". . . if poetry is the little myth we make, history is the big myth we live, and in our living, constantly remake" (p. xii).

Lilburn, of course, understands the "nature of things" even less than Jefferson. The moral universe he has created around himself is patently false and self-vindicating, and he cannot see past it to the actual world. He sees only the roles in which he has cast the inhabitants of his imagination, roles which, of course, the people around him fail to play. Lilburn's error—perhaps the "type" of all error—is solipsism. His fate suggests that the process of "justifying" may just as easily destroy as redeem, may as easily distort and hide as reveal and clarify. But if consciousness may as readily be trapped in a solipsistic circle of illusion as freed to act in the "real" world, how, then, may one find a set of values or definition of self which is not a cleverly disguised deadfall? How may one "find sanctions" without committing an elaborate form of suicide?

Warren has always answered this question rather cryptically with the single word "knowledge." In *Brother to Dragons* R.P.W. explicitly rejects the usual sense of the word in favor of "some new and better definition," at the nature of which he only hints:

> . . . knowing is,
> Maybe, a kind of being, and if you know,
> Can really know, a thing in all its fullness,

Then you are different, and if you are different,
Then everything is different, somehow, too. (pp. 127–28)

It is evident here that Warren means a special kind of knowledge which extinguishes self and transcends the simplistic gestalt of ordinary perception, a knowledge which brings contact with the actual other, not with one's own projected symbol-world. His images for such an experience have nearly always been drawn from religion: Moses on the mountain, Saul on the road to Damascus, or backwoods Southern Protestants violently struck down by grace. In *Brother to Dragons*, however, that kind of knowledge seems to be synonymous with the final sense of the word "love" and is implied when Warren (through Lucy Lewis) equates "love" with (successful) "definition":

> . . . [love] is all you have.
> It is all you can bring with you to the inhabited silence.
> For if love's anything, it is the thing
> That, once existing, may not be denied,
> *For it is definition*, and denial
> Is death, but is
> That death in which you may not ever lie down.
>   (p. 174, italics mine)

Like Lilburn's sadistic self-indulgence, then, love may provide that moment of "glory" of "Pentecostal intuition" through which the value of all things becomes known. If sheer intensity of feeling may stand for meaning—or bestow meaning—then "love" creates the very possibility of "knowing" (in the special sense in which it must be taken in the work). And if more is possible, if solipsism can be broken, love may be the bridge, even the contact itself, which provides the sense of the "thing in all its fullness." The New Critical vocabulary of aesthetic experience seems relevant here: love bestows what the New Critics claimed that art provides, a "concrete" sense of the "world's body." To *know* requires a putting aside of our ordinary and essentially solipsistic games, our symbolic role-playing and projections, in a transcendent moment of *appreciation* (in the root sense of the word) of some part of the Not-me, of the actual other. Such self-transcending glimpses of the world provide the certitude or "reality" which the mind craves, and thus they provide a new definition of self.

To love means, therefore, to create a private moral universe which is not mere illusion but accommodates, at one end of the scale, the sources of our "guilt" and "despair"—the experience of pain. Such a vision must account for and yet transcend that common denominator and only certitude of experience. Love is consequently a revelation, an excruciating "searing" of the self which creates both world and self anew. Jack Burden touches very briefly on the idea of love's transforming power in one of his less successful philosophical flights in *All the King's Men*: ". . . in the act of loving somebody, [you] become real, cease to be a part of the uncreated clay and get the breath of life in you and rise up."[17] But the idea is dramatized, forcefully, for the first time by Warren in *Brother to Dragons*.

The profound transformation which occurs in R.P.W. accounts for (and is dramatized by) the contrast between his first visit to the site of the Lewis tragedy and the second, the episode with which the book closes. In the first visit, which ends with the terrifying encounter with the snake, the scene is colored by an agitation and confused yearning which are different in degree but not in kind from Lilburn's:

> . . . A fellow of forty, a stranger, and a fool,
> Red-headed, freckled, lean, a little stooped,
> Who yearned to be understood, to make communication,
> To touch the ironic immensity of afternoon with meaning,
> To find and know my name and make it heard,
> While the sun insanely screamed out all it knew,
> Its one wild word:
> *Light, light, light!*
> And all identity tottered to that remorseless vibration.
>   (pp. 26–27)

While this assessment is attributed to the farmer who owns the old Lewis place, the judgment is also R.P.W.'s and an ironic echo of Lilburn's only speech a few pages earlier—an anguished cry at the extinction of all "light" in his life (pp. 23–24).

On the second visit the scene is completely altered, its objects shrunken and unterrifying: the "jungle convolvement and visceral delight" have vanished, and the landscape no longer throbs with menace like the forest in *Heart of Darkness*. "For that's the way I had remembered it," R.P.W. comments; "But no, it's not like that. At least, not now,/And never was, I guess, but in my head" (p. 207). The change, then, is not merely seasonal (it being winter on this second occasion), but a reflection of changes in the observer. Inexplicably, all the previously threatening aspects of the scene have been transformed into a vision of peace and normality. The Black Snake is present again in the imagination of the poet, but in its natural dimensions, and snug underground in winter hibernation. That specter of what the unconscious may hold has, in short, been reduced to "natural," unmetaphysical proportions. All the terror it held for him has been dissipated.[18]

The implicit explanation for this transformation, of course, lies in the structure of the work, in everything that has transpired earlier in the action. The whole process of coming to terms with Lilburn's crime has involved the acknowledgement of the monster *as self* and not as terrifying alien. The scene is therefore the culmination, dramatically, of a process of understanding and acceptance. But in the subsequent lines Warren uncharacteristically adduces as a second explanation a cause essentially *out-side* the structure of the work. He moves abruptly to a description of another winter scene in his own life—a first kiss and the belated discovery of love in the beginning (one must presume) of his relationship with Eleanor Clark:

> . . . I stand
> Amid the brown leaves and snow. I lift up my eyes
> Beyond the bluff and the flat land farther
> To where the river gleams. Its gleam is cold.
> And I think of another bluff and another river.
> I think of another year and another winter.
> I think of snow on the brown leaves, and below
> That other bluff, how cold and far was light on that
> northern river.
> I think how her mouth and mine together
> Were cold on the first kiss. (pp. 208–209)

This event, apparently as important in the life of the artist as in the life of the man,[19] becomes, through this sudden retrospective glance, the center of the work, the mysterious redeeming event which the action both explores and dramatizes: the phoenix-like renewal of self. In Jefferson's parallel "redemption," his change and the causes of it are spelled out more fully: in the "incandescence of the heart's great flare," Jefferson asserts, ". . . all creation validates itself,/For whatever you create, you create yourself by it,/And in creating yourself you will create/The whole wide world and gleaming West anew" (p. 195). But Warren's summary of his own transformation penetrates without elaboration to the heart of the mystery: "Since then," he says simply, "I have made new acquaintance with the nature of joy" (p. 209).

Notes

1. The story may be pieced together from fragmentary accounts, beginning with "The Way It Was Written," *New York Times Book Review*, 23 Aug. 1953, p. 6, and the *Paris Review* interview with Ralph Ellison and Eugene Walter, "The Art of Fiction XVIII: Robert Penn Warren," reprinted in *Robert Penn Warren: A Collection of Critical Essays*, ed. John L. Longley, Jr. (New York: New York Univ. Press, 1965), pp. 18–45, and continuing through Richard B. Sale, "An Interview in New Haven with Robert Penn Warren," *Studies in the Novel*, 2 (1970), 340–41, and Jean Crawford, "A Conversation with Robert Penn Warren," *Vanderbilt Alumnus*, March-April 1970, p. 21. The author's nine-year effort is alluded to briefly in the work itself.

2. Warren's phrase in an interview, "Some Important Fall Authors Speak For Themselves," *New York Herald Book Review*, 11 Oct. 1953, p. 11.

3. Warren has mentioned this period of change and reassessment in several places, but his discussion with Richard B. Sale is probably the fullest account. In the *Paris Review* interview, Warren mentioned in passing that ". . . in the last ten years or a little more the personal

relation to my writing changed. I quit writing poems for ten years. . . . I didn't finish one for several years, they felt false. Then I got back at it, and that is the bulk of what I've done since . . ." (pp. 28–29).

4. Although without suggesting the underlying causes, George P. Garrett has vigorously asserted the significance of *Brother to Dragons* as a watershed in Warren's career: "More than anything else, this work managed to bring together the concerns and themes which had separately haunted his poetry and his prose. For any study of his whole work it is crucial. For a consideration of Warren as poet, it marks a turning point. . . . In a sense, then, after *Brother to Dragons*, Warren was liberated, free to turn to something new if he chose to, equally free to carry along with him whatever he wished from his own poetic experience"—"The Recent Poetry of Robert Penn Warren," in Longley, p. 227. Monroe K. Spears has also noted the change and remarked that while it occurred at a time when many other poets were beginning to write more "open" or "confessional" poetry, "it is equally plain that the change was the end product of an internal development. . . ."—"The Latest Poetry of Robert Penn Warren," *Sewanee Review*, 78 (1970), 348. See also George Core, "In the Heart's Ambiguity: Robert Penn Warren as Poet," *Mississippi Quarterly*, 22 (1969), 314–15.

5. *Brother to Dragons: A Tale In Verse and Voices* (New York: Random House, 1953), p. 2. Subsequent references to this text will be by page number only in the body of the text.

6. While other critics have recognized *Brother to Dragons* as a turning point in Warren's career, R. H. Chambers, III, was the first to insist upon the importance of the autobiographical elements to the meaning of the work: "The long poem is the writer's 'crisis' book, his turning point. . ."—and furthermore, ". . . to be fully understood, *Brother to Dragons* must be read, in part at least, autobiographically." What Chambers cites as "*the* crucial point in Warren's career" is, of course, the period of his divorce and remarriage during the composition of *Brother to Dragons*. See "Robert Penn Warren: His Growth as a Writer," Diss. Brown 1969, pp. 6, 17, 21–23, *et passim*.

7. In the only article to focus specifically on the role of "R.P.W." in the work, Dennis M. Dooley asserts that "RPW's spiritual progress *parallels* the spiritual progress of Jefferson"—"The Persona RPW in Warren's *Brother to Dragons*," *Mississippi Quarterly*, 25 (1971), 19–30, italics mine. My own position here is only slightly at odds with Dooley's; I think his account of the change in character of R.P.W. substantially correct and a significant contribution to the critical debate on the work.

8. The role of Jefferson has been described perceptively by Frederick P. W. McDowell in the first lengthy study of the work, "Psychology and Theme in *Brother to Dragons*," published in PMLA in 1955; reprinted in Longley, pp. 197–222.

9. Victor Strandberg argues to the contrary that R.P.W. has "the most comprehensive and objective perspective of anyone in the story," and sees him as "the spokesman for modern man"; R.P.W., he insists, "always speaks in a temperate voice, urging understanding, acknowledgement and acceptance. . . ." In *A Colder Fire: The Poetry of Robert Penn Warren* (Lexington: Univ. of Kentucky Press, 1965), pp. 143, 149, *et passim*.

10. In a review of *Brother to Dragons, Partisan Review*, 21 (1954), 208–12.

11. *A Colder Fire*, p. 151.

12. The best brief account of these changes in Jefferson's character is still Charles H. Bohner's in *Robert Penn Warren* (New York: Twayne, 1964), pp. 118–25. According to John L. Stewart, Warren himself intended that Jefferson's confrontation with Meriwether Lewis be the turning point of the poem—*The Burden of Time: The Fugitives and Agrarians* (Princeton: Princeton Univ. Press, 1965), p. 512.

13. Victor Strandberg discusses these same images and the "naturalistic considerations" to which they give rise, but concludes that "Warren's answer to the problem of cosmic darkness is, in the end, theological."—*A Colder Fire*, pp. 160–62. This seems to me to beg the question.

14. In 1951, during the time he was composing *Brother to Dragons*, Warren published

his famous essay on Conrad in which he wrote (ostensibly describing Conrad's beliefs) that man lives with the necessity to "justify himself . . . to idealize himself and his actions into moral significance of some order, to find sanctions." Even though in one sense man remains "purely a creature of nature, an animal of black egotism and savage impulses" who can rest on "no revealed values and look forward to neither individual immortality nor racial survival," he must create values "in order to exist"—" 'The Great Mirage': Conrad and *Nostromo*," *Selected Essays* (New York: Random House, 1958), pp. 43–45.

15. "Conrad and *Nostromo*," p. 45.

16. Frederick P. W. McDowell's brief gloss of this idea of Warren's is very useful: "every act . . . implies a choice among motives for it to become the act, implies a resolving of 'the essential polarity of possibility' contained within it. The act has a finality 'in the mere fact of achieved definition,' therefore, a degree of purity and simplification at variance with its confused intent."—"Psychology and Theme in *Brother to Dragons*," in Longley, p. 213.

17. *All the King's Men* (New York: Harcourt, Brace and Co., 1946), p. 299.

18. Dennis M. Dooley's essay established the functional nature of the two "digressions" describing the author's visits to Rocky Hill, but much remains to be cleared up concerning their precise role in the unfolding of the story. See his "The Persona RPW in *Brother to Dragons*," 19–30.

19. John L. Stewart, who is personally acquainted with the artist, remarks of this period in Warren's life: "he had, as he suggested in *Brother to Dragons*, lived out some personal version of his great fable and had come to terms with himself." *The Burden of Time*, p. 523.

"Notes on the Revised Version of *Brother to Dragons*"

Richard G. Law[*]

Coming on the heels of Warren's third *Selected Poems* and after yet another fine volume of verse, *Now and Then: Poems, 1976–1978,* the new version of *Brother to Dragons*[1] offers persuasive evidence that the artist must be counted among the major poetic voices of the century. Indeed, such a claim could be made on the strength of his work in the last decade alone. The late blooming of Warren's poetic power is one of the remarkable events of our literary history. Within that larger story, the transformation of the original *Brother to Dragons* (1953), itself a landmark, through several dramatic versions and back again into a long, unclassifiable "Tale in Verse and Voices," promises to become one of the richest sources of information about Warren's later career. Even more than the writer's long tinkering with the materials of *All the King's Men,* the evolution of *Brother to Dragons* will provide a view of Warren's stylistic development, his changing sense of the relation of form and content, and his growing mastery over the recalcitrance of language. And unlike the final dramatic version of *All the King's Men,* the present version of *Brother to Dragons* represents a culmination of a long process. The new version is not, perhaps, the most interesting, but it is the *best* version, the text on which the poet may well rest his case for our attention and for history's laurels.

The new version is likely to enhance rather than revise our view of Warren's achievements. Moreover, the original *Brother to Dragons* occupies such a prominent place in the Warren canon that it will not be easily supplanted by the new. Coinciding with crucial events in the writer's private life and signaling also the re-emergence of his interest in poetry, the first *Brother to Dragons* will continue to preoccupy both critics and biographers. While that text carried forward early experiments with technique begun in such poems as "History" and "The Ballad of Billie Potts," the first version also signaled a departure from Warren's own early aesthetic premises and an opening up of new territories in the

[*]This essay was written specifically for this volume and is published here for the first time by permission of the author.

210

poetry. The loose, informal, open-ended, personal meditation which has become the trademark of his late work appeared there for the first time.

The new version, separated from the dense and intriguing context of the original, will necessarily excite less attention. While there are significant differences of emphasis, subtle shifts of meaning and implication in the present work, most of the changes are excisions. The verse has been pared, tightened, slightly subdued; something of the somber austerity of the late poetry has been infused into a work famous for its shrill and "improbable" rhetoric, its sprawling range and cacophony, and Olympian tactlessness. Some of those qualities which led Leslie Fiedler to characterize the work as "Senecan" are still in evidence, however. The violence, sententiousness, and redundancy are still abundant, and Jefferson still addresses the maimed shade of Meriwether Lewis as "Crack-Head" (p. 108). *Brother to Dragons* remains probably the least understood of Warren's works, and a number of changes appeared intended to rectify critical misconceptions. Warren does his best to suggest that the issues of *Brother to Dragons* are not reducible to adages about Original Sin and that Jefferson's character is not, as many have supposed, impugned in the work. Jefferson's opening speech is vastly improved and clarified by the shift in emphasis from Enlightenment optimism about the perfectibility of man to an image of baffled introspection—the self confronted in the mirror. This image, possibly a borrowing from "The Ballad of Billie Potts," appears often enough in Warren's work to constitute a kind of gloss on the difficulty of self-definition, the danger of narcissism (or solipsism), and the elusiveness of knowledge in general. Moreover, as Warren has remarked elsewhere, his work frequently reflects an interest in the way the psychology of individual characters may "mirror" the "society they are living in, so the story of the society is reflected in the *personal* stories . . . and the other way around too: society . . . enacts these private dramas."[2] The social or cultural implications of *Brother to Dragons* have yet to receive adequate treatment.

In the same passage of Jefferson's opening speech, the language of the original demands attention rather too stridently; the imagery dominates rather than reinforces the sense of what Jefferson says:

> The boast—it was the boast
> That split my heart, the boast which I, in in my late
> Last year, made, while my heart still hugged some hope
> That life had spoken and I'd heard it speak.
> It was that boast that split my heart. It split it
> As the vernal enlargement of life's green germ will split
> The dry acorn. My heart, it was only my heart—
> That old, earth-fallen acorn, dry, but postulating
> Green germ and joy and the summer shade. . . .[3]

The revised text has been improved and simplified:

What else had I in age to cling to,
Even in the face of knowledge?
I tried to bring myself to say:
Knowledge is only incidental, hope is all—
Hope, a dry acorn, but some green germ
May split it yet, then joy and the summer shade. (p. 5)

In both versions, the acorn metaphor presages the affirmation of life which Jefferson will make at the end—an attitude which, implicitly, the character "R.P.W." shares. In the scene of his second visit to the Lewis place, as he is about to leave, he stoops and picks up some pig-nuts to take with him (p. 131), an unconscious testimony, perhaps, to the stirring of hope's "green germ" within him. The image is important and worthy of attention in both versions, but it is more effective in the revised version largely because it is so much less obvious.

The revision here is characteristic of the new version, where the poet seems more confident that the language will do its job on the reader without recourse to violence. On the other hand, where real obstacles to understanding existed in the original, the poet has been to some pains to explain himself or to provide help for the reader. The division of the action into relatively self-contained sections offers useful clues to the rhythm and structure of the work—in marked contrast to the divisions of the dramatic version,[4] which obscured rather than clarified the movement of ideas.

In keeping with the dramatic version, the character of Lucy Lewis is made to share—in her "evilest dream" at least—some small part of her son's sadistic impulses (p. 54). It is a minor complication, however, which leaves her essential role in the action unchanged. Meriwether Lewis's role is enlarged, his status as Jefferson's "near-son" emphasized, and his silent presence insisted upon from the beginning. His brief but intense exchanges with Jefferson provide the necessary dramatic preparation for the accusations he hurls at his surrogate father in Section V. That confrontation had represented perhaps the weakest scene in the original, and, while the present version is far from perfect, it seems both more plausible and less contrived than the first.

In the new version, the tragic "matter of Kentucky," as the historical core of the tale might be called, has been returned to its proper medium. The ax-slaying, the event which provides the occasion for the nightmarish *agon* of the work, is shocking enough to preclude easy attention to the subtleties of Warren's argument; in the dramatized versions, the sensationalism (to say nothing of the elaborate stage business) simply overwhelms the commentary. And this particular action, unfortunately (as the writer pointed out in the original) *requires* the commentary: "the action here is not explained/By anything in the action." Moreover, many of the best lyrical, meditative, and even aphoristic passages do not succeed as spoken dialogue. The remarkable evocation of the continent glittering with ice and the channel-cat dozing in the black waters of the Mississippi (p. 94 of the original), one of the most memorable passages in Warren's poetry, is delivered in the play by a chorus of rustics.[5] Retold, however, as a "Tale in Verse and Voices," the commentary—and even the most improbable "dialogue"—is able to hold its own, so that our attention is focused, as it should be, on the attempt to find significance even in the senselessness of Lilburne's crime. The present form emphasizes what Warren might call the "inwardness" of the issues; it is a form which is more cerebral than the dramatic versions, and, at the same time (because the reader's mind is its own best director), offers more scope to the deeper levels of the imagination. The obstacles to public presentation of such an action are obviously enormous. The characters seldom "interact" in the usual sense; they inhabit private, "inward landscapes." Other selves exist for them chiefly as personifications of their own inner needs—they touch only fitfully, much as searchlights sporadically intersect. As Warren has explained in his Foreword, the characters have only a tenuous existence, appearing and disappearing as "their urgencies of argument swell and subside." Indeed, for the work to succeed, the background, the minutely realized natural setting and seasonal rhythms, as well as the characters themselves, should have no life beyond what the language gives them in the moving spotlight of the argument—an argument which, after all, the writer is having with himself.

Ultimately, the unity of the action of *Brother to Dragons* depends upon the impression of a single mind, troubled, mercurial, and profoundly skeptical, engaged in tortuous but determined battle. The new version restores and enhances that impression in ways that the dramatic version could not.

But not all the changes are improvements. One set of revisions, visible chiefly in the expanded introduction and the change of the victim's name from "George" (the name in the records) to the purely fictional "John," represents a wary bow in the direction of Boynton Merrill's *Jefferson's Nephews: A Frontier Tragedy*, a scholarly account of the background and events of the Lewis crime published by Princeton University Press in 1976. Some of the recent reviews (as well as Merrill's own condescending note about the historicity of *Brother to Dragons*) object to Warren's departures from the records of the Lewis case. These protests reflect (though in far milder terms than those aroused by William Styron's *The Confessions of Nat Turner*) a prevailing hostility to *fictional* accounts which presume to make serious statements about the past—or present—condition of humanity. Irvin Ehrenpreis, in his review of the new version, may be taken as a spokesman for what is apparently a widely held attitude:

> One may ask . . . whether a plain historical account, even in my few words, is not more absorbing than Warren's self-indulgent, highly reflexive work. It would take a most

> dramatic discussion of the problem of original sin to hold us
> better than a bare chain of startling but true events. . . .
> When an author supports his moral doctrine by a mixture of
> fact, speculation, and invention, it cannot seem sturdy.[6]

Ehrenpreis's objection is not the throwback to Ranke's confident epistemology that it may seem, but represents rather a new and precise sense of genre created, apparently, by the success of the hybrid form of literature and journalism employed by Mailer, Capote, and a host of New Journalists. The kind of historical fiction-making practiced by Warren ought not be banished from the world by critical edict, but examined on its own terms. In fact, the whole issue of "historicity" in works such as this deserves a thorough going-over, and perhaps the new version of *Brother to Dragons* will provide the occasion for such a debate.

Warren makes it as clear as possible, both in his introductory comments and within the text itself, where he openly invents the missing pieces of his puzzle, that his aim is not simply to show how it *really* was (*wie es eigentlich gewesen*) at Rocky Hill the night of Sunday, December 15, 1811. Warren is after bigger game. Even in his youthful excursion into history-writing, *John Brown: The Making of a Martyr*, Warren was less interested in the "Truth" of history than in the way the "truths" which comprise the record come into being. The writer's aim, if we may believe his introduction, has to do with exploring the relationship of personal myth—including the "little myth" which is the poem—to history, the "big myth we live, and in our living, constantly remake" (p. xiii). Merrill's account of the Lewis tragedy, meticulous as it appears, fails to dispose of all the *factual* uncertainties in the case, let alone the large uncertainties of motive, meaning, and value. Such a "failure," if it is one, is no fault of Merrill but is due rather to the intrinsic and proper limitations of his inquiry. This competent and scholarly summation of the records tells us a great deal about the texture, composition, and origin of the amber enclosing the specimen, but tells us little of the creature within it. Warren's account speculates intelligently not only upon the savage-looking life-form within the amber but the face reflected in it as well. Are we not served, and served well, by both accounts?

Few would dispute that Warren is a better, more versatile, and technically accomplished poet now than in 1953, when the first version of *Brother to Dragons* appeared. But the special virtues of that work are not everywhere compatible with the austerer qualities of his recent verse. It was partly the range of feeling and experience, expressed in an astonishing, omnivorous style, which excited the admiration of poets like Lowell, Jarrell, and Delmore Schwartz. Vulgar, banal, and elevated by turns, the poem lived by its extravagant contrasts, counterpoints, and surprises. There remain raw surfaces in the work which neither long staring nor mature understanding can soften or mellow; there are, in short, still occasions proper to the sustained shrillness of the early style. But the poet's achievement in *both* versions was to encompass in a single work—and in meaningful dramatic relationship—a full sense of the horror of Lilburne's crime and the grave, affectionate reminiscence of his own father. One must look a long time for a larger definition of the human possibilities.

Notes

1. Published in New York by Random House, 1979. I refer to this text hereafter by page number only in the body of the text. Permission to quote has been kindly granted by the publisher.

2. "Robert Penn Warren: An Interview," in Marshall Walker, *Robert Penn Warren: A Vision Earned* (New York: Barnes & Noble, 1979), p. 248.

3. *Brother to Dragons: A Tale in Verse and Voices* (New York: Random House, 1953), pp. 5–6. Quoted by permission of Random House, Inc.

4. I refer to the text, *Brother to Dragons: A Play in Two Acts*, published in *Georgia Review*, 30 (1976), 65–138.

5. *Brother to Dragons: A Play*, p. 105.

6. "The Long and the Short of It," (review of *Brother to Dragons* and *Now and Then: Poems, 1976-1978*) in *New York Review of Books*, 21 Feb. 1980, p. 27.

"Sacramental Vision: The Poetry of Robert Penn Warren"

A. L. Clements*

For the abundance, range, variety, and high achievement in both fiction and poetry, one thinks back to Lawrence and Hardy for comparisons with Robert Penn Warren. There are important differences too, to be sure. Whereas Hardy wrote most of his poetry only after he abandoned novel-writing, Warren, who published his first book of poems a few years before his first novel, has continued to write in both genres throughout his lifetime, his tenth novel, *A Place To Come To*, being published the same year as his eleventh volume of poetry, *Selected Poems 1923–1975* (1977). (That this is his third *Selected Poems*—previous ones appeared in 1944 and 1966—is in itself an extraordinary mark of accomplishment.) And whereas Lawrence, who produced magnificent poetry as well as bald assertions wigged out typographically in the shape of printed poems, will always be acclaimed a greater novelist than poet, Warren may finally be considered a better poet than novelist, especially if literary honors and awards are any sign of judgment to come. His first major recognition was the Pulitzer Prize for *All the King's Men* (1946), but in the past twenty years the awards, a long list of them, have been for his poetry: another Pulitzer in 1957, followed by the National Book Award, the Edna St. Vincent Millay Prize, the Bollingen Prize, the Van Wyck Brooks Award, and the Copernicus Award from the Academy of American Poets, among other recognitions. And one may reasonably expect other equally and more prestigious awards to follow.

In addition to his poetry and novels, Warren (like Lawrence) has published numerous other books: a play, short stories, biographies, influential criticism and textbooks, editions of other poets, and historical work, so that some critics consider him the most accomplished and distinguished living American man of letters. It is fortunate to have this other body of writing because, among other reasons, much of Warren's own poetry may best be regarded in the light of his own articulate

*Reprinted with permission from the *South Atlantic Bulletin*, 43, No. 4 (1978), 47–65. Copyright © 1978, South Atlantic Modern Language Association.

216

criticism. We are familiar with his view that a poem is an organic system of relationships and that the poetic quality should not be understood as consisting in one or more elements taken in isolation but rather in relation to each other and to the total organization, the *structure*, of the poem. Decades ago, Warren opposed theories of "pure" poetry, which tend to legislate out of poetry certain elements that might qualify or contradict the original impulse of the poem.[1] He has, furthermore, always sought some connection between "my central and obsessive concern with 'poetry' . . . and the 'real' world." In an interview published in *Writers at Work*, he describes poetry as "a vital activity . . . related to ideas and life."[2] His essay on Coleridge records the view that ". . . the truth is implicit in the poetic act as such . . . the moral concern and the aesthetic concern are aspects of the same activity, the creative activity, and . . . this activity is expressive of the whole mind."[3] And his most recent essay, *Democracy and Poetry* (1975), observes that the central "fact" of poetry is the concept of the self, which he defines as "in individuation, the felt principle of significant unity," *significant* implying both continuity and responsibility: that is, "the self as a development in time, with a past and a future" and "the self as a moral identity, recognizing itself as capable of action worthy of praise or blame . . . What poetry most significantly celebrates is the capacity of man to face the deep, dark inwardness of his nature and his fate."[4] Thus his expository prose spells out what we recognize in his fiction and poetry to be his major triune theme of self, time, and moral responsibility, and reveals what for him is the vital purpose of poetry.

With this critical focus from his own essays, we may more clearly and pertinently review Warren's prolific poetic career, a career that is divisible into three distinct periods: 1923–1943, 1943–1960, and 1960–1975. Many poems of each period have a decidedly philosophic and religious content, being preoccupied with his major tripartite theme as well as with guilt and innocence, love and the imagination, death and rebirth. But Warren avoids dogmatism, often minimizes explicit commentary, qualifies ironically, balances tensions. His poetry moves over the years toward "sacramental vision," expressed increasingly in sequences and in the "principle of interrelatedness."

II

Warren's latest volume of poetry, *Selected Poems 1923–1975*, reprints 23 of the 42 poems published in *Selected Poems 1923–1943*, which was largely composed of *Thirty-six Poems* (1935) and *Eleven Poems on the Same Theme* (1942). Astute critic that he is, Warren has made essentially the right choices. Reminders of his association with the Fugitives, of the Ransom and Tate manners, of the Metaphysicals (particularly Donne and Marvell), and Eliot-like devices and diction remain,

beside his own distinctive signature. Common to this poetic company are
the much discussed complexity of attitude, psychological subtlety, strong
dramatic sense, textural density, abrupt transitions and shifts of tone, jux-
taposition of abstract, meditative lines and concrete colloquial passages,
and even metrical alternation from smooth to harsh and from tight to
loose lines; most of these being modes of contrast, tension, and inclusion.
Lines from the powerful early poem on the death of the poet's mother,
"The Return: An Elegy," illustrate some of these characteristics:

It will be the season when milkweed blossoms burn.

The old bitch is dead
what have I said!
I have only said what the wind said . . .

turn backward turn backward O time in your flight
and make me a child again just for tonight
good lord he's wet the bed come bring a light . . .

Warren has kept ten of the *Eleven Poems on the Same Theme*, but
these have been radically re-arranged and interspersed among the eleven
poems remaining from *Thirty-six Poems*. Nevertheless, groups of juxtaposed poems, most very formally patterned, emerge and, together with
"Mexico Is A Foreign Country: Four Studies in Naturalism" (originally
Five Studies), adumbrate a developing interest in writing and arranging
thematically and technically echoic poems into sequences (much more
about that later). The opening lines alone of "Monologue at Midnight,"
"Picnic Remembered," and the much explicated and anthologized
"Bearded Oaks," for example, reveal a ready similarity of setting and subject. "Terror," "Pursuit," "Original Sin: A Short Story," and "Crime,"
still another group, are not only "on the same theme" but so uniformly
dense, minimally generalized, and tightly organized in the successive
images of their formal stanzas that F. O. Matthiessen in his 1944 review
and Victor Strandberg on the very first page of his 1965 book on Warren's
poetry remarked upon the "obscurity" of these and other poems. Today
we do not see them quite so. The "you" at the center of each of the four
poems has in "Terror" "no adequate definition of terror." This poem pictures an age of neurotic anxieties and a world spending itself in its own
destruction, repeating "The crime of Onan, spilled upon the ground,"
while genuine terror seems a pre-condition for salvation. The wholly non-
committed person, the one with the "darling and inept" terrors, equally
as guilty as the sensation-seeking destroyers of self and the world, sees
nothing, heeds nothing, does not "ask tonight where sleeps/That head
which hooped the jewel Fidelity"—that is, is faithful to nothing; on the
other hand, "the conscience-stricken stare/Kisses the terror."

"Pursuit" also concerns search for meaning, in particular "The secret
you are seeking" to eradicate deeply-buried pain. You cannot buy the

secret with charitable purchases, so you take your pain to a doctor, the usurper of priest and poet, who does not know you carry your pain very deep inside you. Hence his prescription: "you simply need a change of scene." Seeking the secret in Florida, you consider nature in the form of the flamingo; that form, returning no answer, takes the shape of a question. Looking for the answers from the other guests, even from the innocent child, is finally fruitless. You are thus left sitting alone, "which is the beginning of error," for "solution, perhaps, is public, despair personal." Though you will continue fruitless wandering, unless you see the inwardness of your disease, there may yet be a palliative, hope maybe, and even perhaps rebirth through commitment to some external support: "the little old lady in black . . . rattles her crutch, which may put forth a small bloom, perhaps white," "perhaps" being a frequent qualifier in Warren's poetry. His perception of the human condition does not permit expectations of vast or easily affected changes.

In "Crime" Warren ironically invites us to "Envy the mad killer," because he, with a kind of childlike innocence, has buried his crime, cannot even remember it. Nor can he "formulate the delicious/And smooth convolution of terror, like whipped cream." In "Original Sin: A Short Story" the pursuing "you" of "Pursuit" becomes the pursued; "the nightmare," original sin, is now the pursuer and cannot be buried. As in "Pursuit," changing places does not alter the darkness in the very nature of man, the partially fixed and inherited capacity for evil and irrationality. "There must be a new innocence for us to be stayed by," but this poem does not "endeavor definition." Naive utopianism and easy panaceas evaporate when to the tentativeness of "may . . . small . . . perhaps" and the restraint and qualification of other poems, like "Ransom," is added the knowledge that the nightmare is never entirely lost.

The most ambitious, longest, and best poem from *Selected Poems 1923–1943* still is "The Ballad of Billie Potts," still placed at the head of the selection, but now slightly revised. Many of Warren's persistent essential themes inform the poem, a structural unit that integrates a colloquial narrative section and a choric, meditative section, an effective combination of Warren's strong story-telling and speculative abilities. These themes and the double-thread form appear in *At Heaven's Gate* and *All the King's Men*, novels nearly contemporaneous with the poem, and propose a view of reality as dialectical process rather than static perfection. Uniting contrary impulses and discordant elements, "The Ballad" is rich, gritty, funny, pitiful, and tragic, and (together with "Mexico Is A Foreign Country," a poem of hearty and humorous coarseness) it marked a breaking away from the mannered, purely intellectualized modes that were popular some decades ago.

The story element of "The Ballad of Billie Potts," based on material Warren heard in his youth and acquiring mythic proportions through his treatment, concerns an inn-keeping family: Big Billie Potts, his "dark and little" wife, and their son, Little Billie, "A clabber-headed bastard with snot in his nose," who have a lucrative side-business of robbing their former customers on the road. Little Billie attempts to commit a robbery himself, fails at it, is wounded and, for safety's sake, is sent out West by his parents. The Prodigal returns ten years later but is not recognized by his parents, who sink a hatchet into his head for his money and then learn too late what they have done. Such is the simple narrative outline. But the various thematic implications are not as easily set down. The lines

> (There was a beginning but you cannot see it.
> There will be an end but you cannot see it. . . .)

suggest a recurrent interest of Warren's: man's predicament of lacking sufficient knowledge in time. The context of these lines indicate that the beginning is with the father, a variation on the doctrine of Original Sin. Little Billie tries to escape West and find himself; but as seen in other poems you cannot escape what is always pursuing you, and you must stay, face responsibility, and earn definition.

> There is always another name and another face . . .
> The name and the face are you.
> The name and the face are always new . . .
> For they have been dipped in the redeeming blood.
> For they have been dipped in Time.

In this sacramental vision, a man in Time cannot know the end, cannot know until he is out of Time. But, another edge to the irony, a man can be redeemed only in Time. The poem remarks that innocence, associated by Warren with childhood as it always mythically is associated, was lost long ago, and it concludes with this image of "you, wanderer, back,"

> To kneel in the sacramental silence of evening
> At the feet of the old man
> Who is evil and ignorant and old,
> To kneel
> With the little black mark under your heart,
> Which is your name,
> Which is shaped for luck,
> Which is your luck.

As in "Original Sin," Warren affirms the need for a new innocence, but again he does not here attempt definition. There are only "hints and guesses" and the direction taken in the poems of Warren's middle and late periods.

III

In the decade after *Selected Poems 1923–1943*, Warren was preoccupied with writing and publishing several volumes of fiction and his "novel in verse," *Brother to Dragons* (1953). He returned to the "short" form in *Promises: Poems 1954–1956*, widely regarded as more successful than the experimental *You, Emperors, and Others: Poems 1957–1960*. After considerably reducing this later volume for *Selected Poems 1923–1966*, Warren has made further cuts so that only about half of *You, Emperors, and Others* now appears in *Selected Poems 1923–1975*. Still, unsatisfactory poems remain, such as "Switzerland" and especially "Man in the Street" with its jarring jingling rimes. "Mortmain," one of several groups of poems, is the most effective and moving in *You, Emperors*, its subject being the poet's father and the father's death, developed in five poems with a shifting time scheme that proceeds achronologically from the 1950s to the 1880s. On the whole, however, *You, Emperors* must be regarded as a largely failed experiment, Warren's least impressive book of poetry.

Except for the very short last poem, "The Necessity for Belief," all of the extraordinary *Promises* has been reprinted in *Selected Poems 1923–1975*. The subject of childhood and Warren's bent for twofoldness are again evident in *Promises*, which is divided into two sections. The first and smaller section, "To a Little Girl, One Year Old, in a Ruined Fortress," dedicated to his daughter, has a Mediterranean setting in a season which moves from summer toward autumn. The second, longer section, "Promises," dedicated to his son, is itself of a twofold nature: most of these poems draw their material from Warren's recollections of his childhood in Kentucky during the early years of this century, and other poems are addressed and applicable to his son. The basic subject matter of childhood helps give thematic continuity to the book's quest for self-discovery, contemporary childhood contrasting and interacting with recollected childhood, and encourages a ranging from intense personal feelings to historical and universal implications.

In his criticism of "The Rime of the Ancient Mariner," Warren writes that there are two themes, the primary theme of sacramental vision or of "One Life" and the secondary theme of the imagination; sacramental vision and the imagination are construed as distinguishable aspects of the same reality. He approaches the secondary theme through the symbol of different kinds of light, discussing the constant contrast between moonlight, symbolizing the imagination, and sunlight, symbolizing the "mere reflective faculty" which, Coleridge said, partakes of "Death." Warren points out that in the poem the good events occur under the aegis of the moon, and the bad events, under that of the sun. The issue is a bit complicated in that the operation and effect of the imagination can be both joyous and terrifying. In his own poetry, Warren makes similar use of light imagery and the themes of sacramental vision and imagination, though he often substitutes starlight for moonlight in his later poetry.

Recollections are present imaginings of the past. In "Court-Martial," written in short couplets and triplets, the speaker recalls his grandfather's story of the hangings of bushwhackers during the Civil War. "I see him now, as once seen." The grandfather and grandson sit in the shade of an evergreen, "withdrawn from the heat of the sun," the light of which dapples the objects under the boughs. The old cavalryman's story is itself a recollection—a history, in one sense, the significance of which the speaker tries to discover:

> I sought, somehow, to untie
> The knot of History,
> For in our shade I knew
> That only the Truth is true,
> That life is only the act
> To transfigure all fact,
> And life is only a story
> And death is only the glory
> Of the telling of the story,
> And the *done* and the *to-be-done*
> In that timelessness were one
> Beyond the poor *being done*.

While raising questions concerning History, Truth, Time, the poem suggests that the final reality is somehow involved with the imagination. Just after the old man has concluded his story and before the poem ends, the speaker turns away and sees his grandfather, "not old now—but young," riding out of the sky. This is imagined in detail: the saddle, the cavalry boots, the hanged men with outraged faces taking shape behind the rider. The poem concludes:

> The horseman does not look back.
> Blank-eyed, he continues his track,
> Riding toward me there,
> Through the darkening air.
>
> The world is real. It is there.

What, considered in its context, is the world referred to in the last line; what is the referent of "there"? The world external to the mind or the world as transfigured by the deific imagination? The answer may well be both. But internal considerations lead to the conclusion that "world" and "there" refer in a special sense to the world shaped by the speaker's imagination: History, Truth, and Time are functions of the creative imagination, which has a value-giving capacity. The external world or natural order is devoid of values. Taken by itself, there is no one thing in the natural order that is better than any other thing. The poem (and particularly the line, "life is only a story") does not empty reality of its content; it makes it clear that the content is given value and meaning by the imagination.

Just as in this poem of recollection so in "Lullaby: Smile in Sleep" the theme of imagination as a kind of ultimate, transcendental (in Kant's sense) shaping force finds expression. Lulling his infant son, the speaker says "You will dream the world anew." Awake, the boy in years to come will see a violent world, the truth perverted, and love betrayed; thus is his obligation greater to "Dream perfection": the more imperfect the world the greater is the human need for perfection. The image serves to re-create and to perfect imperfect reality and gives "our hope new patent to/Enfranchise the human possibility./Grace undreamed is grace forgone./Dream grace, son." The tension of lullaby juxtaposed against images of violence is resolved in the last stanza:

> There's never need to fear
> Violence of the poor world's abstract storm.
> For now you dream Reality.
> Matter groans to touch your hand.
> Matter lifts now like the sea
> Toward that cold moon that is your dream's command.
> Dream the power coming on.

The implications are clear: as the moon influences the sea, so the dream or image, which is the working of the imagination, shapes inferior matter. Warren's conception of the imagination is precisely Coleridgean. The imagination organizes what otherwise would be chaotic sensation, and, contrariwise, it anchors the reason in images of sensation, so that the imagination repeats "in the finite mind . . . the eternal act of creation in the infinite I am." The primary imagination creates the world and the self; the secondary imagination is the value-creating capacity; and one knows by creating.

The child as well as the poem is a "promise"; both renew the world. In Warren, childhood has much of the same prominence and significance that it does in Henry Vaughan and Thomas Traherne. The Infant Boy at Midcentury, we read in a poem of that title, enters "our world at scarcely its finest hour . . . in the year when promises are broken," when the need for renewal is great. Thus the poet has attempted to order and set down meanings wrung from early experience as a legacy to the child. Though there will be "modification of landscape . . . And expansion, we trust, of the human heart-hope, and hand-scope," Warren does not sentimentally anticipate vast changes or changes easily effected. The poems of recollection present images of a violent and terror-ridden world: a summer storm bringing havoc to a county; the founding fathers in their defects; some unidentifiable evil terrifying another county; a father murdering his entire family. The same dark and hidden forces that, submerged, lie waiting to spring and do spring in one generation do not simply disappear in the next. Thus

> The new age will need the old lies, as our own more than
> once did;
> For death is ten thousand nights—yes, it's only the process

> Of accommodating flesh to idea, but there's natural distress
> In learning to face Truth's glare-glory, from which our eyes
>   are long hid. ("Infant Boy at Midcentury")

The need of finding Truth to live by is related to Warren's pervasive theme of the need for self-definition; he who has discovered and defined himself in finding a Truth by which to live an integrated life can face "the awful responsibility of Time."

The difficult problem of truth-finding is further complicated by the elusiveness of the meanings of experiences. Such elusiveness preoccupies several poems: "Dark Woods," "Country Burying (1919)," "School Lesson . . . ," "Dark Night of the Soul," and others. In "The Dogwood," the second section of "Dark Woods," the speaker is walking in, not merely stopping by, the dark woods at night. These were the woods of his childhood. Now suddenly he comes across a dogwood tree, "White-floating in darkness . . . white bloom in dark air." He experiences a mixture of feelings: first joy, and then wrath so that he would have struck the tree if a stick had been handy.

> But one wasn't handy, so there on the path then, breath scant,
> You stood, you stood there, and oh, could the poor heart's
>   absurd
> Cry for wisdom, for wisdom, ever be answered? Triumphant,
> All night, the tree glimmered in darkness, and uttered
>   no word.

This object of white in dark should, it seems to the speaker, have held the key to meaning; but the speaker remains outside the still moment, not entering into intuitive illumination. As with other tree imagery, the dogwood in the night, a contrast of opposites, is both a symbol of reality and of the speaker's wish for insight into it.

It is this insight, resulting in the silent state of being "blessed past joy or despair" (from "Boy's Will . . .") that the poems, finally, move toward. On the word "blessedness," which in its different grammatical forms appears repeatedly in the later poetry, Walter Stace remarks: "Whatever may be the root and derivation of this word in common language, it is now a wholly religious and mystical word, and not a part of the common naturalistic vocabulary at all."[5] The ultimate symbolizandum of Warren's poetry, as of all religious language, is the mystical or transcendental or peak experience. That this is so is clearly evidenced in the sacramental vision and the principle of interrelatedness of the more recent poems of *Tale of Time: New Poems 1960–1966, Incarnations: Poems 1966–1968, Audubon: A Vision* (1969), *Or Else—Poem/Poems 1968–1974,* and "Can I See Arcturus from Where I Stand? Poems 1975."

IV

While a number of pieces have been moved to *Or Else*, only six poems from Warren's previous four volumes have not been reproduced in *Selected Poems 1923-1975*, more than half of which (188 of 325 pages) consists of poems written between 1960-1975, clear and accurate recognition by Warren himself of the general superiority of his later poems over his earliest work. He has been increasingly both a more prolific poet and a remarkably better one.

These four recent volumes as well as "Can I See Arcturus From Where I Stand?," the ten new poems published in *Selected Poems 1923-1975*, demonstrate both poetic continuity and development in a poetry stylistically more lucid, firm, and powerful, with somewhat less tentativeness and qualification. The strokes are bolder and yet the nuances more subtle and various, usually through a directness of poetic narrative, more frequent use of the long line, and added emphasis on the colloquial, though sometimes the language is plainly too flat. Warren's later poetry is less metaphysically knotty and dense than his early work but no less complex in significance. He can still delight us with echoes of the Metaphysical manner, with "glittering ambiguity" and a "more complex/Version of Zeno's paradox" ("Paradox" in "Can I See Arcturus . . ."), but that of course was never his own major mode so much as a part of a more various, inclusive style and of his insight into a diverse range of writers and traditions. His later poetry is intellectual without being intellectualized, with few exceptions idea not being purposelessly substituted for image. Warren is now as accomplished at presenting descriptive images which "effortlessly" expand into metaphor and meaning as he is at developing narrative, always his great strength. Exceptionally vivid descriptions and extraordinarily pleasing sounds frequently appear as integral parts of a poem's progress (see, for example, "Forever O'Clock" and "Composition in Gold and Red-Gold" in *Or Else*). The later poems are generally less formally arranged in meter, line length, and rime, but Warren has developed enormous skill in the syntax of the sentence, the placement of the words in the line, the use of spacing, and the rhythms thereby and otherwise produced. While he takes radical risks in language, thought, and structure, the poetry achieves seemingly stunningly simple and often powerfully direct effects.

Many of Warren's later poems are remarkable for the quality of unanticipated yet just and engaging, sometimes overwhelmingly effective and memorable last lines. The ring, reason, and rhythm of these last lines remain long after reading within the reader's memory. It will not do to quote only a few lines in illustration. For (and herein lies the principle of interrelatedness), the lines must be taken and understood in context, and by "context" is meant not only the poem of which the last line or lines are a part, but also the sequence of which the poem is a part, the volume of which the sequence is a part, and the total body of Warren's poetry of which any one volume is a part. This principle of interrelatedness functions as the major formal and technical aspect of his more recent poetry as well as a major semantic dimension of his sacramental vision and the subsumed central themes of time, self, responsibility, love, death, rebirth, and joy.

Since the publication in 1942 of *Eleven Poems On The Same Theme*, Warren has been writing in groups of poems, increasingly so from *Promises* on, as just a glance at the table of contents in *Selected Poems 1923–1975* readily though only partially indicates. Not only grouping and repeated subjects and thematic concerns but also full sequences with the recurrence of certain words and images conduce to the sense of continuity and integration. *Audubon: A Vision* reads as a single long poem composed of shorter poems. And in a foreword, Warren has said exactly that about *Or Else*: "this book is conceived as a single poem composed of a number of shorter poems or sections or chapters." Simplifying slightly, *Or Else*, preoccupied with remembrance of things past ("Time is the mirror into which you stare"), begins in summer, progresses soon thereafter from very frequent images of snow to thaw near the end of the book, from death to rebirth, from parent to self to son and blessedness ("For what blessing may a man hope for but/An immortality in/The loving vigilance of death?"), from uncertainty about the self (*"Is this really me?"*) to rediscovery of the self. The words *dream* and *see* (and their grammatical variations) keep reappearing, often associated with the past, the imagination, and sacramental vision. Images of mountains and especially of stars ("Man lives by images," we read in "Reading Late At Night, Thermometer Falling," a marvelous and moving poem on Warren's father) abound in this volume. They do also in "Can I See Arcturus From Where I Stand?" which has eight of its ten poems star-lit or night-set and which takes its epigraph, "Is *was* but a word for wisdom, its price?" from a poem in *Or Else*.

Warren employs a number of other means for indicating interrelatedness both within and between sequences and volumes. For example, in the later poetry, he vastly increases the number of run-on lines, not only from line to line but also between stanzas, sections, and even whole poems within a sequence. For another example, *Tale of Time*, which asserts "To know is, always, all," has one poem in the title sequence that ends with the question "What is love?"; the next poem concludes "You have not answered my question." The answer or rather one answer comes two volumes later in *Audubon: A Vision*, in the poem "Love and Knowledge," which tells us about the birds Audubon painted that

> He put them where they are, and there we see them:
> In our imagination.

And then the poem concludes:

> What is love?
>
> One name for it is knowledge.

Knowledge here being Audubon's loving, creative, imaginative apprehension and rendering of his birds and perhaps also the viewers', "our," imaginative perception.

Added significance and purpose obtain in Warren's poetic sequences because his metaphysic regards reality as relational or interrelated. As *Incarnations* reads, "Truth lives only in relation," and from one of the Arcturus poems: "you are a part/Of everything, and your heart bleeds far/Beyond the outermost pulsar." (It is now an ecological truism that everything is ultimately connected to everything else; science has finally confirmed what poets and mystics have intuited and experienced—actually sensed and felt—for centuries.) Like the world's body, each poem is itself an organic system of relationships, and each poem, as each creature, object, and event in the world, has full meaning, value, and being not separately in isolation from but interdependently in relation to all others. Form and content, especially in Warren's later work, are themselves inextricably interwoven.

In "Holy Writ," from *Tale of Time*, the biblical Samuel, concerned about his "son," expresses a view of time to be found throughout Warren's poetry and novels too:

> I am the past time, am old, but
> Am, too, the time to come, for I,
> In my knowledge, close my eyes, and am
> The membrane between the past and the future,
>   am thin, and
> That thinness is the present time, the membrane
> Is only my anguish, through which
> The past seeps, penetrates, is absorbed into
> The future, through which
> The future bleeds into, becomes, the past even before
> It ceases to be
> The future.

Earlier in the same volume, Warren had written that "Truth"

> Is all. But
> I must learn to speak it
> Slowly, in a whisper.
> Truth, in the end, can never be spoken aloud,
> For the future is always unpredictable.
> But so is the past . . .   ("Insomnia")

In *Incarnations* we read that "The world"

Is fruitful, and I, too,
In that I am the father
Of my father's father's father. I,
Of my father, have set the teeth on edge. But
By what grape? I have cried out in the night.

("The Leaf")

Similarly, in *All the King's Men*, Jack Burden, who comes to realize that "all times are one time" and "nothing is ever lost," says "I eat a persimmon and the teeth of a tinker in Tibet are put on edge." The allusion in both the poetry and prose is of course to the biblical "the fathers have eaten a sour grape and their children's teeth are set on edge" (Jer. 31:29; Ezek. 18:2), which is one succinct formulation of the doctrine of Original Sin. "All times are one time" in the sense that, as Samuel's words suggest, any event in time is meaningful only in relation to past and future events. The past is not separate and completed in itself but an ever-developing part of a changing present and future. Once this knowledge is learned, one's individual life and all life may be seen to fall into coherent and inevitable patterns which give meaning to the past, present, and future. We all have and are a multiplicity of fathers because we inherit all of the past and we bequeath our lifetime.

Warren's conception of the self parallels his view of time: a past self or a past life is never simply over, for the past exists not only as past but simultaneously with the present in the sense that, being a part of the present self, it influences the present, as it and the present shape the future. Hence the importance and recurrence in Warren's work of history, recollecting the past, childhood, relationships between generations. Warren further distinguishes between two selves: a surface, spurious, temporal self and a deeper, essential, and eternal (that is, timeless) self (Warren has used the terms "ideal" and "regenerate" self). The first self or ego is one's conception of oneself, the role one assumes and is assigned to play, the known created object, not the knowing, imaginative, creative Act. As shown, for example, by "Interjection #5: Solipsism and Theology," with its repeated "Wild with ego," the ego is a prideful sense of separate existence, a rather abstract and conventional notion of oneself rather than the actual, concrete, living reality. To be in touch with this latter nontemporal real self, which paradoxically develops only in time and in vital relation to community, is to be blessed. Warren writes of Jean Jacques Audubon:

His life, at the end, seemed—even the anguish—simple.
Simple, at least, in that it had to be,
Simply, what it was, as he was,
In the end, himself and not what
He had known he ought to be. The blessedness!—

To wake in some dawn and see,
As though down a rifle barrel, lined up
Like sights, the self that was, the self that is, and there,
Far off but in range, completing that alignment, your fate.

Hold your breath, let the trigger-squeeze be slow and steady.

The quarry lifts, in the halo of gold leaves, its noble head.

This is not a dimension of Time.
("The Sign Whereby He Knew")

Various succinct though incomplete expressions of Warren's complex
sacramental vision appear throughout his poetry, such as in the prob-
lematic, prosy "Interjection #4" from *Or Else*:

If blood
Was shed, it was, in a way, sacramental, redeeming . . .
Dear God, we pray
To be restored to that purity of heart
That sanctifies the shedding of blood.

More clearly and certainly: "we are all one flesh," "The world/Is a
parable and we are/The meaning," "do you truly, truly,/Know what flesh
is, and if it is . . . really sacred?" from *Incarnations*, one of whose
epigraphs is from Nehemiah 5, "Yet now our flesh is as the flesh of our
brethren." And "have you . . . eaten the flesh of your own heart?" and
"the dream of the eating of human flesh" from *Tale of Time*. The last
phrase is from the title poem "Tale of Time," which centrally concerns
the death of the speaker's mother, just as many of Warren's later poems
dwell or touch upon death. "Tale of Time" also provides this fuller expression of sacramental vision:

But the solution: You
Must eat the dead.
You must eat them completely, bone, blood, flesh, gristle, even
Such hair as can be forced. You
Must undertake this in the dark of the moon, but
At your plenilune of anguish.

Immortality is not impossible,
Even joy.

History, all time, and the cruel, inescapable fact of death are to be incorporated in and by the living. Acceptance, indeed affirmation, of the past
and of change or transience, is essential to successful self definition, that
is, to knowing one's deep, regenerate self, that "unself which was self,"
"that darkness of sleep which/Is the past, and is/The self." Self-

knowledge, in turn, gives direction to the future and induces in one, as in Audubon, a capacity more fully to love and sympathize.

Self-knowledge, however, is never completed; it is a process of continuous becoming because the self is always in the process of becoming a new self, of coming into new relations with others. "You are not you," one of Warren's novels reads, "except in terms of relation to other people." Self-knowledge is difficult because the self is not so much just a knowable object but rather a series of relations in time. Hence the necessity of sacramentally eating the dead, incorporating the past and all time in a kind of communion, to discover one's larger, eternal self and thereby attain "Immortality . . . Even joy."

Something of the principle of interrelatedness as method and of an end of sacramental vision appears in *Or Else* in the remarkable "Interjection #2: Caveat":

> Necessarily, we must think of the
> world as continuous, for if it were
> not so I would have told you, for I have
> bled for this knowledge, and every man
> is a sort of Jesus . . .

The poem moves from a prosy "metaphysical" beginning on continuity and discontinuity to contrasting plain, subtle statement, even understatement, describing a highway under construction with miles of crushed rock and recommending that you "fix your eyes firmly on/one fragment of crushed rock," highway and fragment becoming metaphors for continuity and discontinuity. At first the rock "only/glows a little," then it glitters and vibrates, the earth underfoot twitches,

> the bright sun
> jerks like a spastic, and all things seem to
> be spinning away from the univer-
> sal center that the single fragment of
> crushed rock has ineluctably become. . . .

> at last, the object screams

> in an ectasy of

> being.

The poem leads suddenly to overwhelming vision, makes us see. In other words, another aspect of Warren's sacramental vision obtains in the illuminated, imaginative perceptions into reality as joyous and sacred, when "every/Ulcer in love's lazaret may, like a dawn-stung gem, sing—or even burst into whoops of, perhaps, holiness," as we read in "There's A Grandfather's Clock In The Hall," a poem which attains grace beyond the reach of art.

At times the divine is seen as incarnate in the world. In such perfect moments, or epiphanic spots of time, ordinary, everyday events and entities appear extraordinary and transcendent, become charged through the creative imagination with enormous physical, emotional, and spiritual meanings, are more fully created or brought into fuller being. "All the things of the universe," as Whitman says, "are seen as perfect miracles." Or as Zen puts it, "How marvelous, how supernatural, I draw water and carry wood!" Emerson also, as Warren remarks in his sequence "Homage to Emerson," "thought that significance shines through everything." Examples abound in Warren's later poetry, often associated with images of light, such as the exceptionally fine "Two Poems About Suddenly and a Rose" from the sequence "Delight" in *Tale of Time*, which lead us to see that "The rose dies laughing, suddenly."

"Trying To Tell You Something" and "Brotherhood In Pain," two companion poems in "Can I See Arcturus . . . ," develop the idea that "All things lean at you, and some are/Trying to tell you something," and conclude that any chance object you fix your eyes on will "smile shyly, and try to love you." In *Or Else*, "The mountains lean. They watch. They know" ("Little Boy And Lost Shoe"). In the same volume, the speaker recalls the time he looked at the stars and cried out

> "O reality!" The stars
> Love me. I love them. I wish they
>
> Loved God, too. I truly wish that. ("Stargazing!")

And he remembers

> How once I, a boy, crouching at creekside,
> Watched, in the sunlight, a handful of water
> Drip, drip, from my hand. The drops—they were bright!
> ("Blow, West Wind")

Not uncharacteristically, Warren concludes this poem with a balancing ironic tension, "But you believe nothing, with the evidence lost." Nevertheless, sacramental vision exists also in present time without irony or contradiction. From *Incarnations*, we read

> When there is a strong swell, you may, if you surrender to it,
>   experience
> A sense, in the act, of mystic unity with that rhythm. Your
>   peace is the sea's will.

This poem, "Masts at Dawn," indicating that imaginative loving (an act of enlightened loving apprehension) leads to seeing the incarnate divine, concludes "We must try/To love so well the world that we may believe, in the end, in God." And, finally, this instance of "dream"-like or imaginative, illuminated, joyful vision beyond the rational knowing of the "mere reflective faculty," with the consequent "perfect stillness," from *Audubon*:

The world declares itself. That voice
Is vaulted in—oh, arch on arch—redundancy of joy, its end
Is its beginning, necessity
Blooms like a rose. Why,

Therefore, is truth the only thing that cannot
Be spoken?

It can only be enacted, and that in dream,
Or in the dream become, as though unconsciously, action . . .

He walked in the world. He was sometimes seen to stand
In perfect stillness, when no leaf stirred.
                    ("The Sign Whereby He Knew")

If Warren's poetry thus affirms life and its moments of perfect stillness, it does so only after its journey through the valley of the suffering and the dead, only after spending its season in hell. Audubon comes to his vision some time after witnessing the violent death by hanging of a woman and her two sons, described with precise detail. He who "felt the splendor of God . . . , loved the world . . . and wrote: " 'in my sleep I continually dream of birds' " knew also that the world "though wicked in all conscience is *perhaps* as good as worlds unknown." Affirmation thus obtains through the tentativeness of the italicized qualifier *perhaps* and after various means of balanced ironic tension. Similarly, *Incarnations* contains both the long poetic sequence "Internal Injuries," which concerns the death by execution of a convict and the death by automobile accident of his mother, and also such balancing *seemingly* contradictory yet all "true" statements as "The world means only itself," "the world is a metaphor," "the world is a parable and we are the meaning," and "only Nothingness is real and is a sea of light," this last being one of several expressions of the mystical *via negativa* to be found in Warren's poetry. A good number of poems in *Or Else* and several poetic sequences in *Tale of Time* likewise centrally involve violence and death, including one death by suicide. In short, Warren's joyful, interrelated, sacramental vision is not an easy or facilely optimistic one but one gained through judicious qualification and hard, unblinking, recurrent recognition, even a pervasive sense, of pain, darkness, and death. Thus *Incarnations*: "The terror is, all promises are kept. Even happiness"; "and there is no joy without some pain." The rose dies laughing, suddenly.

All items listed above belong in the world
In which all things are continuous,
And are parts of the original dream which
I am now trying to discover the logic of. This
Is the process whereby pain of the past in its pastness
May be converted into the future tense

Of joy. ("I Am Dreaming of a White Christmas . . ."
                    in *Or Else*.)

V

We may say finally of Warren exactly what he has written of Audubon: "He yearns to be able to frame a definition of joy." And exactly what he has written of Flaubert:

> his heart
> burst with a solemn thanksgiving to God for
> the fact he could perceive the worth of the
> world with such joy. ("Flaubert in Egypt" in *Or Else*)

For Warren knows, as Yeats has written:

> When such as I cast out remorse
> So great a sweetness flows into the breast
> We must laugh and we must sing,
> We are blest by everything,
> Everywhere we look upon is blest.

In Warren's later poems, the sense of human limitations is as strong as in his early poems, but the sense of the possibilities of joy and blessedness is somewhat greater. His poems point to and progress toward the joyous and blessed experience in which lies the perfect repose of silence. "Silence, in timelessness, gives forth/Time, and receives it again" ("The True Nature of Time"). *Incarnations* contains the prayer "Forgive us—oh, give us!—our joy," this one subsequent statement among many on rebirth, "There comes a time for us all when we want to begin a new life," and near the end of the volume these lines, "Light rises . . . All, all/Is here, no other where. The heart, in this silence, beats." *Or Else* contains a poem, "Interjection #8," that describes the ubiquitous and "unsleeping principle of delight." *Audubon* concludes with the perfect stillness of Audubon and the petition "Tell me a story of deep delight." And *Tale of Time* ends with a sequence of poems entitled "Delight." Warren's poetry, like much poetry of great or important poets, begins in pain, makes its progress through darkness to death, and then, perfectly aware of the often inexplicable violence and suffering that human flesh is heir to, through its earned and integrated vision ends in rebirth, truth, selfhood, even joy.

Notes

1. "Pure and Impure Poetry," *Selected Essays* (New York: Random House, 1958), pp. 22 *et passim*.

2. *Writers at Work*, ed. Malcolm Cowley (New York: Viking Press, 1959), p. 192.

3. "A Poem of Pure Imagination: An Experiment in Reading," *The Rime of the Ancient Mariner* (New York: Reynal and Hitchcock, 1946), p. 103. See also his "Knowledge and the Image of Man" in *Robert Penn Warren: A Collection of Critical Essays*, ed. John L. Longley, Jr. (New York: New York Univ. Press, 1965), pp. 237–46.

4. *Democracy and Poetry* (Cambridge: Harvard Univ. Press, 1975), pp. xii–xiii, 31.

5. *Time and Eternity* (Princeton: Princeton Univ. Press, 1952), p. 104.

INDEX